Bible Passages That Can Influence Your Life

by
Dorothy Scott

1663 L*IBERTY* D*RIVE*, S*UITE* 200
B*LOOMINGTON*, I*NDIANA* 47403
(800) 839-8640
WWW.A*UTHOR*H*OUSE*.COM

This book is a work of non-fiction. Unless otherwise noted, the author and the publisher make no explicit guarantees as to the accuracy of the information contained in this book and in some cases, names of people and places have been altered to protect their privacy.

© 2005 Dorothy Scott. All Rights Reserved.

No part of this book may be reproduced, stored in a retrieval system, or transmitted by any means without the written permission of the author.

First published by AuthorHouse 01/25/05

ISBN: 1-4184-1219-8 (e)
ISBN: 1-4184-1218-X (sc)
ISBN: 1-4184-1217-1 (hc)

Library of Congress Control Number: 2003095829

Printed in the United States of America
Bloomington, Indiana

This book is printed on acid-free paper.

This book is dedicated to God who inspires me on a daily basis through Bible passages that touch and influence my life. He has provided me with wonderful family, friends and co-workers. These wonderful people have supported me, listened to me or have given me feedback throughout the writing process. They did this regardless of whether my interpretations were similar to theirs, or not.
I feel truly blessed!
D. S.

Special Thanks go to Bev,
who spent many long hours helping to edit this.

Foreword

In much the same way that Reality shows allow the observer to take a glimpse into another person's life, thoughts and decisions, this book allows you a very candid, enlightening glimpse into my personal and spiritual life. The Reality show doesn't just portray the strengths of the person observed. It also portrays the weaknesses, as does this book. Reading the Bible on a daily basis has positively enriched my life in ways that go far beyond literal interpretation.

Although this book has the potential of being controversial, it is not my intent to offend any person, group or religious belief. I feel obliged to honestly express how the selected Bible passages have influenced my life and would be negligent, as an author and a Christian, to do anything less.

It's my desire for readers of all ages and religious backgrounds to find that reading the Bible never becomes outdated and continues to hold personal significance for all types of readers of the new millennium.

D.S.

Bible Passages That Can Influence Your Life

Would you believe that a fable got me started reading the Bible? In 1980, someone said something to me about, "god helps him who helps himself," and referred to it being in the Bible. I had heard this saying over the years, but realized it contradicted some other things I had read in the Bible. I looked through the Concordance at the back of my Bible but couldn't find this passage anywhere. Perplexed, I decided the only way I would know if it was in the Bible was for me to read it from cover to cover for myself. Now, this decision wasn't based solely on my frustration about this quote. I had a neighbor who quoted different contradictory things from the Bible, as well. I figured that I needed to read the Bible to see what God really said about the topics the neighbor kept referring to. I get concerned when people quote passages from the Bible out of context, making them sound the way they want.

Well, it's twenty-three years later and I have completely read the Bible from cover to cover sixteen plus times. "God helps him who helps himself," is not in it anywhere! Actually, the Bible says that we are supposed to turn to God for our every need, trusting that He will provide for us (paraphrased.)

I was frustrated as I continued to hear people quote this, because I couldn't figure out where people got it. Most of the people who used this quote, said it as if they thought it came from the Bible. Well, I finally have closure on this...after all this time!

I was reading some *Aesop's Fables* to my students. They have to be able to identify the moral of a story for a test they have in the spring. I decided that I could help them be more successful on the test if I had them identify the morals from *Aesop's Fables*. Well, after reading "*Hercules and the Wagoner*," I finally realized where "god helps him who helps himself" came from. It's from this fable! The moral written for this fable is "Self help is the best help" and "Heaven helps those who help themselves."

When they are talking about god, they aren't talking about God. They are talking about the mythological character, Hercules. I bet most people haven't the slightest idea that they are quoting a fable instead of the Bible.

This may seem like a trivial thing, but it has been a confusing issue to me for twenty-three years and now it's resolved! I feel so relieved and wanted to share this with others. Actually, this has really worked out well in the long run. If it hadn't been for my inability to find this quote in the Bible, I might not have been motivated to read the Bible from cover to cover. I enjoy reading it so much that I continue to read it from cover to cover again and again. Every time I read it, I get something new out of it.

Particular passages in the Bible have really influenced my life and have molded my relationship with God. I felt led to share these with you, since they may have a similar impact on your life, as well.

Whenever someone quotes Bible passages, it's really good to read them for yourself. You should read a portion before and after the passage. This helps you know if people are pulling these passages from the Bible out of context, distorting the meaning by making it sound the way they want.

I use the King James Bible for my quotes which tends to spell things somewhat differently than we do (example: labour for labor). In order to keep the passages just as they are in the Bible, I use the exact spellings, punctuation, capitalizations or lack thereof in order to not alter the passage. I do attempt to explain what these passages mean to me, or I describe how they have influenced my life.

I'm not a minister and don't profess to be one, but I feel that reading the Bible can influence your life, as well. Will it impact your life in exactly the same way? Probably not, the Bible is a very personal thing. If 1,000 different people read the Bible, there would be 1,000 different interpretations. Every time I read the Bible, passages I have read before often mean something totally different to me, depending on what is going on in my life at the time. God uses the Bible as a means of communicating His personal message for each and every one of us.

Reading the Bible may seem like a major undertaking for some of you. Actually, after you get through the "thee's" and "thou's," it's not as difficult to understand as you might think. A chapter in the Bible isn't like a chapter in a novel. A Bible chapter is generally about one to two columns long. It's hardly ever longer than a page or two, at most. I read at least one to two chapters a day for about 10-15 minutes. It takes me an anywhere from one year to two years to read the Bible from cover to cover, depending on how many chapters I read each day. It's so rewarding that you might consider reading it yourself! The quiet time I have with God each day as I read the Bible, sets a positive tone for my day and my life.

I was just beginning to read the New Testament when I started writing this book. That's why the New Testament is written first and the Old Testament is written afterward. After I finished writing the book, I had thought about cutting and pasting the Old Testament first but realized it wouldn't work. As I wrote the book, I made comments about passages and referred back to them at other times. If I put the Old Testament in the beginning, some of the comments I share with you would be out of sequence. I am hoping that leaving the book in this order doesn't cause a problem for anyone. If it does, I apologize in advance, but still feel this book has many redeeming qualities, more significant than whether the Old Testament is listed first or second.

The passages in *italics* are from the Bible. Otherwise, they are my personal comments on how these passages have influenced my life. I also try to capitalize any reference to God/Jesus out of respect, which makes it easier for you to follow who is speaking or being spoken to. I may group similar passages from the Bible together so that you have an approximate idea of how many times God stresses a particular topic. The sheer number of times that God has had something mentioned in the Bible has led me to make changes in my life. Although you may not relate to these passages in the same ways I have, the reader can be influenced by the Bible in a way that is personally significant to them.

....

Then was Jesus led up of the Spirit into the wilderness to be tempted of the devil. And when He had fasted forty days and forty nights, He was afterward an hungered. And when the tempter came to Him, he said, If Thou be the Son of God, command that these stones be made bread. But He answered and said, It is written, Man shall not live by bread alone, but by every Word that proceedeth out of the Mouth of God. Matthew, Chapter 4, verses 1-4.

When I was a child, I saw a big bowl of my mother's home-made butterscotch pudding sitting on the kitchen cupboard. I looked around and couldn't see anyone, so I sneaked over to the bowl and ran my finger around the side of the bowl. I ever so carefully got a small amount of pudding on my pudgy finger and licked it off.

I thought I was going to get off "Scott free" but I didn't realize there were spies about and a bounty on pudding thieves. After being told the pudding had to be thrown out because I had gotten germs all over it, my consequence was to be sent to my room. Instead of being remorseful for what I did, my thoughts were, "If I had known the pudding would be thrown out, I would have eaten a whole bunch instead of a little bit. That would have made my consequence much more worthwhile."

I gave in to these temptations and lost my perspective of right and wrong and I hadn't even been fasting for forty days like Jesus. In fact, I had eaten a filling lunch but still was vulnerable to the lure dangled in front of me. Now some might think that this isn't a major sin but don't realize that Satan works in very subtle ways to get us to rationalize our actions. He is able to lead us astray without our ever realizing it. Fortunately for me, Jesus didn't give in to the temptations for food, status or power that we often fall prey to.

Here are some related passages:

*Then the devil taketh Him up into the holy city, and setteth Him on a pinnacle of the temple, And saith unto Him, If Thou be the Son of God, cast Thyself down: for it is written, He shall give His angels charge concerning Thee; and in their hands they shall bear Thee up, lest at any time Thou dash Thy foot against a stone. Jesus said unto him, It is written again, thou shalt not tempt the Lord thy God. Matthew, Chapter 4, verses 5-7.

*Again, the devil taketh Him up into an exceeding high mountain, and showeth Him all the kingdoms of the world, and the glory of them: And saith unto Him, all these things will I give Thee, if Thou wilt fall down and worship me. Then saith Jesus unto him, Get thee hence, Satan: for it is written, Thou shalt worship the Lord thy God, and Him only shalt thou serve. Matthew, Chapter 4, verses 8-10.

....

And Jesus, walking by the sea of Galilee, saw two brethren, Simon called Peter, and Andrew his brother, casting a net into the sea: for they were fishers. And He saith unto them, Follow Me and I will make you fishers of men. And they straightway left their nets, and followed Him. Matthew, Chapter 4, verses 18-20.

I remember getting a round hot pad called a "Round Tuit." It's a gag gift you give to people who always answer that they will do things when they get "around to it." I realize that the disciples didn't even know Jesus, but when He asked them to be fishers of men, the disciples dropped everything, no questions asked. In contrast, here I am needing a "Round Tuit" saying by my actions, "Well, I'm busy right now, God, but I might talk to others about the impact You've left on my life when I get around to it."

Here are some related passages:

And going on from thence, He saw other two brethren, James the son of Zebedee, and John his brother, in a ship with Zebedee their father, mending their nets, and He called them. And they immediately left the ship and their father and followed Him. Matthew, Chapter 4, verses 21-22.

And another of His disciples said unto Him, Lord, suffer me first to go and bury my father. But Jesus said unto him, Follow Me; and let the dead bury their dead. Matthew, Chapter 8, verses 21-22.

And as Jesus passed forth from thence, He saw a man, named Matthew, sitting at the receipt of custom: and He saith unto him, Follow Me, And he arose, and followed Him. Matthew, Chapter 9, verse 9.

So when they had dined, Jesus saith to Simon Peter, Simon, son of Jonas, lovest thou Me more than these? He saith unto Him, Yea, Lord; Thou knowest that I love Thee. He saith unto him, Feed My lambs. He saith unto him again the second time, Simon, son of Jonas, lovest thou Me? He saith unto Him, Yea, Lord: Thou knowest that I love Thee. He saith unto him, Feed My sheep. He saith unto him the third time, Simon, son of Jonas, lovest Thou Me? Peter was grieved because He said unto him the third time, Lovest thou Me? And he said unto Him, Lord, Thou knowest all things; Thou knowest that I love Thee. Jesus saith unto him, Feed My sheep. John, Chapter 21, verses 15-17.

....

And He opened His Mouth, and taught them, saying, Blessed are the poor in spirit: for theirs is the kingdom of heaven. Blessed are they that mourn: for they shall be comforted. Blessed are the meek: for they shall inherit the earth. Blessed are they which do hunger and thirst after righteousness: for they shall be filled. Blessed are the merciful: for they shall obtain mercy. Blessed are the pure in heart: for they shall see God. Blessed are the peacemakers: for they shall be called the children of God. Blessed are they which are persecuted for righteousness' sake: for theirs is the kingdom of heaven. Blessed are ye, when men shall revile you, and persecute you, and shall say all manner of evil against you falsely, for My sake. Rejoice, and be exceeding glad: for great is your reward in heaven: for so persecuted they the prophets which were before you. Matthew, Chapter 5, verses 2-12.

I picture this as a pep talk with Jesus as the coach of a team of Christians. He might say something like, "Of course there are teams that get ahead because they do unethical things, and the ones focused on playing a good honest game on earth don't get ahead. I know the team takes a hit for playing the game ethically and sometimes gets laughed at. I know you definitely don't rake in the big bucks and status the way other players do. I promise that you will have your compensation in heaven for all your hard work and sacrifice on My behalf. Your efforts never go unnoticed and will be repaid. Keep up the good work and don't let the world get you down!"

Here is a related passage:

*And every one that hath forsaken houses, or brethren, or sisters, or father, or mother, or wife, or children, or lands, for My Name's sake, shall receive an hundredfold, and shall inherit everlasting life. Matthew, Chapter 19, verse 29.

....

Ye are the light of the world. A city that is set on a hill cannot be hid. Neither do men light a candle, and put it under a bushel, but on a candlestick: and it giveth light unto all that are in the house. Let your light so shine before men, that they may see your good works, and glorify your Father which is in heaven. Matthew, Chapter 5, verses 14-16.

I've kept my relationship with God hidden under a bushel for most of my life. I'm not much for walking door to door to talk to strangers about God. I haven't done much to try to actively convert people. I guess writing this book isn't any big-time "shining" when you think about it. I'm sharing this information in a low risk fashion. I need to make more of an attempt to take the risks that God needs me to on His behalf. I guess I have to start somewhere and this is it. I will see where God leads me from here.

....

Ye have heard that it was said by them of old time, Thou shalt not commit adultery: But I say unto you, That whosoever looketh on a woman to lust after her hath committed adultery with her already in his heart. Matthew, Chapter 5, verses 27-28.

This makes me think of when I am attracted to particular male movie stars and have thought inappropriate things that only God knows about. He also knows all the times that I think mean, hateful things about other people. Of course, no one else knows these things except for God and me, but I just stuff them under my spiritual rug like someone who can't find a dustpan. God sees what I think and what's under my rug, so I need to start "cleaning house" soon!

....

Ye have heard that it hath been said, An eye for an eye, and a tooth for a tooth: But I say unto you, That ye resist not evil: but whosoever shall smite thee on thy right cheek turn to him the other side also. Matthew, Chapter 5, verses 38-39.

When frustrated with someone who has been rude or insensitive to me, it's really easy for me to say something back, displaying less than Christian behavior. I may not say something rude, but if I pull an attitude, harboring hatred or resentment toward that person, I haven't genuinely turned the other cheek. It's important for me to remember to turn my feelings over to God when these occasions arise.

....

Ye have heard that it hath been said, Thou shalt love thy neighbor, and hate thine enemy. But I say unto you, Love your enemies, bless them that curse you, and pray for them which despitefully use you, and persecute you: That ye may be the children of your Father which is in heaven: for He maketh His sun to rise on the evil and on the good, and sendeth rain on the just and on the unjust. For if ye love them which love you, what reward have ye? do not even the publicans the same? Matthew, Chapter 5, verses 43-46.

God isn't asking me to ignore hurtful and spiteful things that people do because I am a Christian. He is asking me to go further than that. He wants me to be nice to them in return, despite their actions and to pray for them. I think we are much better examples of our beliefs when we don't stoop to the same level as others, but it's difficult at times. God can take care of my pride if I ask Him to, making me a better example of how He works in my life.

....

Take heed that ye do not your alms before men, to be seen of them: otherwise ye have no reward of your Father which is in heaven. Therefore when thou doest thine alms, do not sound a trumpet before thee, as the hypocrites do in the synagogues and in the streets, that they may have glory of men. Verily I say unto you, They have their reward. But when thou doest alms, let not thy left hand know what thy right hand doeth: That thine alms may be in secret: and thy Father which seeth in secret Himself shall reward thee openly. Matthew, Chapter 6, verses 1-4.

This passage makes me very aware that I need to be discreet about giving to the church and other charities. I remember that there was a time in my life that I routinely did favors and nice things for others. What I really was waiting for was a "thank you" or what I call a "Good Dorothy." I was waiting for someone else to tell me what a wonderful person I was as if to validate my existence here on earth.

I realize my goal as a Christian is to do nice things discreetly. So now I do them for God and not the "Good Dorothy's". The good works we do for others shouldn't be to show off or to prove to others what good Christians we are. They should be out of our love for Jesus.

....

And when thou prayest, thou shalt not be as hypocrites are: for they love to pray standing in the synagogues and in the corners of the streets, that they may be seen of men. Verily I say unto you, They have their reward. But thou, when thou prayest, enter into thy closet, and when thou hast shut thy door, pray to thy Father which is in secret: and thy Father which seeth in secret shall reward thee openly. Matthew, Chapter 6, verses 5-6.

God wants me to be discreet when I pray, as well. I shouldn't do it in a way that attracts other people's attention, especially when to do so might put me in the position to gain the respect or admiration of others. My prayers aren't for personal gain but are my personal communication with God.

....

But when ye pray, use not vain repetitions, as the heathen do: for they think that they shall be heard for their much speaking. Matthew, Chapter 6, verse 7.

I get caught up in thinking that I'm saying these wonderful prayers, but I recognize that they don't mean anything if I'm daydreaming about situations at work or what I need to get at the store. I realize that when I say the same prayers over and over without thinking about what I'm saying to God, they ARE vain repetitions! God doesn't want me just going through the motions when I pray. He wants any communication I have with Him to be meaningful enough to focus on it.

Here is a related passage:

*This people draweth nigh unto Me with their mouth, and honoureth Me with their lips; but their heart is far from Me. But in vain they do worship Me, teaching for doctrines the commandments of men. Matthew, Chapter 15, verses 8-9.

....

For if ye forgive men their trespasses, your heavenly Father will also forgive you: But if ye forgive not men their trespasses, neither will your Father forgive your trespasses. Matthew, Chapter 6, verses 14-15.

Every time I pray, I ask God to forgive all of my sins, but do I do the same? I find myself harboring resentment towards others instead of letting it go. I find that if I hold onto hatred, anger or resentment, which eats at me, I'm not the example that God wants me to be in my everyday life. I can set a better Christian example by forgiving others, letting God take the resentment away when I ask Him. One of the best ways I have to let my "light shine" for God is by being an example of how He works in my life.

....

Moreover when ye fast, be not, as the hypocrites, of a sad countenance: for they disfigure their faces, that they may appear unto men to fast. Verily I say unto you, They have their reward. But thou, when thou fastest, anoint thine head, and wash thy face, That thou appear not unto men to fast, but unto thy Father which is in secret: and thy Father which seeth in secret, shall reward thee openly. Matthew, Chapter 6, verses 16-18.

I remember when I was little, the neighbor kids and I would gloat in front of others by saying things like, "Ha, ha, ha. I have a new bike and you don't!" These statements were to bring about the envy of some and the admiration of others. Well, as Christians, we are tempted to "show off" for the very same reasons.

I realized through this passage that God doesn't want me to be a martyr, getting the attention of others when I fast or do things for Him. That draws too much attention to me. There's the possibility that I might get caught up in trying to be a "Show off Christian" so others will see how pious I am.

I fast on Ash Wednesday and Good Friday, because it's my way of trying to focus on all the suffering Jesus went through for us. When I fast, I need to make sure not to draw undue attention to myself. That's exactly what would happen if I sat with others at work and made it very apparent that I wasn't eating anything. Now I develop a plan to do it in a manner that doesn't let anyone else know what I'm doing.

The feeling I get when we read the Bible is that anything we do for God should be done privately. Drawing attention to ourselves and what we are doing for Him is counterproductive. It takes away from our gesture for God and should be done out of pure love and not for the attention we can milk out of it!

....

Lay not up for yourselves treasures upon earth, where moth and rust doth corrupt, and where thieves break through and steal: But lay up for yourselves treasures in heaven, where neither moth nor rust doth corrupt, and where thieves do not break through nor steal: For where your treasure is, there will your heart be also. Matthew, Chapter 6, verses 19-21.

I think my faith in Jesus is like a savings account, but the bank isn't here on earth, it's in heaven. My belief in Jesus is the minimum investment a Christian has to make to get this special savings account. This investment can lie there dormant, with no additional deposits made and eventually be put in the inactive file. Or I can make deposits by the things I do as an example of how Jesus works in my life.

Now, thieves can steal the money from banks on earth, but the only one who will take away the "money" from my heavenly account is me, by leading a worldly life that leads me astray. If I'm planning on having a good "nest egg" built up in my Salvation account, then I should be more focused on leading a Christian life, reflecting this goal.

Here is a related passage:

*Again, the kingdom of heaven is like unto treasure hid in a field; the which when a man hath found, he hideth, and for joy thereof goeth and selleth all that he hath, and buyeth that field. Again, the kingdom of heaven is like unto a merchant man, seeking goodly pearls: Who, when he had found one pearl of great price, went and sold all that he had and bought it. Matthew, Chapter 13, verses 44-46.

....

> *No man can serve two masters: for either he will hate the one, and love the other; or else he will hold to the one, and despise the other. Ye cannot serve God and mammon [wealth, riches and possessions]. Matthew, Chapter 6, verse 24.*

I have tried to be a "Have My Cake and Eat It Too Christian," but it just doesn't work that way. I thought I could balance my faith like a teeter totter, with Jesus on one side and getting ahead in my job, having nice things and a decent bank account on the other side. Well, what I have found is that when my focus is on getting ahead in my job, possessions and wealth; the worldly end of the teeter totter goes up.

I was pleased by the growth I saw in these worldly areas, but when I looked back on the other side of the teeter totter, I saw Jesus sitting there at the bottom of my priorities. Although I've tried various ways to maintain a balance to have my cake and eat it too, it just doesn't work. I need to make the necessary changes to have Jesus on top as my primary goal. When I do this, the job, possessions and wealth are at the bottom of my priorities which doesn't really seem to matter much, because Jesus provides for my every need.

Here is a related passage:

> **No servant can serve two masters: for either he will hate the one, and love the other; or else he will hold to the one, and despise the other. Ye cannot serve God and mammon. Luke, Chapter 16, verse 13.*

....

These are some of my most favorite Bible verses. In fact, I love this passage so much that I asked the minister to say this at my wedding. It is long but it's wonderful!

> *Therefore I say unto you, Take no thought for your life, what ye shall eat, or what ye shall drink; nor yet for your body, what ye shall put on. Is not the life more than meat, and the body than raiment? Behold the fowls of the air: for they sow not, neither do they reap, nor gather into barns; yet your heavenly Father feedeth them. Are ye not much better than they? Which of you by taking thought can add one cubit unto his stature? And why take ye thought for raiment? Consider the lilies of the field, how they grow; they toil not, neither do they spin: And yet I say unto you, That even Solomon in all his glory was not arrayed like one of these. Wherefore, if God so clothe the grass of the field, which to day is, and tomorrow is cast into the oven, shall He not much more clothe you, O ye of little faith? Therefore take*

no thought, saying, What shall we eat? or, What shall we drink? or, Wherewithal shall we be clothed? (For after all these things do the Gentiles seek:) for your heavenly Father knoweth that ye have need of these things. But seek ye first the kingdom of God, and His righteousness; and all these things shall be added unto you. Take therefore no thought for the morrow: for the morrow shall take thought for the things of itself. Sufficient unto the day is the evil thereof. Matthew, Chapter 6, verses 25-34.

This passage has been instrumental in a major change in my relationship with God. Most people have some type of vice. Various people drink, some have affairs, others use drugs, but mine is my need to be in control. It's really difficult for me to not be in total control of all aspects of my life, as well as, other situations that arise. I remember how I used to plan, calculate and budget every single cent. I would do this a month in advance, fretting over my finances the rest of the month. Although, this might be good for someone who spends too much money, it wasn't good for me because I wasn't letting God be in control of my life.

I think people with control issues are probably great people to have on committees, because they make sure all the details are taken care of. It's not always a blessing to be that much in control of things. When I'm in total control of everything in my life, I'm not trusting God to take care of me because I'm too busy trying to plan everything. It's kind of like I'm saying, "Wait in the wings, God. Let me see what I can do first and if I can't figure it out, then I'll turn to You for help." Everything I read in the Bible states repeatedly that God wants me to turn to Him for everything. That's why I'm writing this book. It's to show people that God doesn't say, "God helps him who helps himself." God wants us to turn to Him in all things (paraphrased).

Control also played a part in my eating problem. I used to be around 70-80 pounds heavier. I always figured that I could lose the weight if I went on my "good diet" and stuck with it. I joined about every weight loss group around and several times, at that! I went on my "good diet" and found it wasn't productive either. Then I sat down in my bedroom one day and said, "I give up, God. I'm always going to be heavy. God, if you want me to ever be thin, You'll have to take care of it because I can't,"…and you know what, He did!

From that moment on, the desire for sweets and great quantities of food were taken away from me. I didn't do anything, in and of myself. God did it all! This all happened because I asked God to take care of it. I guess this was probably one of the first times I had really given up my control. The reason I said this prayer wasn't because I was expecting God to take all my weight away. I was just giving up and was turning it all over to God because I didn't want to worry about being heavy anymore. He used this miracle to turn my life around and to show me that He needs to be the One in control of my life, not me.

If God takes care of things in nature, He will surely take care of me and all my needs. I find that when I'm not spending so much time trying to be in control of situations and people, I have much more time to spend focusing on God and my family. That's because I'm trusting God to take care of situations that arise. Now, this isn't to say I don't slip into that control mode, at times. It's my vice. I think Satan knows that anytime I'm in my control mode, I'm using the "I's" and "Me's" to make things happen. In other words, I'm controlling situations, which means I'm not focusing on God. I'm glad God takes the time to keep reminding me that I need to turn to Him in all things.

There is a similar passage to this that will be included elsewhere in the book. Sometimes I include those passages separately because there is something significant that I would like to share at that time. Other times, I include additional or related Bible verses below the passage. I find it interesting to compare other passages with similar topics.

Here is a related passage:

And when they had sent away the multitude, they took Him even as He was in the ship. And there were also with Him other little ships. And there arose a great storm of wind, and the waves beat into the ship, so that it was now full. And He was in the hinder part of the ship, asleep on a pillow: and they awake Him, and say unto Him, Master, carest thou not that we perish? And He arose, and rebuked the wind, and said unto the sea, Peace, be still. And the wind ceased, and there was a great calm. And He said unto them, Why are ye so fearful? how is it that ye have no faith? And they feared exceedingly, and said one to another, What manner of Man is this, that even the wind and the sea obey Him? Mark, Chapter 4, verses 36-41.

....

Give not that which is holy unto the dogs, neither cast ye your pearls before swine, lest they trample them under their feet, and turn again and rend you. Matthew, Chapter 7, verse 6.

When I was in high school there were lots of different groups of kids. Well, they called one of these groups the "dopers" mainly because their lives revolved around recreational drugs, losing sight of all else. As a Christian, I value my faith in Jesus above all else (my pearls.) I could have walked into the crowd of "dopers" and told them that Jesus has positively influenced my life in ways that I would like to share with them. Do you think I would get a warm response? You're right; they would tell me to get out of there and give me a hard time, not being open to any of the things that I wanted to share with them.

My faith in Jesus is better shared with those who might possibly be open to listening to me. Now that doesn't mean that I am not to share my faith with those who use recreational drugs or have worldly lifestyles. I can choose my timing wisely and approach those people one-on-one, at a time where I think they might be more receptive. If I really want to share my relationship with Jesus, I will try to maximize my potential of successfully doing this.

Here is a related passage:

> *And whosoever shall not receive you, nor hear your Words, when ye depart out of that house or city, shake off the dust of your feet. Verily I say unto you, It shall be more tolerable for the land of Sodom and Gomorrha in the day of judgment, than for that city. Matthew, Chapter 10, verses 14-15.*

....

> *For the Son of Man is Lord even of the Sabbath day. And when He was departed thence, He went into their synagogue: And, behold, there was a man which had his hand withered. And they asked Him, saying, Is it lawful to heal on the Sabbath days? that they might accuse Him. And He said unto them, What man shall there be among you, that shall have one sheep, and it fall into a pit on the Sabbath day, will he not lay hold on it, and lift it out? How much then is a man better than a sheep? Wherefore it is lawful to do well on the Sabbath days. Matthew, Chapter 12, verses 8-12.*

This was of special interest to me. I had read in several different sections in the Bible that we aren't to do work on the Sabbath. This isn't something my particular church promotes, but it's written in the Bible in so many places that I figured God wants people to pay attention to it. I don't really think it matters to God whether people choose Saturday or Sunday to worship Him, as long as we choose one of the days to abstain from work while focusing on Him and relaxing. My impression is that God realized some people are workaholics and need some down time. If people worked on the Sabbath and didn't have a family day to relax and worship together, each family member might be likely to go off in a different direction.

Bible Passages That Can Influence Your Life

I had a dilemma a few years ago that relates to this passage. When I went to visit my elderly grandparents after church, I wanted to do household jobs that they couldn't do but didn't want to go against the Bible by working on the Sabbath. This passage solved that dilemma, because Jesus said that it was alright to help someone on the Sabbath. After realizing this, I was able to help my grandparents and not feel like I was compromising my beliefs.

Sometimes the related passages that I list below the main entry refer to the same general topic. Other times the related passages that are below the main entry sound almost identical. I feel it's important for the reader to see these even though they may sound redundant. Many of the disciples were with Jesus and got an opportunity to see and experience some of the same things. They shared these observations from their perspective as God led them to write portions of the Bible. Although these accounts may differ somewhat in wording, they are especially significant because they show that Jesus really did exist and is not a figment of someone's imagination.

Here are some related passages:

*And it came to pass also on another Sabbath, that He entered into the synagogue and taught: and there was a man whose right hand was withered. And the scribes and Pharisees watched Him, whether He would heal on the Sabbath day; that they might find an accusation against Him. But He knew their thoughts, and said to the man which had the withered hand, Rise up, and stand forth in the midst. And he arose and stood forth. Then said Jesus unto them, I will ask you one thing; Is it lawful on the Sabbath days to do good, or to do evil? to save life, or to destroy it? And looking round about upon them all, He said unto the man, Stretch forth thy hand. And he did so: and his hand was restored whole as the other. And they were filled with madness; and communed one with another what they might do to Jesus. And it came to pass in those days, that He went out into a mountain to pray, and continued all night in prayer to God. And when it was day, He called Him His disciples: and of them He chose twelve, whom also He named apostles. Luke, Chapter 6, verses 6-13.

*And the ruler of the synagogue answered with indignation, because that Jesus had healed on the Sabbath day, and said unto the people, There are six days in which men ought to work: in them therefore come and be healed, and not

on the Sabbath day. The Lord then answered him, and said, Thou hypocrite, doth not each one of you on the Sabbath loose his ox or his ass from the stall, and lead him away to watering? And ought not this woman, being a daughter of Abraham, whom Satan hath bound, lo, these eighteen years, be loosed from this bond on the Sabbath day? And when He had said these things, all His adversaries were ashamed: and all the people rejoiced for all the glorious things that were done by Him. Luke, Chapter 13, verses 14-17.

*And behold, there was a certain man before him which had the dropsy. And Jesus answering spake unto the lawyers and Pharisees, saying, Is it lawful to heal on the Sabbath day? And they held their peace. And He took him, and healed him, and let him go; And answered them, saying, Which of you shall have an ass or an ox fallen into a pit, and will not straightway pull him out on the Sabbath day? And they could not answer Him again to these things. Luke, Chapter 14, verses 2-6.

If thou turn away thy foot from the Sabbath, from doing thy pleasure on My holy day; and call the Sabbath a delight, the holy of the LORD, honourable; and shalt honour Him, not doing thine own pleasure, nor speaking thine own words: Then shalt thou delight thyself in the LORD; and I will cause thee to ride upon the high places of the earth, and feed thee with the heritage of Jacob thy father: for the Mouth of the LORD hath spoken it. Isaiah, Chapter 58, verses 13-14.

....

Then was brought unto Him one possessed with a devil, blind, and dumb: and He healed him, insomuch that the blind and the dumb both spake and saw. And all the people were amazed, and said, Is not this the Son of David? But when the Pharisees heard it, they said, This Fellow doth not cast out devils, but by Beelzebub the prince of the devils. And Jesus knew their thoughts, and said unto them, Every kingdom divided against itself is brought to desolation; and every city or house divided against itself shall not stand: And if Satan cast out Satan, he is divided against himself; how shall then his kingdom stand? And if I by Beelzebub cast out devils, by whom do your children cast them out? therefore they shall be your judges. But if I cast out devils by the Spirit of God, then the kingdom of God is come unto you. Or else how can one enter into a strong man's house, and spoil his goods, except he first bind the strong man? and then he will spoil his house. He that is not with Me is against Me; and he that gathereth not with Me scattereth abroad. Wherefore I say unto you, All manner of sin and blasphemy shall be forgiven unto men: but the blasphemy against the Holy Ghost shall not be forgiven unto men. And whosoever speaketh a word against the Son of Man, it shall be forgiven him: but whosoever speaketh against the Holy Ghost, it shall not be forgiven him, neither in this world, neither in the world to come. Matthew, Chapter 12, verses 22-32.

I found that my students had their limits. They may have tolerated someone calling them names and teasing them, but once someone said something hateful about their Mother, it put the situation in a whole other ballpark. Well, I think Jesus is responding in a similar fashion. I think He's saying something like, "O.K. I may have put up with you saying stupid things like I must be Satan, because I am able to heal the deaf and dumb. It really doesn't make any sense to start with. A house divided against itself will fall, so Satan couldn't cast himself out.

"You're just looking for things to confuse people and discredit the miracles that I do to prove that I'm your Savior. Well, I may have tolerated you belittling Me, but I sure won't tolerate you belittling the Holy Ghost. I'm warning you now; if you continue to do that, you will live to regret it because it's intolerable! Although you don't know it yet, I'm here to save you from your sins, but people who say hateful things against the Holy Ghost won't even get a second chance. They will lose any hope for Salvation. Don't say I didn't warn you!"

....

Therefore speak I to them in parables; because they seeing see not; and hearing they hear not, neither do they understand. And in them is fulfilled the prophecy of Esaias, which saith, By hearing ye shall hear, and shall not understand; and seeing ye shall see, and shall not perceive: For this people's heart is waxed gross, and their ears are dull of hearing, and their eyes they have closed; lest at any time they should see with their eyes, and hear with their ears, and should understand with their heart, and should be converted, and I should heal them. But blessed are your eyes, for they see: and your ears, for they hear. For verily I say unto you, That many prophets and righteous men have desired to see those things which ye see, and have not seen them; and to hear those things which ye hear, and have not heard them. Matthew, Chapter 13, verses 13-17.

I've walked up to a child who was upset. I had planned to distract them from their anger by telling them the class was going to do something fun like cook or do a craft, but they were so angry that they couldn't hear what I was going to tell them. When they saw me approaching, they covered their ears and started making sounds to block out anything I might say. I usually walk away thinking that it's their loss, because they miss out on the fun activity that I was going to tell them about.

It's a shame that there are still some who aren't open to hearing that Jesus is our Savior. They are the ones who will miss out on the opportunity for Salvation, which is sad. It's difficult to get through to people when they have deliberately closed their minds, eyes and ears to what we have to share.

....

Another parable put He forth unto them, saying, The kingdom of heaven is likened unto a man which sowed good seed in his field: But while men slept, his enemy came and sowed tares [weeds] among the wheat, and went his way. But when the blade was sprung up, and brought forth fruit, then appeared tares also. So the servants of the householder came and said unto him, Sir, didst not thou sow good seed in thy field? from whence then hath it tares? He said unto them, An enemy hath done this. The servants said unto him, Wilt thou then that we go and gather them up? But he said, Nay; lest while ye gather up the tares ye root up also the wheat with them. Let both grow together until the harvest: and in the time of harvest I will say to the reapers, Gather ye together first the tares, and bind them in bundles to burn them: but gather the wheat into my barn. Matthew, Chapter 13, verses 24-30.

Then Jesus sent the multitude away, and went into the house: and His disciples came unto Him, saying, Declare unto us the parable of the tares of the field. He answered and said unto them, He that soweth the good seed is the Son of Man; The field is the world; the good seed are the children of the kingdom; but the tares are the children of the wicked one; The enemy that sowed them is the devil; the harvest is the end of the world; and the reapers are the angels. As therefore the tares are gathered and burned in the fire; so shall it be in the end of this world. The Son of Man shall send forth His angels, and they shall gather out of His kingdom all things that offend, and them which do iniquity; And shall cast them into a furnace of fire: there shall be wailing and gnashing of teeth. Then shall the righteous shine forth as the sun in the kingdom of their Father. Who hath ears to hear, let him hear. Matthew, Chapter 13, verses 36-43.

This is also like when you make popcorn. Pretend all the fully popped kernels are those who believe Jesus is their Savior and try to lead their lives accordingly. The unpopped kernels or "Old Maids" are those who have fallen prey to Satan's enticements to live a worldly life. After you pop the popcorn, you debate whether to pick out all the "Old Maids," since there are quite a few, or to leave them in.

Some of the popcorn kernels are partially popped, but you decide to count them as "Old Maids," because they really aren't the same as fully popped popcorn. This is similar to people who know Jesus is our Savior, but don't put any effort into praying or leading a life that reflects their love for Him. You think about it and decide to dump all the popcorn into a paper bag to eat rather than pulling the "Old Maids" out. That symbolizes both Christians and non-Christians living together on earth.

The fully popped popcorn is chosen and is removed from the bag, representing the Christians who will be chosen and will have Salvation in heaven. All the "Old Maids" and partial "Old Maids" will be discarded when you throw the paper bag into the garbage can. This represents those with a worldly focus who will be going to hell. I don't know about you, but I don't want be discarded like an "Old Maid Christian," so I need to live my life accordingly.

Here is a related passage:

*Again, the kingdom of heaven is like unto a net, that was cast into the sea, and gathered of every kind: Which, when it was full, they drew to shore, and sat down, and gathered the good into vessels, but cast the bad away. So shall it be at the end of the world: the angels shall come forth, and sever the wicked from among the just, And shall cast them into the furnace of fire: there shall be wailing and gnashing of teeth. Matthew, Chapter 13, verses 47-50.

....

Another parable spake He unto them; The kingdom of heaven is like unto leaven, which a woman took, and hid in three measures of meal, till the whole was leavened. Matthew, Chapter 13, verse 33.

I'm not really sure what this means but will explain what it makes me think of. It reminds me of an office that I worked in for the government, some years ago. When I first started working there, the group of ladies I had break with, spent a lot of time complaining and harping about unproductive issues. After I felt more comfortable and mentioned my faith in Jesus, I found that some of those ladies opened up about their faith, as well, and the tone of our breaks seemed to change. They seemed kinder to each other and our discussions weren't focused around unproductive issues and griping.

I think Christians have the ability to be a positive influence through their example, even though it may seem insignificant at the time. This may set the foundation for spiritual growth in someone, similar to how the flour grew from a little bit of yeast.

....

This Bible passage is when Jesus walked on the water to meet the boat with the disciples on it.

> *But straight way Jesus spake unto them, saying, Be of good cheer; it is I; be not afraid. And Peter answered Him and said, Lord, if it be Thou, bid me come unto Thee on the water. And He said, Come. And when Peter was come down out of the ship, he walked on the water, to go to Jesus. But when he saw the wind boisterous, he was afraid; and beginning to sink, he cried, saying, Lord, save me. And immediately Jesus stretched forth His hand, and caught him, and said unto him, O thou of little faith, wherefore didst thou doubt? And when they were come into the ship, the wind ceased. Then they that were in the ship came and worshipped Him, saying Of a Truth Thou art the Son of God. Matthew, Chapter 14, verses 27-33.*

After God allowed me to experience the miracle of losing 75 pounds of excess weight, my church was having a garage sale. I looked at my big clothes and thought I probably should keep them in case I gained all the weight back. The thought was in my head that I wasn't trusting God to take care of me. I was virtually saying, "God I'm going to keep these big clothes just in case you don't continue to take care of my weight problem." This realization made a major difference in my life. I decided to get rid of the big clothes immediately. I definitely don't want to start sinking like Peter did when He wasn't trusting Jesus to take care of him.

Here is a related passage:

And Jesus said unto them, Because of your unbelief: for verily I say unto you, If ye have faith as a grain of mustard seed, ye shall say unto this mountain, Remove hence to yonder place; and it shall remove, and nothing shall be impossible to you. Matthew, Chapter 17, verse 20.

....

While He yet spake, behold, a bright cloud overshadowed them: and behold a Voice out of the cloud, which said, This is My beloved Son, in Whom I am well pleased: hear ye Him. And when the disciples heard it, they fell on their face, and were sore afraid. Matthew, Chapter 17, verses 5-6.

You know how famous football players and movie stars are on commercials endorsing particular products they like, so others will come to know how good they are? Well, this is an endorsement from God so the disciples of Jesus would know how good He is. His is an endorsement that defies all explanation.

It makes me wonder what God's endorsement of me would be. "This is one of my supposed followers, Dorothy. She is a 'Back Seat Driver Christian,' telling others how they should live their lives as Christians, unwilling to do the same. It would have been nice to count her as one of My flock, but she backed away from opportunities that I have given her to share her faith. So sad."

....

And Jesus called a little child unto Him, and set him in the midst of them. And said, Verily I say unto you, Except ye be converted and become as little children, ye shall not enter into the kingdom of heaven. Whosoever therefore shall humble himself as this little child, the same is greatest in the kingdom of heaven. And whoso shall receive one such little child in My Name receiveth Me. But whoso shall offend one of these little ones which believe in Me, it were better for him that a millstone were hanged about his neck, and that he were drowned in the depth of the sea. Woe unto the world because of offences! for it must needs be that offences come; but woe to that man by whom the offence cometh! Matthew, Chapter 18, verses 2-7.

Take heed that ye despise not one of these little ones; for I say unto you, That in heaven their angels do always behold the face of My Father which is in heaven. Matthew, Chapter 18, verse 10.

Usually, I interpret this passage to mean that we should have the faith of a little child in order to go to heaven. This time, this passage was saying to me that the people who abuse children physically, sexually and emotionally better beware because God doesn't want anyone hurting children under any circumstances. I noticed that there are exclamation marks used in this passage a couple of times and I don't see them used much in the Bible. I take it to mean that Jesus is emphatically telling people to beware not to harm children.

It's so sad. The court systems are full of children who have been neglected and abused in one form or another. What's even worse is that some of these children have been abused by their own family members who are supposed to love them and protect them from harm.

What can we do as Christians? We can make an effort to not become so desensitized to the needs of abused children because we see it so frequently in the news. We can support legislators to enact laws to make it more difficult for the court system to let out pedophiles, rapists and aggressive criminals. We can mentor a child who appears to need a little extra attention. Going to read or play games with children in the Women's Shelters can be beneficial, because these children need someone in their corner.

We can encourage our children to include others who appear to be loners. This helps not only the isolated child, but it teaches our children to be sensitive to the needs of others instead of being "I", "Me" focused. The list of things we could do is endless.

Here is a related passage:

Then said He unto the disciples, It is impossible but that offences will come: but woe unto him, through whom they come! It were better for him that a millstone were hanged about his neck, and he cast into the sea, than that he should offend one of these little ones. Luke, Chapter 17, verses 1-2.

....

Moreover if thy brother shall trespass against thee, go and tell him his fault between thee and him alone: if he shall hear thee, thou hast gained thy brother. But if he will not hear thee, then take with thee one or two more, that in the mouth of two or three witnesses every word may be established. And if he shall neglect to hear them, tell it unto the church: but if he neglect to hear the church, let him be unto thee as an heathen man and a publican. Verily I say unto you, Whatsoever ye shall bind on earth shall be bound in heaven: and whatsoever ye shall loose on earth shall be loosed in heaven. Matthew, Chapter 18, verses 15-18.

God doesn't want us to give up on people easily, but we are to follow a progression from approaching them privately to publicly, if necessary. First, we are to have a confidential talk with the person who is going down the wrong path. If that doesn't work, we are to get others to help. It reminds me of something that I've seen on TV where loved ones gather together for an "Intervention" to tell a drug user that they need to go through drug rehab for their sake and all those who care about them. If that doesn't work, we are to turn to the church for support to confront this person. If nothing works, we have to cut our losses, disassociating ourselves from that person so that we don't inadvertently get caught up in their lifestyle.

....

Again I say unto you, That if two of you shall agree on earth as touching any thing that they shall ask, it shall be done for them of My Father which is in heaven. For where two or three are gathered together in My Name, there am I in the midst of them. Matthew, Chapter 18, verses 19-20.

This reminds me of the saying: Two heads are better than one. Well, in this passage two people praying are better than one and it's a situation of: the more the merrier. So when I'm concerned about someone's health, I call my church's prayer chain and raise my hand during the Joys and Concerns portion of the church service.

Of course, God answers prayers in whatever way He determines is best. Sometimes it isn't always the way we had hoped things would turn out. Although it may be difficult to understand, I ultimately need to have faith in God's decisions and timing for everything.

....

Then came Peter to Him, and said, Lord how oft shall my brother sin against me, and I forgive him? till seven times? Jesus saith unto him, I say not unto thee, Until seven times: but, Until seventy times seven. Therefore is the Kingdom of heaven likened unto a certain king, which would take account of his servants. And when he had begun to reckon, one was brought unto him, which owed him ten thousand talents. But forasmuch as he had not to pay, his lord commanded him to be sold, and his wife, and children, and all that he had, and payment to be made. The servant therefore fell down, and worshipped him, saying, Lord, have patience with me, and I will pay thee all. Then the lord of that servant was moved with compassion, and loosed him and forgave him the debt. But the same servant went out, and found one of his fellowservants, which owed him an hundred pence: and he laid hands on him, and took him by the throat, saying, Pay me that thou owest. And his fellowservant fell down at this feet, and besought him, saying, Have patience with me, and I will pay thee all. And he would not: but went and cast him into prison, till he should pay the debt. So when his fellowservants saw what was done, they were very sorry, and came and told unto their lord all that was done. Then his lord, after that he had called him, said unto him, O thou wicked servant, I forgave thee all that debt, because thou desirest me. Shouldest not thou also have had compassion on thy fellowservant, even as I had pity on thee? And his lord was wroth, and delivered him to the tormentors, till he should pay all that was due unto him. So likewise shall My heavenly Father do also unto you, if ye from your hearts forgive not every one his brother his trespasses. Matthew, Chapter 18, verses 21-35.

God forgave us all our sins by sending His son, Jesus, to die for us and to arise again. Just think of all the humiliation Jesus had to go through for us. After all of that torment, Jesus asked God to forgive everyone involved in His crucifixion. I have a lot of nerve holding onto petty grudges against other people. It makes me feel like I am the first servant who is forgiven his large debt (all my sins) and I'm not showing the same forgiveness to others who have done so much less. This reminds me that I need to be more forgiving and tolerant of others because I don't want to be delivered unto the tormentors on The Last Day.

Here is a related passage:

*But I say unto you, that whosoever is angry with his brother without a cause shall be in danger of the judgment: and whosoever shall say to his brother, Raca [worthless], shall be in danger of the council: but whosoever shall say, Thou fool, shall be in danger of hell fire. Therefore if thou bring thy gift to the altar, and there rememberest that thy brother hath aught against thee: Leave there thy gift before the altar, and go thy way; first be reconciled to thy brother, and then come and offer thy gift. Matthew, Chapter 5, verses 22-24.

....

And, behold, one came and said unto Him, Good Master, what good thing shall I do, that I may have eternal life? and He said unto him. Why callest thou Me good? There is none good but One, that is, God: but if thou wilt enter into life, keep the Commandments. He saith unto Him, Which? Jesus said, Thou shalt do no murder, Thou shalt not commit adultery, Thou shalt not steal, Thou shalt not bear false witness, Honour thy father and thy mother: and, Thou shalt love thy neighbour as thyself. The young man saith unto Him, All these things have I kept from my youth up: what lack I yet? Jesus said unto him, If thou wilt be perfect, go and sell that thou hast, and give to the poor, and thou shalt have treasure in heaven: and come and follow Me. But when the young man heard that saying, he went away sorrowful: for he had great possessions. Then said Jesus unto His disciples, Verily I say unto you, That a rich man shall hardly enter into the kingdom of heaven. And again I say unto you, It is easier for a camel to go through the eye of a needle, than for a rich man to enter into the kingdom of God. When His disciples heard it, they were exceedingly amazed, saying, Who then can be saved? But Jesus beheld them, and said unto them, With men this is impossible; but with God all things are possible. Matthew, Chapter 19, verses 16-26.

Now, it can be easy to ignore this passage and think that this just doesn't pertain to me because I'm not rich. Being rich is a relative thing. (I wanted to say some corny thing about all your relatives coming around if you were rich. Forgive me, but I couldn't resist!) Don't you think those from a Third World Country would think that American's on welfare are rich? We have so much, but don't realize it when we compare ourselves to others who seem to have so much more.

I think it's about how all our stuff and the desire for more stuff, money or wealth interfere with our total focus on God. Everything we couldn't bear to put in a Salvation Army, Goodwill or other charitable bin has some control on us. Its importance has worked a very subtle wedge in our relationship with God.

I was trying to think about which things might be excluded from this. First, I thought about my toothbrush, because it seems like an essential item. Then I thought that the disciples didn't have toothbrushes when they followed Jesus. If Jesus told me I needed to follow Him and be willing to give up my toothbrush I would need to, no questions asked.

Next, I thought about my shoes, because I thought they were essential. I realize having 27-35 pairs of shoes in my closet right now for casual, work or dress wear throughout the year is highly questionable. Well, I looked in the Bible and found this passage:

And the people asked Him, saying, What shall we do then? He answereth and saith unto them, He that hath two coats, let him impart to him that hath none; and he that hath meat, let him do likewise. Luke, Chapter 3, verses 10-11.

I think this is a good rule of thumb. I don't know much about the philosophy of those who write books about simplifying your life by giving up things, but it seems this passage would support the general principal of how things become too important to us. There is no way I want the extra pairs of shoes I own to become a wedge in my relationship with God.

I was just thinking that if I could get my shoes down to one pair of tennis shoes instead of five different types, a pair of dress shoes, etc. and give the rest to a charitable organization, I would be more in-tune with what God wants for me.

Here are some related passages:

*And a certain ruler asked Him, saying, Good Master, what shall I do to inherit eternal life? And Jesus said unto him, Why callest thou Me good? none is good, save One, that is, God. Thou knowest the Commandments, Do not commit adultery, Do not kill, Do not steal, Do not bear false witness, Honour thy father and thy mother. And he said, All these have I kept from my youth up. Now when Jesus heard these things, He said unto him, Yet lackest thou one thing: sell all that thou hast, and distribute unto the poor, and thou shalt have treasure in heaven: and come, follow Me. And when he heard this, he was very sorrowful: for he was very rich. And when Jesus saw that he was very sorrowful, He said, How hardly shall they that have riches enter into the kingdom of God! And they that heard it said, Who then can be saved? And He said, The things which are impossible with men are possible with God. Luke, Chapter 18, verses 18-27.

*Trust not in oppression, and become not vain in robbery: if riches increase, set not your heart upon them. Psalm, Chapter 62, verse 10.

....

This is the reply of Jesus to the chief priests who were asking Him questions, trying to trick Him.

> *But what think ye? A certain man had two sons; and he came to the first, and said, Son go work today in my vineyard. He answered and said, I will not: but afterward he repented, and went. And he came to the second, and said likewise. And he answered and said, I go, sir: and went not. Whether of them twain did the will of his father? They say unto Him, the first, Jesus saith unto them, Verily I say unto you, That the publicans and the harlots go into the kingdom of God before you. For John came unto you in the way of righteousness, and ye believed him not: but the publicans and the harlots believed him:; and ye, when ye had seen it, repented not afterward, that ye might believe him. Matthew, Chapter 21, verses 28-32.*

Jesus makes a pretty bold statement here, saying that the commonly despised tax collectors (publicans) and the prostitutes will go to heaven, because they believed in Jesus when John the Baptist told them. I'm glad God is no respecter of status, but I'm concerned about the second brother who is a "Dragging Your Feet Christian."

When his father asks him, he spouts off (paraphrased), "Sure, I'll help you, Dad," but he never did what he promised to do. Actually, that seems worse than being honest and saying, "I'm sorry, I can't do it right now," because at least people can plan accordingly and not depend on that person to accomplish the task. I do this when I read how we're supposed to share our love for Jesus with those who might not know Him. I say, "Sure I will, God. I really love You and I want to do whatever it is that You want." Do I do it? Nope. I just plan to share my faith with others, but I'm still dragging my feet.

Well, the father in this parable forgave the son who said he wouldn't do it but changed his mind and did it after all, but that wasn't the case for the other son. I don't want God saying, "Dorothy said she'd share her faith, but did she? Yeah, she wrote this book, but she never went out of her comfort zone and really took any risks. What would have happened if Jesus never took the risks to be humiliated, crucified and rise from the grave? He went through all of that for her and she thinks she can fool Me. She says that she's only too glad to help out, but doesn't do a single thing. I've got her number!"

....

And Jesus answered and spake unto them again by parables, and said, The kingdom of heaven is like unto a certain king, which made a marriage for his son, And sent forth his servants to call them that were bidden to the wedding: and they would not come. Again, he sent forth other servants, saying, Tell them which are bidden, Behold, I have prepared my dinner: my oxen and my fatlings are killed, and all things are ready: come unto the marriage. But they made light of it, and went their ways, one to his farm, another to his merchandise: And the remnant took his servants, and entreated them spitefully, and slew them. But when the king heard thereof, he was wroth: and he sent forth his armies, and destroyed those murderers, and burned up their city. Then saith he to his servants, The wedding is ready, but they which were bidden were not worthy. Go ye therefore into the highways, and as many as ye shall find, bid to the marriage. So those servants went out into the highways, and gathered together all as many as they found, both bad and good: and the wedding was furnished with guests. And when the king came in to see the guests, he saw there a man which had not on a wedding garment: And he saith unto him, Friend, how camest thou in hither not having a wedding garment? And he was speechless. Then said the king to the servants, Bind him hand and foot, and take him away, and cast him into the outer darkness; there shall be weeping and gnashing of teeth. For many are called, but few are chosen. Matthew, Chapter 22, verses 1-14.

    I guess I'm on a party theme. This passage is about a wedding, but when I went to explain this, the thought in my mind is to compare it to a surprise birthday party for your boss.

    This is a black tie affair and you've sent out invitations to all your co-workers, asking them to R.S.V.P. It's several days before the party, but only a few people have called to say they are coming. You have reserved this big banquet hall and have paid for the caterers. Getting nervous, you call the people who haven't responded. Well, you get one lame excuse after another. You overhear a couple of co-workers in the restroom saying that they are going to a golf tournament that day, but they told you they had a sick family member. You decide very quickly that you can do without friends like that, but your boss will be embarrassed if the banquet hall is almost empty. You don't want him to be humiliated, so you think of a plan, fast!

You decide to go invite the people who work in the stock room and the mail room. They hardly ever interact with your boss, but it's better than having an empty banquet hall. You give them the invitations, with directions to the banquet hall and busy yourself with all the last minute preparations. Now you can relax, because you know the banquet hall will be full of people. You start to realize that these lower status people are more dependable and more deserving than your so-called friends who gave you lame excuses.

On the day of the surprise party you welcome all the loyal stock room and mail room workers. You thank them for coming and tell them where to hide to surprise the boss. Just then, some guy comes in dressed in khaki shorts and a Polo shirt. You ask him what he could have been thinking about when he decided to come dressed like that. You tell him to leave, because he's not welcome at this black tie affair. Those who put some effort in and did what they were supposed to were welcome regardless of their financial or social standing. You don't want a freeloader who doesn't even put the effort into properly getting ready for the party.

Well, sometimes I'm a "Freeloader Christian," too. Jesus asks all of us to put some effort into being one of His chosen few. He even gave His own life for us, so we could be invited to His party in heaven on the Last Day. Otherwise, we wouldn't have qualified for an invitation of that magnitude. Some of us will do our part, although we can never truly earn admission to such a swanky affair. Jesus did that for us. We have a free ride on His coat tails, provided we aren't being an ungrateful freeloader.

Well, Jesus calls each and every one of us, but how many of us come up with reasons why we can't go to church, why we are too busy to pray or too embarrassed to let others know that we are Christian? Well, if we don't respond when He calls us, He will invite others to take our place in Heaven with Him. That's not what I want!

Here is a related passage:

> *Then said He unto him, A certain man made a great supper, and bade many: And sent his servant at supper time to say to them that were bidden, Come; for all things are now ready. And they all with one consent began to make excuse. The first said unto him, I have bought a piece of ground, and I must needs go and see it: I pray thee have me excused. And another said, I have bought five yoke of oxen, and I go to prove them: I pray thee have me excused. And another said, I have married a wife, and therefore I cannot come. So that servant came, and showed his lord these things. Then the master of the house being angry said to his servant, Go out quickly into the streets and*

lanes of the city, and bring in hither the poor, and the maimed, and the halt, and the blind. And the servant said, Lord, it is done as you hast commanded, and yet there is room. And the lord said unto the servant, Go out unto the highways and hedges, and compel them to come in, that my house may be filled. For I say unto you, That none of those men which were bidden shall taste of my supper. Luke, Chapter 14, verses 16-24.

....

But be not ye called Rabbi: for One is your Master, even Christ; and all ye are brethren. And call no man your father upon the earth: for One is your Father, which is in heaven. Neither be ye called masters: for One is your Master, even Christ. Matthew, Chapter 23, verse 8-10.

God wants us to hold Him in highest regard and no other.

....

Woe unto you, scribes and Pharisees, hypocrites! for ye pay tithe of mint and anise and cummin, and have omitted the weightier matters of the law, judgment, mercy, and faith: these ought ye to have done, and not to leave the other undone. Matthew, Chapter 23, verse 23.

Of course we don't give spices when they pass the offering plate around at church. This passage reminds me of some who put large sums of money in as an indicator of their faith in God, yet their daily actions show quite the opposite. Outside of church, they may be critical and judgmental of others, not generous to those less fortunate or unforgiving of others. The thing that matters to God is how we live our lives as examples of His positive influence on us, not how much we put in the offering plate.

Here are some related passages:

*Woe unto you, scribes and Pharisees, hypocrites! For ye make clean the outside of the cup and of the platter, but within they are full of extortion and excess. Thou blind Pharisee, cleanse first that which is within the cup and platter, that the outside of them may be clean also. Matthew, Chapter 23, verses 25-26.

*Woe unto you, scribes and Pharisees, hypocrites! for ye are like unto whited sepulchres, which indeed appear beautiful outward, but are within full of dead men's bones, and of all uncleanness. Even so ye also outwardly appear righteous unto men, but within ye are full of hypocrisy and iniquity. Matthew, Chapter 23, verses 27-28.

*Woe unto you, scribes and Pharisees, hypocrites!
Because ye build the tombs of the prophets, and garnish the
sepulchres of the righteous, And say, If we had been in the days
of our fathers, we would not have been partakers with them in
the blood of the prophets. Matthew, Chapter 23, verses 29-30.*

....

*And many false prophets shall rise, and deceive many.
And because iniquity shall abound, the love of many shall wax
cold. But he that shall endure unto the end, the same shall be
saved. And this Gospel of the kingdom shall be preached in all
the world for a witness unto all nations; and then shall the end
come. Matthew, Chapter 24, verses 11-14.*

Many will try to entice us to believe things that won't lead us to Salvation. They will encourage us to belong to churches that sound like they follow God's Will, but really misconstrue what is said in the Bible. God doesn't want us to be taken in by these people, but wants us to continue to share His Word with others.

Here are some related passages:

**Then if any man shall say unto you, Lo, here is the
Christ, or there; believe it not. For there shall arise false
Christs, and false prophets, and shall show great signs and
wonders; insomuch that, if it were possible, they shall deceive
the very elect. Behold, I have told you before, Wherefore if they
shall say unto you, Behold, he is in the desert; go not forth:
behold, he is in the secret chambers; believe it not. Matthew,
Chapter 24, verses 23-26.*

**But evil men and seducers shall wax worse and worse,
deceiving, and being deceived. But continue thou in the things
which thou hast learned and hast been assured of, knowing
of whom thou hast learned them; And that from a child thou
hast known the Holy Scriptures, which are able to make thee
wise unto Salvation through faith which is in Christ Jesus.
All Scripture is given by inspiration of God, and is profitable
for doctrine, for reproof, for correction, for instruction in
righteousness. 2 Timothy, Chapter 3, verses 13-16.*

**BUT THERE were false prophets also among the
people, even as there shall be false teachers among you who
privily shall bring in damnable heresies, even denying the Lord
that brought them, and bring upon themselves swift destruction.*

And many shall follow their pernicious ways; by reason of whom the Way Of Truth shall be evil spoken of. And through covetousness shall they with feigned words make merchandise of you: whose judgment now of a long time lingereth not, and their damnation slumbereth not. 2 Peter, Chapter 2, verses 1-3.

*Then said the prophet Jeremiah unto Hananiah the prophet, Hear now, Hananiah; The LORD hath not sent thee; but thou makest this people to trust in a lie. Therefore thus saith the LORD; Behold, I will cast thee from off the face of the earth; this year thou shalt die, because thou hast taught rebellion against the LORD. So Hananiah the prophet died the same year in the seventh month. Jeremiah, Chapter 28, verses 15-17.

*And Zephaniah the priest read this letter in the ears of Jeremiah the prophet. Then came the Word of the LORD unto Jeremiah, saying, Send to all them of the captivity, saying, Thus saith the LORD concerning Shemaiah the Nehelamite; Because that Shemaiah hath prophesied unto you, and I sent him not, and he caused you to trust in a lie: Therefore thus saith the LORD; Behold, I will punish Shemaiah the Nehelamite, and his seed: he shall not have a man to dwell among his people: neither shall he behold the good that I will do for My people, saith the LORD; because he hath taught rebellion against the LORD. Jeremiah, Chapter 29, verses 29-32.

....

When the Son of Man shall come in His glory, and all the holy angels with Him, then shall He sit upon the throne of His glory: And before Him shall be gathered all nations: and He shall separate them one from another, as a Shepherd divideth His sheep from the goats: And He shall set the sheep on His right Hand, but the goats on the left. Then shall the King say unto them on His right Hand, Come ye blessed of My Father, inherit the kingdom prepared for you from the foundation of the world: For I was an hungered, and ye gave Me drink: I was a stranger, and ye took Me in: Naked, and ye clothed Me: I was sick, and ye visited Me: I was in prison, and ye came unto Me. Then shall the righteous answer Him, saying, Lord, when saw we Thee an hungered, and fed Thee? or thirsty, and gave Thee drink? When saw we Thee a stranger, and took, Thee in? or naked, and clothed Thee? Or when saw we Thee sick, or in prison, and came unto Thee? And the King shall answer and say unto them, Verily I say unto you, Inasmuch as ye have done it unto one of the least of these My brethren, ye have done it unto Me. Then shall He say also unto them on the left hand, Depart from Me, ye cursed, into everlasting fire, prepared for the devil and his angels: For I was hungered, and ye gave Me no meat: I was thirsty, and ye gave Me no drink: I was a stranger, and ye took Me not in: naked, and ye clothed Me not: sick, and in prison, and ye visited Me not. Then shall they also answer Him, saying, Lord when saw we Thee an hungered, or athirst, or a stranger, or naked, or sick, or in prison, and did not minister unto Thee? Then shall He answer them, saying, Verily I say unto you, Inasmuch as ye did it not to one of the least of these, ye did it not to Me. And these shall go away into everlasting punishment, but the righteous into life eternal. Matthew, Chapter 25, verses 31-46.

We aren't just supposed to say, "I am a Christian so I will have Salvation regardless of my actions." There is a passage in Romans that talks about whether we are saved by our works alone, which is definitely not going to happen.

Neither yield ye your members as instruments of unrighteousness to sin: but yield yourselves unto God as being alive from the dead, and your members as instruments of righteousness to God. For sin shall not have dominion over you: for ye are not under the Law, but under grace. What then? shall we sin, because we are not under the Law, but under grace? God forbid! Romans, Chapter 6, verses 13-15.

We are to be examples of how God works in our lives, not just to those we consider worthy of our attention. We are to include those who are down and out and those that society deems as unworthy.

....

And the angel answered and said unto the women, Fear not ye: for I know that ye seek Jesus, which was crucified. He is not here: for He is risen, as He said. Come see the place where the Lord lay. And go quickly, and tell His disciples that He is risen from the dead; and, behold, He goeth before you into Galilee; there shall ye see Him: lo, I have told you. And they departed quickly from the sepulchre with fear and great joy; and did run to bring His disciples word. Matthew, Chapter 28, verses 5-8.

A little bit ago, I was reading the part of the Bible that makes me the saddest, where they spit on Jesus and mock Him when He's preparing to give His life for our sins…even for those that treated Him so terribly. Now, I'm reading this part which makes me exceedingly happy. I get goose bumps thinking of how amazing it must have been to be there when Jesus had arisen just as He had told them, such wonderful news that defies all explanation!

....

Then He taught them many things by parables, and said to them in His doctrine: Hearken: Behold, there went out a sower to sow. And it came to pass, as he sowed, some fell by the way side, and the fowls of the air came and devoured it up. And some fell on stony ground, where it had not much earth; and immediately it sprang up, because it had no depth of earth: But when the sun was up, it was scorched; and because it had no root, it withered away. And some fell among thorns, and the thorns grew up and choked it, and it yielded no fruit. And other fell on good ground, and did yield fruit that sprang up and increased; and brought forth, some thirty, and some sixty, and some an hundred. And He said unto them, He that hath ears to hear, let him hear. Mark Chapter 4, verses 2- 9.

And He said unto them, Know ye not this parable? and how then will ye know all parables? The sower soweth the Word. And these are they by the way side, where the Word is sown; but when they have heard, Satan cometh immediately, and taketh away the Word that was sown in their hearts. And these are they likewise which are sown on stony ground; who when they have heard the Word, immediately receive it with gladness; And have no root in themselves, and so endure but for a time: afterward, when affliction or persecution ariseth for the Word's sake immediately they are offended. And these are they which are sown among thorns; such as hear the Word, And the cares of this world, and the deceitfulness of riches, and the lusts of other things entering in, choke the Word, and it becometh unfruitful. And these are they which are sown on good ground; such as hear the Word, and receive it, and bring forth fruit, some thirtyfold, some sixty, and some an hundred. And He said unto them, Is a candle brought to be put under a bushel, or under a bed? and not to be set on a candlestick? For there is nothing hid which shall not be manifested; neither was any thing kept secret, but that it should come abroad. If any man have ears to hear, let him hear. Mark, Chapter 4, verses 13-23.

Since many who hear the message of Salvation, start out well-intentioned but are led astray, it's important for me to not take my faith for granted. It's something that needs to be an integral part of my everyday life. I should live my faith outwardly and develop it further so I don't become vulnerable to the influences of others and the world.

Here are some related passages:

*And He spake many things unto them in parables, saying, Behold, a sower went forth to sow; And when he sowed, some seeds fell by the way side, and the fowls came and devoured them up: Some fell upon stony places, where they had not much earth: and forthwith they sprung up, because they had no deepness of earth: and when the sun was up, they were scorched; and because they had no root, they withered away. And some fell among thorns; and the thorns sprung up, and choked them: But other fell into good ground, and brought forth fruit, some an hundredfold, some sixtyfold, some thirtyfold. Who hath ears to hear, let him hear. Matthew, Chapter 13, verses 3-9.

*Hear ye therefore the parable of the sower. When any one heareth the Word of the kingdom, and understandeth it not, then cometh the wicked one, and catcheth away that which was sown in this heart. This is he which received seed by the way side. But he that received the seed into stony places, the same is he that heareth the Word, anon with joy receiveth it; Yet hath he not root in himself, but dureth for a while: for when tribulation or persecution ariseth because of the Word, by and by he is offended. He also that received seed among the thorns is he that heareth the Word; and the care of this world, and the deceitfulness of riches, choke the Word, and he becometh unfruitful. But he that received seed into the good ground is he that heareth the Word, and understandeth it; which also beareth fruit, and bringeth forth, some an hundredfold, some sixty, some thirty. Matthew, Chapter 13, verses 18-23.

....

> *He answered and said unto them, Give ye them to eat. And they say unto Him, Shall we go and buy two hundred penny worth of bread, and give them to eat? He saith unto them, How many loaves have ye? Go and see. And when they knew, they say, Five, and two fishes. And He commanded them to make all sit down by companies upon the green grass. And they sat down in ranks, by hundreds, and by fifties. And when He had taken the five loaves and the two fishes, He looked up to heaven, and blessed, and brake the loaves, and gave them to His disciples to set before them: and the two fishes divided He among them all. And they did all eat, and were filled. And they took up twelve baskets full of the fragments, and of the fishes. And they that did eat of the loaves were about five thousand men. Mark, Chapter 6, verses 37-44.*

I had always enjoyed reading about this miracle that Jesus did, but I was really surprised when I was reading the Bible and found there was another time Jesus fed the multitudes. At first, I thought it was a different disciple telling about the loaves and fishes and was just off on some of the basic facts a little. Then after reading the Bible many times, I realized it was Mark who told about the first feeding of the five thousand and he was the same one who told about the feeding of four thousand. These were two different, but similar miracles that Jesus did.

> *In those days the multitude being very great, and having nothing to eat, Jesus called His disciples unto Him, and saith unto them, I have compassion on the multitude, because they have now been with Me three days, and have nothing to eat: And if I send them away fasting to their own houses, they will faint by the way: for divers of them came from far. And His disciples answered Him, From whence can a man satisfy these men with bread here in the wilderness? And He asked them, How many loaves have ye? And they said, Seven. And He commanded the people to sit down on the ground: and He took the seven loaves, and gave thanks, and brake, and gave to His disciples to set before them; and they did set them before the people. And they had a few small fishes and He blessed, and commanded to set them also before them. So they did eat, and were filled, and they took up of the broken meat that was left seven baskets. And they that had eaten were about four thousand: and He sent them away. Mark, Chapter 8, verses 1-9.*

This amazed me, but I still figured I must be mistaken. This next passage, also written by Mark, puts the whole thing together.

And He left them, and entering into the ship again departed to the other side. Now the disciples had forgotten to take bread, neither had they in the ship with them more than one loaf. And He charged them saying, Take heed, beware of the leaven of the Pharisees, and of the leaven of Herod. And they reasoned among themselves, saying, It is because we have no bread. And when Jesus knew it. He saith unto them, Why reason ye, because ye have no bread? Perceive ye not yet, neither understand? Have ye your heart yet hardened? Having eyes, see ye not? And having ears, hear ye not? And do ye not remember? When I brake the five loaves among five thousand, how many baskets full of fragments took ye up? They say unto Him, Twelve. And when the seven among four thousand, how many baskets full of fragments took ye up? And they say Seven. And He said unto them, How is it that ye do not understand? Mark, Chapter 8, verses 13-21.

I know, I know! This may not be the most profound religious experience you have ever had. I just thought it was interesting to know that there were two totally different times that Jesus provided food for the multitudes and Mark told about both of them. It influenced me to start reading more in-depth to not miss the details. Then, Jesus refers to both miracles when He asks His Disciples why they were so worried about having enough food; didn't they remember the two recent miracles He had done in their midst?

I guess the lesson I would get out of all of this is to remember that God does so much for me. He provides for my every need. He gets me through all types of situations. Now, do I remember these things when I'm faced with uncertainty? Nope! Just like the disciples, I'm too quick to fret and worry about things, forgetting God will provide for all my needs and take care of me, if I let Him.

Here are some related passages:

*When Jesus then lifted up His Eyes, and saw a great company come unto Him, He saith unto Phillip, whence shall we buy bread, that these may eat? And this He said to prove Him: for He Himself knew what He would do. Philip answered Him, Two hundred pennyworth of bread is not sufficient for them, that every one of them may take a little. One of His disciples, Andrew, Simon Peter's brother, saith unto Him, There is a lad here, which hath five barley loaves, and two small fishes: but what are they among so many? And Jesus said, Make the men sit down. Now there was much grass in the place, So the men sat

down, in number about five thousand. And Jesus took the loaves; and when He had given thanks, He distributed to the disciples, and the disciples to them that were set down; and likewise of the fishes as much as they would. When they were filled, He said unto His disciples, Gather up the fragments that remain, that nothing be lost. Therefore they gathered them together, and filled twelve baskets with the fragments of the five barley loaves, which remained over and above unto them that had eaten. Then those men, when they had seen the miracle that Jesus did, said, This is of a Truth that Prophet that should come unto the world. *John, Chapter 6, verses 5-14.*

*Then Jesus said unto them, Take heed and beware of the leaven of the Pharisees and the Sadducees. And they reasoned among themselves, saying, It is because we have taken no bread. Which when Jesus perceived, He said unto them, O ye of little faith, why reason ye among yourselves because ye have brought no bread? Do ye not yet understand, neither remember the five loaves of the five thousand, and how many baskets ye took up? Neither the seven loaves of the four thousand, and how many baskets ye took up? How is it that ye do not understand that I spake it not to you concerning bread, that ye should beware of the leaven of the Pharisees and of the Sadducees? Then understood they how that He bade them not beware of the leaven of bread, but of the doctrine of the Pharisees and of the Sadducees. *Matthew, Chapter 16, verses 6-12.*

....

And they come to Jerusalem: and Jesus went into the temple, and began to cast out them that sold and bought in the temple, and overthrew the tables of the moneychangers, and the seats of them that sold doves; And would not suffer that any man should carry any vessel through the temple. And He taught, saying unto them, Is it not written, My house shall be called of all nations the house of prayer? but ye have made it a den of thieves. *Mark, Chapter 11, verses 15-17.*

I think this passage shows a time where even Jesus says through His actions, "Enough Is Enough!" It really got me thinking. Generally, I hide behind my Christian faith to justify my passive interactions. In this instance, Jesus didn't handle the situation in a passive manner. It leads me to believe there are times that stronger actions are needed to get the point across! Anything less than that would be condoning the inappropriate behavior or situation.

This reminds me of a Cultural Diversity training my husband arranged for co-workers. They were talking about being in a situation where someone is putting down others whether for racial, gender, sexual reasons or otherwise. They said to just stand there and not say anything is the same as participating in the put-downs, because our lack of action condones that behavior. They said people should actually take a stand and tell the ones making the rude comments that we find them objectionable and would prefer that they discontinue them immediately.

Now, the passive side of me that doesn't want to stand out in a crowd has to come to terms with this one. Not only am I drawing attention to myself, I am also risking the possibility that someone may get angry with me or disapprove of my opinion. Jesus took an active stand on an important issue and I think that I need to work on being able to confront people who are belittling others, despite my insecurities. Jesus didn't stop and think, "Now, if I tell them to quit selling all their wares in the church, they may be angry with Me. Maybe I shouldn't risk this because they might not like Me anymore." He took action because He knew it was wrong! I need to take action because I know belittling others is wrong!

Here are some related passages:

And Jesus went into the temple of God, and cast out all them that sold and bought in the temple, and overthrew the tables of the moneychangers, and the seats of them that sold doves, And said unto them, It is written, My house shalt be called the house of prayer; but ye have made it a den of thieves. Matthew, Chapter 21, verses 12-13.

And He went into the temple, and began to cast out them that sold therein, and them that bought; Saying unto them, It is written, My house is the house of prayer: but ye have made it a den of thieves. Luke, Chapter 19, verses 45-46.

And the Jew's passover was at hand, and Jesus went up to Jerusalem, And found in the temple those that sold oxen and sheep and doves, and the changers of money sitting: And when He had made a scourge of small cords, He drove them all out of the temple, and the sheep, and the oxen; and poured out the changers' money, and overthrew the tables; And said unto them that sold doves, Take these things hence; make not My Father's house an house of merchandise. And His disciples remembered that it was written, The zeal of Thine house hath eaten Me up. John, Chapter 2, verses 13-17.

> *And Jesus, answering saith unto them, Have faith in God. For verily I say unto you, That whosoever shall say unto this mountain, Be thou removed, and be thou cast into the sea; and shall not doubt in his heart, but shall believe that those things which he saith shall come to pass; he shall have whatsoever he saith. Therefore I say unto you, What things soever ye desire, when ye pray, believe that ye receive them, and ye shall have them. Mark, Chapter 11, verses 22-24.*

This reminds me of how I ask God to take care of me, but I'm really establishing a plan in my mind of how to handle the situation or I'm continuing to worry about it. It's like I'm saying, "God, I want You to handle this situation but just in case You don't take care of me, I will have a 'Plan B' ready or worry until it's resolved." It's just like telling God I don't really trust Him to take care of me. I need to be much more aware of displaying total trust in God to take care of my needs, concerns and my family.

Here are some related passages:

> **If any of you lack wisdom, let him ask of God, that giveth to all men liberally, and upbraideth not; and it shall be given him. But let him ask in faith, nothing wavering. For he that wavereth is like a wave of the sea driven with the wind and tossed. James, Chapter 1, verses 5-6.*

> **Jesus answered and said unto them, Verily I say unto you, If ye have faith, and doubt not, ye shall not only do this which is done to the fig tree, but also if ye shall say unto this mountain, Be thou removed, and be thou cast into the sea; It shall be done. And all things, whatsoever ye shall ask in prayer, believing, ye shall receive. Matthew, Chapter 21, verses 21-22.*

> **And I say unto you, Ask, and it shall be given you; seek, and ye shall find; knock, and it shall be opened unto you. For every one that asketh receiveth; and he that seeketh findeth; and to him that knocketh it shall be opened. If a son shall ask bread of any of you that is a father, will he give him a stone? or if he ask a fish, will he for a fish give him a serpent? Or if he shall ask an egg, will he offer him a scorpion? If ye then, being evil know how to give good gifts unto your children: how much more shall your heavenly Father give the Holy Spirit to them that ask Him? Luke, Chapter 11, verses 9-13.*

Ask, and it shall be given you; seek, and ye shall find; knock, and it shall be opened unto you: For every one that asketh receiveth; and he that seeketh findeth: and to him that knocketh it shall be opened. Or what man is there of you whom if his son ask bread, will he give him a stone? Or if he ask a fish, will he give him a serpent? If ye then, being evil, know how to give good gifts unto your children, how much more shall your Father which is in heaven give good things to them that ask Him? Matthew, Chapter 7, verses 7-11.

And they shall no more be a prey to the heathen, neither shall the beast of the land devour them; but they shall dwell safely, and none shall make them afraid. And I will raise up for them a plant of renown, and they shall be no more consumed with hunger in the land, neither bear the shame of the heathen any more. Thus shall they know that I the LORD their God am with them, and that they, even the house of Israel, are My people, saith the Lord GOD. And ye My flock, the flock of MY pasture, are men, and I am your God, saith the Lord GOD. Ezekiel, Chapter 34, verses 28-31.

....

And when ye stand praying, forgive, if ye have aught against any: that your Father also which is in heaven may forgive your trespasses. But if ye do not forgive, neither will your Father which is in heaven forgive your trespasses. Mark, Chapter 11, verses 25-26.

This passage makes me think I'm a "Hold Grudges Against Others Christian," because I remember insensitive or hurtful things people have done to me. God doesn't want me to hold onto these feelings. I'm sure I have done my share of insensitive and hurtful things to others in my life. I sure don't want to be judged by God with the same harsh standards that I impose on others.

....

Master, Moses wrote unto us, If a man's brother die, and leave his wife behind him, and leave no children, that his brother should take his wife, and raise up seed unto his brother. Now there were seven brethren: and the first took a wife, and dying left no seed. And the second took her, and died, neither left he any seed: and the third likewise. And the seven had her, and left no seed: last of all the woman died also. In the resurrection therefore, when they shall rise, whose wife shall she

> be of them? for the seven had her to wife. And Jesus answering said unto them, Do ye not therefore err, because ye know not the Scriptures, neither the power of God? For when they shall rise from the dead, they neither marry, nor are given in marriage; but are as the angels which are in heaven. Mark, Chapter 12, verses 19-25.

This was really interesting to me, especially because I have remarried and my first husband was not a very nice person. This is a relief, because now I know we won't be in heaven joined with our past or present spouses.

Here is a related passage:

> *Then came to Him certain of the Sadducees, which deny that there is any resurrection; and they asked Him, Saying, Master, Moses wrote unto us, If any man's brother die, having a wife, and he die without children, that his brother should take his wife, and raise up seed unto his brother. There were therefore seven brethren: and the first took a wife, and died without children. And the second took her to wife, and he died childless. And the third took her; and in like manner the seven also: and they left no children, and died. Last of all the woman died also. Therefore in the resurrection whose wife of them is she? for seven had her to wife. And Jesus answering said unto them, The children of this world marry, and are given in marriage: But they which shall be accounted worthy to obtain that world, and the resurrection from the dead, neither marry, nor are given in marriage: Neither can they die any more: for they are equal unto the angels; and are the children of God, being the children of the resurrection. Now that the dead are raised, even Moses showed at the bush, when he calleth the Lord the God of Abraham, and the God of Isaac, and the God of Jacob. For He is not a God of the dead, but of the living: for all live unto Him. Then certain of the scribes answering said, Master, Thou hast well said. Luke, Chapter 20, verses 27-39.

. . . .

> And as touching the dead, that they rise: have ye not read in the book of Moses, how in the bush God spake unto him, saying, I am the God of Abraham, and the God of Isaac, and the God of Jacob? He is not the God of the dead, but the God of the living: ye therefore do greatly err. Mark, Chapter 12, verses 26-27.

This passage causes me to refocus my thinking. Once I'm dead there isn't anything I can do to earn Salvation. Rather than focus on what it's going to be like in heaven, I need to focus on how my life reflects my belief in God, right now, here on Earth so I get to heaven.

....

And one of the scribes came, and having heard them reasoning together, and perceiving that He had answered them well, asked Him, Which is the first Commandment of all? And Jesus answered him, The first of all the Commandments is: Hear, O Israel; The Lord our God, is one Lord: And thou shalt love the Lord thy God with all thy heart, and with all thy soul, and with all thy mind, and with all thy strength: this is the first Commandment. And the second is like, namely this, Thou shalt love thy neighbor as thyself. There is none other Commandment greater than these. Mark, Chapter 12, verses 28-31.

I'm reminded that I can't be a "Just When It's Convenient Christian." I'm to make my faith a priority. God wants me to treat others nicely, even if...Even if they are rude to me...Even if they get the job I wanted...Even if they have more money than I do and didn't deserve it...Even if they take advantage of me...Even if they are hateful...Even if they talk down to me...Even if they make really poor lifestyle choices...Even if they cut in front of me on the freeway...Even if they don't believe the way I do...Even if they are a telemarketer and don't let me off the phone when I want to get off. (I really have to work on this one!) If I get caught up in being resentful, rude or hateful, I'm not being the example that God wants me to be of how He works in my life.

Here is a related passage:

*Then one of them, which was a lawyer, asked Him a question, tempting Him, and saying, Master, which is the great Commandment in the Law? Jesus said unto him, Thou shalt love the Lord thy God with all thy heart, and with all thy soul, and with all thy mind. This is the first and great Commandment. And the second is like unto it, Thou shalt love thy neighbour as thyself. On these two Commandments hang all the Law and the prophets. Matthew, Chapter 22, verses.35-40.

....

And He said unto them in His Doctrine, Beware of the scribes, which love to go in long clothing, and love salutations in the marketplaces, And the chief seats in the synagogues, and the uppermost rooms at feasts: Which devour widows' houses, and for a pretence make long prayers: these shall receive greater damnation. Mark, Chapter 12, verses 38-40.

This reinforces that God wants us to live our faith. We are to be good examples of this faith in all that we do, not just at church by doing showy things so others think we are righteous. Our faith in God should be something that is an integral part of our daily lives, tempered with discreetness and humility.

Here is a related passage:

*Then spake Jesus to the multitude, and to His disciples, Saying, The scribes and the Pharisees sit in Moses' seat: All therefore whatsoever they bid you observe, that observe and do; but do not ye after their works: for they say, and do not. For they bind heavy burdens and grievous to be borne, and lay them on men's shoulders; but they themselves will not move them with one of their fingers. But all their works they do for to be seen of men: they make broad their phylacteries, and enlarge the borders of their garments, And love the uppermost rooms at feasts, and the chief seats in the synagogues. Matthew, Chapter 23, verses 1-6.

....

And Jesus sat over against the treasury, and beheld how the people cast money into the treasury: and many that were rich cast in much. And there came a certain poor widow, and she threw in two mites, which make a farthing. and He called unto Him His disciples, and saith unto them, Verily I say unto you, That this poor widow hath cast more in, than all they which have cast into the treasury: For all they did cast in out of their abundance; but she of her want did cast in all that she had, even all her living. Mark, Chapter 12, verses 41-44.

I get very self-righteous thinking about how I do nice things for people and donate to the needy. I was on a work mission with our church's youth group in Juarez, Mexico. Someone in the group told us how they were going to leave behind their clothes to donate to the people of that community. I thought about it awhile and decided it was a nice thing to do. So, I looked at things I didn't mind donating. Basically, they were the things more worn and less desirable. Then this passage flashed back in my mind, and I realized I was only giving to others out of my excess where it still felt comfortable. I was not giving to others out of my need. It took me a long time and a lot of prayer with God as I agonized over this-mostly because my favorite nightgown was in my suitcase.

If I had just left a few things to donate to the people of the community, no one would have been the wiser. If I had donated everything I owned except my favorite nightgown, no one would have even known, but God and I knew. The thing that bothered me the most was how long it took before I was finally willing to leave all my things for the needy. It showed me how worldly I had become. That certain possessions mattered to me, appalled me, because I had always prided myself in being a "Good Christian."

Obviously, we can fool ourselves. I'm so thankful that God provided this opportunity for personal growth. I still find it easier to give to others out of the excesses of my time, money and possessions. I have to be reminded that I'm not truly giving until I give out of my need, or at least closer to it.

Here are some related passages:

*And He looked up, and saw the rich men casting their gifts into the treasury. And He saw also a certain poor widow casting in thither two mites. And He said, Of a Truth I say unto you, that this poor widow hath cast in more than they all: For all these have of their abundance cast in unto the offerings of God: but she of her penury hath cast in all the living that she had. Luke, Chapter 21, verses 1-4.

*But this I say, He which soweth sparingly shall reap also sparingly; and he which soweth bountifully shall reap also bountifully. Every man according as he purposeth in his heart, so let him give; not grudgingly, or of necessity; for God loveth a cheerful giver. And God is able to make all grace abound toward you; that ye, always having all sufficiency in all things, may abound to every good work. 2 Corinthians, Chapter 9, verses 6-8.

*And above all things have fervent charity among yourselves: for charity shall cover the multitude of sins. Use hospitality one to another without grudging. 1 Peter, Chapter 4, verses 8-9.

*For the poor shall never cease out of the land: therefore I command thee, saying Thou shalt open thine hand wide unto thy brother, to thy poor, and to thy needy, in thy land. Deuteronomy, Chapter 15, verse 11.

*He that giveth unto the poor shall not lack: but he that hideth his eyes shall have many a curse. Proverbs, Chapter 28, verse 27.

....

> *And she brought forth her firstborn Son, and wrapped*
> *Him in swaddling clothes, and laid Him in a manger: because*
> *there was no room for them in the inn. Luke, Chapter 2, verse 7.*

Royalty usually are shown living in castles or expensive mansions. I think it's difficult for today's royalty to move around without lots of Paparazzi following them everywhere. It's to the point that they can't even go for a walk without people snapping their picture. Customers buy up these magazines, because they are in awe of royalty or celebrities, of one kind or another.

Jesus came into this world in very humble surroundings. There was no fanfare or notoriety, unless you figure an angel notifying the shepherds and a star guiding the wise men, fits into this category. Jesus lived a humble life. He didn't live in a castle with great wealth and servants even though He could have chosen to. In fact, He didn't even own property.

> *And Jesus saith unto him, The foxes have holes, and the*
> *birds of the air have nests; but the Son of Man hath not where to*
> *lay His head. Matthew, Chapter 8, verse 20.*

He could have chosen to lead the good life, but chose poverty and persecution for me. Do I deserve it? No way! Nothing I ever do will be anything close to earning all that Jesus went though on my behalf. The only thing I can do is make sure that I'm not just a "Holiday Christian," only focusing on God or only attending church on religious holidays. The only way I can thank Him is by trying to live my life as an example, so others can come to know Him as I do.

....

> *Take ye heed, watch and pray: for ye know not when the*
> *time is. For the Son of Man is as a man taking a far journey,*
> *who left his house, and gave authority to his servants, and to*
> *every man his work, and commanded the porter to watch. Watch*
> *ye therefore: for ye know not when the master of the house*
> *cometh, at even, or at midnight, or at the cockcrowing, or in the*
> *morning: Lest coming suddenly he find you sleeping. And what*
> *I say unto you I say unto all, Watch. Mark 13, verses 33-37.*
> *There is a similar passage in Luke, Chapter 12, verses 42-47.*

This passage helps me realize that I'm supposed to live the life God wants, all the time. I could have a more self-involved attitude where

I wanted to be worldly now, focusing my time and attention on earning the most I could, attending all-night parties, living life in the fast lane, with heavy drinking and recreational drugs. Thinking I could focus my attention on my faith later on in life.

I might not ever get a second chance to do that. I could be in an accident five minutes from now or the world could end. Who knows? Only God does and I may never get another chance to turn my life around.

Do you think the owner will continue to employ the servant who fell asleep while he was supposed to guard the owner's home? I doubt it. Well, God wants us to live the life of a Christian all the time, not sometime later, when we feel like settling down a little more. That time may never come.

This is in no way meant to imply people who have lived their lives in the fast lane can't go to heaven. The operative word is "lived." This means the person has made a choice to change their life around because of their faith in Jesus and start living the life of a Christian. None of us knows when God is going to come for us, so we can't put off these choices indefinitely. We need to put a lot of prayerful thought into whether we think God would be pleased with the life we are leading?

Here are some related passages:

*Heaven and earth shall pass away, but My Words shall not pass away. But of that day and hour knoweth no man, no, not even the angels of heaven, but My Father only. Matthew 24, verses 35-36.

*Watch therefore: for ye know not what hour your Lord doth come. But know this, that if the goodman of the house had known in what watch the thief would come, he would have watched, and would not have suffered his house to be broken up. Therefore be ye also ready: for in such an hour as ye think not the Son of Man cometh. Who then is a faithful and wise servant, whom his lord hath made ruler over his household, to give them meat in due season? Blessed is that servant, whom his lord when he cometh shall find so doing. Verily I say unto you, That he shall make him ruler over all his goods. But and if that evil servant shall say in his heart, My lord delayeth his coming; And shall begin to smite his fellowservants, and to eat and drink with the drunken; The lord of that servant shall come in a day when he looketh not for him, and in an hour that he is not aware of, And shall cut him asunder, and appoint him his portion with the hypocrites: there shall be weeping and gnashing of teeth. Matthew, Chapter 24, verses 42-51.

Watch therefore, for you know neither the day nor the hour wherein the Son of Man cometh. Matthew, Chapter 25, verse 13.

Let your loins be girded about, and your lights burning; And ye yourselves like unto men that wait for their lord, when he will return from the wedding; that when he cometh and knocketh, they may open unto him immediately. Blessed are those servants, whom the lord when he cometh shall find watching: verily I say unto you, that he shall gird himself, and make them to sit down to meat, and will come forth and serve them. And if he shall come in the second watch, or come in the third watch, and find them so, blessed are those servants. And this know, that if the goodman of the house had known what hour the thief would come, he would have watched, and not have suffered his house to be broken through. Be ye therefore ready also: for the Son of Man cometh at an hour when ye think not. Luke, Chapter 12, verses 35-40.

And the Lord said, Who then is that faithful and wise steward, whom his lord shall make ruler over his household, to give them their portion of meat in due season? Blessed is that servant, whom his lord when he cometh shall find so doing. Of a Truth I say unto you, that he will make him ruler over all that he hath. But and if that servant say in his heart, My lord delayeth his coming; and shall begin to beat the menservants and maidens, and to eat and drink, and to be drunken; The lord of that servant will come in a day when he looketh not for him, and at an hour when he is not aware, and will cut him in sunder, and will appoint him his portion with the unbelievers. And that servant which knew his lord's will, and prepared not himself, neither did according to his will, shall be beaten with many stripes. But he that knew not, and did commit things worthy of stripes, shall be beaten with few stripes. For unto whomsoever much is given, of him shall be much required: and to whom men have committed much, of him they will ask the more. Luke, Chapter 12, verses 42-48.

And when He was demanded of the Pharisees, when the kingdom of God should come, He answered them and said, The kingdom of God cometh not with observation: Neither shall they say, Lo here! or, lo there! for, behold the kingdom of God is within you. And He said unto the disciples, The days will come, when ye shall desire to see one of the days of the Son of Man, and ye shall not see it. And they shall say to you, See here; or, see there: go not after them, nor follow them. Luke, Chapter 17, verses 20-23.

*And as it was in the days of Noe [Noah], so shall it be also in the days of the Son of Man. They did eat, they drank, they married wives, they were given in marriage, until the day that Noe entered into the ark, and the flood came, and destroyed them all. Likewise also as it was in the days of Lot; they did eat, they drank, they bought, they sold, they planted, they builded; But the same day that Lot went out of Sodom it rained fire and brimstone from heaven, and destroyed them all. Even thus shall it be in the day when the Son of Man is revealed. Luke, Chapter 17, verses 26-30.

*And they asked Him, saying, Master, but when shall these things be? and what sign will there be when these things shall come to pass? And He said, Take heed that ye be not deceived: for many shall come in My Name, saying, I am Christ; and the time draweth near: go ye not therefore after them. And when ye shall hear of wars and commotions, be not terrified: for these things must first come to pass; but the end is not by and by. Luke, Chapter 21, verses 7-9.

*Heaven and earth shall pass away: but My Words shall not pass away. But of that day and that hour knoweth no man, no, not the angels which are in heaven, neither the Son, but the Father. Mark, Chapter 13, verses 31-32.

*But the day of the Lord will come as a thief in the night; in the which the heavens shall pass away with a great noise, and the elements shall melt with fervent heat, the earth also and the works that are therein shall be burned up. Seeing then that all these things shall be dissolved, what manner of persons ought ye to be in all holy conversation and godliness, Looking for and hasting unto the coming of the day of God, wherein the heavens being on fire shall be dissolved, and the elements shall melt with fervent heat? 2 Peter, Chapter 3, verses 10-12.

*But I would not have you to be ignorant, brethren, concerning them which are asleep, that ye sorrow not, even as others which have no hope. For if we believe that Jesus died and rose again, even so them also which sleep in Jesus will God bring with Him. For this we say unto you by the Word of the Lord, that we which are alive and remain unto the coming of *the Lord shall not prevent them which are asleep. For the Lord Himself shall descend from heaven with a shout, with the voice of the archangel, and with the trump of God: and the dead in Christ shall rise first: Then we which are alive and remain shall be caught up together with them in the clouds, to meet the Lord in the air: and so shall we ever be with the Lord. Wherefore comfort one another with these Words. 1 Thessalonians, Chapter 4, verses 13-18.*

....

And He entered into one of the ships, which was Simon's and prayed Him that He would thrust out a little from the land. And He sat down and taught the people out of the ship. Now when He had left speaking, He said unto Simon, Launch out into the deep, and let down your nets for a draught. And Simon answering said unto Him, Master, we have toiled all the night, and have taken nothing: nevertheless at Thy Word I will let down the net. And when they had this done, they enclosed a great multitude of fishes: and their net brake. And they beckoned unto their partners, which were in the other ship, that they should come and help them. And they came, and filled both the ships, so that they began to sink. When Simon Peter saw it, he fell down at Jesus' knees saying, Depart from me; for I am a sinful man, O Lord. For he was astonished, and all that were with him, at the draught of the fishes which they had taken: And so was also James, and John, the sons of Zebedee, which were partners with Simon. And Jesus said unto Simon, Fear not; from henceforth thou shalt catch men. Luke, Chapter 5, verses 3-10.

Jesus impressed me when He turned the work of these three gentlemen from being fishers, who supply man's human needs, to being fishers of men, who supply man's spiritual needs. I think Jesus wants us to be fishers of men too. We need to each listen to the instincts that He gives us about this so we can do His will.

....

But I say unto you which hear, Love your enemies, do good to them which hate you, Bless them that curse you, and pray for them which despitefully use you. And unto him that smiteth thee on the one cheek offer also the other; and him that taketh away thy cloak forbid not to take thy coat also. Luke, Chapter 6, verses 27-29.

I used to get caught up in being angry and resentful when people were rude or insensitive to me. I can't say that I don't ever get caught up in those human emotions anymore. Fortunately, these passages will pop into my mind in the middle of those feelings.

I realize that God wants me to pray for these people rather than waste my time being angry with them. I think anger can be a very counterproductive emotion, at times. I remember a time when I was working under a very insensitive-demanding supervisor. I was almost to the point of tears at work when I went into the bathroom because I didn't want anyone to see me crying. This passage popped into my mind, so I prayed for the supervisor and for God to bless her. I was only expecting God to make me feel better so I could leave the restroom without anyone realizing I had been crying.

When I left the bathroom after saying that quick prayer, not only did I feel relieved but the supervisor was much nicer to me. I really wasn't expecting that to happen. Since it happened this way the first time, I have gone to the bathroom to pray many times over the years. Every time I have done this, the situation was much better afterward. It's amazing to see how God is personally involved in our lives.

It's important that I do not respond to these people in like manner. Coming back with an equally hateful or insensitive remark isn't being the example God wants me to be of how He works in my life. When I pray for these people, I'm putting them in God's very capable hands. Actually, it would be wonderful if these hurtful or rude people would have their lives turned around by God who can cause miraculous changes in anyone.

Here are some related passages:

*Bless them which persecute you: bless, and curse not. Romans, Chapter 12, verse 14.

*Recompense to no man evil for evil. Provide things honest in the sight of all men. If it be possible, as much as lieth in you, live peaceably with all men. Romans, Chapter 12, verses 17-18.

*Therefore if thine enemy hunger, feed him; if he thirst, give him drink: for in so doing thou shalt heap coals of fire on his head. Be not overcome of evil, but overcome evil with good. Romans, Chapter 12, verses 20-21. There is also a similar passage in Matthew, Chapter 5, verse 44.

*And if any man will sue thee at the law, and take away thy coat, let him have thy cloak, also. And whosoever shalt compel thee to go a mile, go with him twain. Give to him that asketh thee, and from him that would borrow of thee turn not away. Matthew, Chapter 5, verses 40-42.

*The disciple is not above his Master, nor the servant above his Lord. It is enough for the disciple that he be as his Master, and the servant as his Lord. If they have called the Master of the house Beelzebub, how much more shall they call them of His household? Matthew, Chapter 10, verses 24-25.

....

Give to every man that asketh of thee; and of him that taketh away thy goods ask them not again. Luke, Chapter 6, verse 30.

I think God wants us to give freely to those in need. I'm not sure about the interpretation of the second part of this passage. I have taken it to be an answer to a dilemma I have with giving to others. I think there is a fine line between empowering and enabling. There are times when a person gives to others and it empowers them, giving them a hand-up to be the best they can be. Then there are times where you give to others and it creates an enabling dependency that is counterproductive and isn't healthy for that person. So I don't give to people I think are going to use the money to buy another bottle or to people who are deliberately trying to take advantage of me or scam me.

I'm not sure that's what the second part of this passage was really saying and I apologize if I'm misleading anyone, but that's the way I have taken it. A good rule of thumb is to trust the instincts that God gives you. I try to let those instincts guide me in giving. Don't forget giving isn't only of our money. Sometimes giving is by treating others with respect or taking the time to listen to their story whether you've heard similar stories a million times over. Giving of your time by being there for someone else when they need someone in their corner can be a much more powerful thing than any monetary gift. Sometimes people who are down and out just need a hand-up, a little respect and a smile or two.

(As I read this passage while I'm editing the book, I wonder if God doesn't want us to give even if we think someone is going to buy another bottle. Who are we to say whether our kindness might leave a positive impact on that person which goes far beyond anything we might ever realize. As I said originally, trust the instincts that God gives you on this subject. Those will be right for your situation.)

> *And as ye would that men should do to you, do ye also to them likewise. For if ye love them which love you, what thank have ye? for sinners also love those that love them. And if ye do good to them which do good to you, what thank have ye? for sinners also do even the same. And if ye lend to them of whom ye hope to receive, what thank have ye? for sinners also lend to sinners, to receive as much again. But love ye your enemies, and do good, and lend hoping for nothing again; and your reward shall be great and ye shall be the children of the Highest: for He is kind unto the unthankful and to the evil. Be ye therefore merciful, as your Father also is merciful. Luke, Chapter 6, verses 31-36.*

God is telling us He wants us to be nice, considerate and giving to everyone, especially those who aren't nice, considerate and giving to us. He says it's easy to be giving to people who are nice to us, so that's not very difficult. We are really doing a bigger thing when we are giving to those we don't care for, those who aren't nice to us or those who don't look like people we would ever associate with. I can't say I always do this, but I pray that God gives me the willingness to be the example that He wants me to be to others, especially those I'm reluctant to interact with.

> *Judge not, and ye shall not be judged: condemn not, and ye shall not be condemned: forgive, and ye shall be forgiven: Give, and it shall be given unto you, good measure, pressed down, and shaken together, and running over, shall men give into your bosom. For with the same measure that ye mete withal it shall be measured to you again. Luke, Chapter 6, verses 37-38.*

This message reminds me that I would NOT want God to judge me by the same standards I use to judge other people. I'm very thankful that He reminds me of this, because I often find myself being critical or judgmental of others.

When we genuinely give to others out of our need, God will always make sure we are provided for. This is a miracle unto itself, similar to the loaves and fishes. I do have some concerns though. There are some supposed churches that promote giving to others as a plan to get financial reward in return. They talk to their parishioners about giving lots of money to the church or to causes in order to get great wealth for their good deeds. Well, this is God we are talking about and He's all-knowing. He can tell when we are genuinely giving to others and when we are giving to others with ulterior motives. You can't con God!

Here are some related passages:

And the scribes and Pharisees brought unto Him a woman taken in adultery; and when they had set her in the midst, they say unto Him, Master, this woman was taken in adultery, in the very act. Now Moses in the Law commanded us, that such should be stoned: but what sayest Thou? This they said, tempting Him, that they might have to accuse Him. But Jesus stooped down, and with His finger wrote on the ground, as though He heard them not. So when they continued asking Him, He lifted up Himself, and said unto them, He that is without sin among you, let him first cast a stone at her. And again He stooped down, and wrote on the ground. And they which heard it, being convicted by their own conscience, went out one by one, beginning at the eldest, even unto the last: and Jesus was left alone; and the woman standing in the midst. When Jesus had lifted up Himself, and saw none but the woman, He said unto her, Woman, where are those thine accusers? hath no man condemned thee? She said, No man, Lord. And Jesus said unto her, Neither do I condemn thee: go, and sin no more. Then spake Jesus again unto them, saying, I am the Light of the World: He that followeth Me shall not walk in darkness, but shall have the Light of Life. John, Chapter 8, verses 3-12.

Therefore thou art inexcusable, O man, whosoever thou art that judgest: for wherein thou judgest another, thou condemnest thyself; for thou that judgest doest the same things. But we are sure that the judgment of God is according to Truth against them which commit such things. And thinkest thou this, O man, that judgest them which do such things, and doest the same, that thou shalt escape the judgment of God? Romans, Chapter 2, verses 1-3.

Judge not, that ye be not judged. For with what judgment: and with what measure ye mete, it shall be measured to you again. Matthew, Chapter 7, verses 1-2.

....

And He spake a parable unto them, Can the blind lead the blind? shall they not both fall into the ditch? Luke, Chapter 6, verse 39.

Sometimes we get into a routine of doing whatever everyone else is doing. If they are going to a particular church, we try it out. If our friends use God's Name in vain, we forget what we learned in Sunday school while we were growing up and start using His Name in vain too. If everyone else is doing it, it must not be all that bad. Right???

We need to make sure the people we choose to follow are those who make choices God would approve of, or we just might be following someone right to Hell (the ditch). That definitely isn't the direction I want to go!

Here is a related passage:

*Let them alone: they be blind leaders of the blind, And if the blind lead the blind, both shall fall into the ditch. Matthew, Chapter 15, verse 14.

. . . .

And why beholdest thou the mote that is in thy brother's eye, but perceivest not the beam that is in thine own eye? Either how canst thou say to thy brother, Brother, let me pull out the mote that is in thine eye, when thou thyself beholdest not the beam that is in thine own eye? Thou hypocrite, cast out first the beam out of thine own eye, and then shalt thou see clearly to pull out the mote that is in thy brother's eye. Luke, Chapter 6, verses 41-42.

From what I have read in the Bible, God doesn't want us to get to the point we EVER feel so self-righteous that we can be critiquing other people's behavior or choices. We need to focus on our own choices and make sure we are being the best example of our faith we can possibly be.

Here is a related passage:

*And why beholdest thou the mote that is in thy brother's eye, but considerest not the beam that is in thine own eye? Or how wilt thou say to thy brother, Let me pull out the mote out of thine eye; and, behold, a beam is in thine own eye? Thou hypocrite, first cast out the beam out of thine own eye; and then shalt thou see clearly to cast out the mote out of thy brother's eye. Matthew, Chapter 7, verses 3-5.

. . . .

Whosoever cometh to Me, and heareth My sayings, and doeth them, I will show you to whom he is like: He is like a man which built an house, and digged deep, and laid the foundation on a rock: and when the flood arose, the stream beat vehemently upon that house, and could not shake it: for it was founded upon a rock. But he that heareth, and doeth not, is like a man that without a foundation built an house upon the earth; against which the storm did beat vehemently, and immediately it fell; and the ruin of that house was great. Luke, Chapter 6, verses 47-49.

I need to make sure that my faith in God has a firm foundation like the house built on rock, because my faith has to withstand all the human temptations that arise. Some of those temptations are very subtle and can let little things into our lives that seem very minor but still shake our foundation. Food has always been one of my bigger vices.

My younger brother has always been very giving and still is. I'm ashamed to say that I took advantage of him when he wasn't even in school yet. Being the youngest and the only boy in the family, he had a piggy bank full of money. When my parents weren't around, I talked him into breaking into his piggy bank to get all his money out to take with us to the movies. Being the generous person that he is, he shared all his money with his older sister. I bought ice cream after ice cream, followed by enough candy bars to make a person sick. He had trusted me, but my ulterior motives interfered with being an example of my faith. Like I said, we have to be careful about the subtle things in life that sneak in and shake our foundation on rock. Something very minor could cause that foundation to crumble!

Here is a related passage:

*Therefore whosoever heareth these sayings of Mine, and doeth them, I will liken him unto a wise man, which built his house upon a rock: And the rain descended, and the floods came, and the winds blew, and beat upon that house; and it fell not: for it was founded upon a rock. And every one that heareth these sayings of Mine, and doeth them not, shall be likened unto a foolish man, who built his house upon the sand: And the rain descended, and the floods came, and the winds blew, and beat upon that house; and it fell: and great was the fall of it. And it came to pass, when Jesus had ended these sayings, the people were astonished at His doctrine. Matthew, Chapter 7, verses 24-28.

....

And He said to them all, If any man will come after Me, let him deny himself, and take up his cross daily, and follow Me. For whosoever will save his life shall lose it: but whosoever will lose his life for My sake, the same shall save it. For what is a man advantaged, if he gain the whole world, and lose himself, or be cast away? Luke, Chapter 9, verses 23-25.

I think God is telling us that we have to be totally dedicated to Him. It's all too easy to get caught up in our daily lives and focus on getting ahead in the world. It's especially difficult since there is so much pressure to try to keep up with the Jones's that we might lose sight of our goal. To paraphrase what Jesus said, "What good is it to have all these worldly things and lose your Salvation in the process? Those that are willing to give up everything, including their worldly lives for Me, will have eternal life in Heaven."

Here are some related passages:

He that loveth father or mother more than Me is not worthy of Me: and he that loveth son or daughter more than Me is not worthy of Me. And he that taketh not his cross, and followeth after Me, is not worthy of Me. Matthew, Chapter 10, verses 37-38.

Then said Jesus unto His disciples, If any man will come after Me, let him deny himself, and take up his cross, and follow Me. For whosoever will save his life shall lose it: and whosoever will lose his life for My sake shall find it. For what is a man profited, if he shall gain the whole world, and lose his own soul? or what shall a man give in exchange for his soul? For the Son of Man shall come in the Glory of His Father with His angels; and then He shall reward every man according to his works. Matthew, Chapter 16, verses 24-27.

....

For whosoever shall be ashamed of Me and of My Words, of him shall the Son of Man be ashamed, when He shall come in His own Glory, and in His Father's, and of the holy angels. Luke, Chapter 9, verse 26.

This relates to a situation that made a major difference in my relationship with God. One time, I was doing something that was an outward sign of my faith. It was in a place where other people could see what I was doing and would have known I am a Christian. I'm ashamed to say that this had made me really uncomfortable.

The thought in my mind shortly after this was about the movie "*American Graffiti*". One of the main characters had been in charge of keeping an eye on a young pre-teen or teenage girl. He had a reputation of being "cool" and didn't like being a glorified babysitter. Later, he and the young lady got to know each other better and became friends. Then there was a point in the movie where he was driving down the main drag and he saw a group of his friends. He realized that they would see him with this young girl and it could hurt his "cool image" if they knew he was babysitting. So he asked his new found friend to duck down in the seat so his other friends wouldn't see her sitting in his car, thus maintaining his reputation.

Well, that's what I was doing with God. I was saying to God, "You are really important to me and I love you a lot, but I don't want other people to know how important You are to me. I want to look 'cool' to others and don't want them to think I'm a religious fanatic. So, God, please duck down so they don't know I'm a Christian."

This movie impacted my life and my relationship with God because it helped me realize that I used to shy away from mentioning anything about God or my faith to anyone. I can't say it's all that easy for me now, because I'm still very weak and have a hard time risking ridicule from others. I do try to say things like, "Boy, God was really looking after you," when there was a miracle in someone's life that they may have overlooked.

When I do this, I'm generally anxious because I never know how anyone is going to respond to these statements. I'm always afraid that they are going to think I'm a fanatic and shy away from me, but I have never received that response from anyone. In fact, people have been very appreciative and it has opened up opportunities for the other person to share their perspective of how God has influenced their life. I need to continue to focus on being more willing to take risks for God. I would never want Him to turn His back on me the way I have done to Him.

....

Then there arose a reasoning among them, which of them should be greatest. And Jesus, perceiving the thought of their heart, took a child, and set him by Him, and said unto them, Whosoever shall receive this child in My Name receiveth Me: and whosoever shall receive Me receiveth Him that sent Me: for he that is least among you all, the same shall be great. Luke, Chapter 9, verses 46-48.

Being a "Self-righteous Christian" too many times to mention, this passage reminds us that we shouldn't get caught up in determining how great we are for all the good things we do in God's Name. That isn't what it's all about. God says, *"For he who is least among you all, the same shall be great."* I need to make sure that I'm focused on living the life God wants for me rather than trying to look pious to others by attaining religious status.

Bible Passages That Can Influence Your Life

....

> *But he, willing to justify himself, said unto Jesus, And who is my neighbour? And Jesus answering said, A certain man went down from Jerusalem to Jericho, and fell among thieves, which stripped him of his raiment, and wounded him, and departed leaving him half dead. And by chance there came down a certain priest that way: and when he saw him, he passed by on the other side. And likewise a Levite, when he was at the place, came and looked on him, and passed by on the other side. But a certain Samaritan, as he journeyed, came where he was: and when he saw him, he had compassion on him, And went to him, and bound up his wounds, pouring in oil and wine, and set him on his own beast, and brought him to an inn, and took care of him. And on the morrow when he departed, he took out two pence, and gave them to the host, and said unto him, Take care of him; and whatsoever thou spendest more, when I come again, I will repay thee. Which now of these three, thinkest thou, was neighbour unto him that fell, among the thieves? And he said, He that showed mercy on him, Then said Jesus unto him, Go, and do thou likewise. Luke, Chapter 10, verses 29-37.*

It makes me think of all the people that need help on the side of the road that I ignore. I have a dilemma. It isn't very safe to be picking up people by the side of the road these days, but I bet there are things I can do to help anyway. I could probably ask them if they need me to call a tow truck or something. That might be risky too. What I have been doing is using my cell phone, at times, to call the highway patrol to tell them the approximate location of the broken down car. I know it's not as big an effort as the Samaritan made, but I think we all need to start someplace. I get too caught up in my own little world and tend to ignore the things that make me uncomfortable or that I really don't want to deal with. I need to be more sensitive to the needs of others, being an example on a regular basis of how God works in my life.

....

> *And it came to pass, as He spake these things, a certain woman of the company lifted up her voice, and said unto Him, Blessed is the womb that bare Thee, and the paps which Thou hast sucked. But He said, Yea rather, blessed are they that hear the Word of God, and keep it. Luke, Chapter 11, verses 27-28.*

God lets me know in this passage that it's not good enough to hear the Word of God. We are supposed to live the life that He suggests. It reminds me of teaching math to children. I would explain a new math concept to nodding heads. I would ask if anyone had a question, but they rarely did. I thought they really understood the concept, but as I walked around the room, I found that although the children thought they understood the concept, they weren't applying it and were lost.

It's pretty easy to hear things in church and feel it's impacted your life. If we are just "Sunday Christians" cussing at other motorists, yelling at our kids or being rude to others the rest of the week, we may not be living our lives as examples of how God works in us.

Here is a related passage:

**For whosoever shall do the will of My Father which is in heaven, the same is My brother, and sister, and mother. Matthew, Chapter 12, verse 50.*

....

For there is nothing covered, that shall not be revealed; neither hid, that shall not be known. Therefore whatsoever ye have spoken in darkness shall be heard in the Light; and that which ye have spoken in the ear in closets shall be proclaimed upon the housetops. And I say unto you My friends, Be not afraid of them that kill the body, and after that have no more that they can do. Luke, Chapter 12, verses 2-4.

I think Jesus was probably talking about the people who were plotting against Him. Those who said all these hateful things about Him in private thought it was private, but God knows all.

I'm not totally sure of God's message in this one. What I think about when I read this passage is more directed to me, personally. It feels like God is saying to me, "You know you profess to be such a good Christian, don't you? But I see when you are gossiping with others and saying less than kind things. You know your actions are supposed to be an example of your faith in Me. You think those things you say in secret are really secret, but I know everything! You ought to think about whether this is really what you want Me to hear coming out of your mouth. Think about it, Dorothy, because I care about you."

....

But he that denieth Me before men shall be denied before the angels of God. And whosoever shall speak a word against the Son of Man, it shall be forgiven him: but unto him that blasphemeth against the Holy Ghost it shall not be forgiven. Luke, Chapter 12, verses 9-10.

Sometimes I feel awkward talking to others about my faith in God. I'm afraid they will shy away from me the same way I want to hide in my house when a particular religious group that has a belief that isn't compatible with mine, comes knocking on my door. I hate it that God sees all the times I'm afraid to risk on His behalf. I want to be a strong Christian He can depend on, not the "Self-serving Christian" who is worried about what others think.

. . . .

And when they bring you unto the synagogues, and unto magistrates, and powers, take ye no thought how or what thing ye shall answer, or what ye shall say: For the Holy Ghost shall teach you in the same hour what ye ought to say. Luke, Chapter 12, verses 11-12.

Jesus is really talking to the disciples and other people, preparing them not to worry about what they should say if they are questioned about their beliefs, because the Holy Spirit will provide the right words for them to say. Well, I have found this is also beneficial for me to bear in mind in all types of situations.

I found myself worrying about a job I really wanted. I remembered that it's all in God's hands no matter which way it turned out. When I realized that, I relaxed knowing He would take care of it.

Shortly before I went for the interview, I said a quick prayer and asked God to take care of the words (meaning the words that come out of my mouth) and my willingness to let Him take care of the words. It was amazing! When I came out of the interview, I reviewed it over and over in my mind, amazed at how the words just flowed out of my mouth. I couldn't believe some of the answers I had given to questions I knew little about or had never thought about before.

I guess I shouldn't have been so amazed. God always takes good care of me and hadn't I just asked Him to take care of the words? Should I have expected any less? Now before stressful situations, I try to remember to ask God to take care of the words and my willingness to let Him take care of the words and He always does!

Here is a related passage:

*And ye shall be brought before governors and kings for My sake, for a testimony against them and the Gentiles. But when they deliver you up, take no thought how or what ye shall speak: for it shall be given you in that same hour what ye shall speak. For it is not ye that speak, but the Spirit of your Father which speaketh in you. Matthew, Chapter 10, verses 18-20.

And one of the company said unto Him, Master, speak to my brother, that he divide the inheritance with me. And He said unto him, Man, who made Me a judge or a divider over you? And He said unto them, Take heed, and beware of covetousness: for a man's life consisteth not in the abundance of the things which he possesseth. And He spake a parable unto them, saying, The ground of a certain rich man brought forth plentifully: And he thought within himself, saying, What shall I do, because I have no room where to bestow my fruits? And he said, This will I do: I will pull down my barns, and build greater; and there will I bestow all my fruits and my goods. And I will say to my soul, Soul, thou hast much goods laid up for many years; take thine ease, eat, drink, and be merry. But God said unto him, Thou fool, this night thy soul shall be required of thee: then whose shall those things be, which thou hast provided? Luke, Chapter 12, verses 13-21.

Our belief in God isn't a "Once a Christian-Always a Christian Guarantee" that once you have it, you always have it regardless of your actions. If it were, people could become a Christian, go rob a bank and shoot someone because they need their next fix, not worrying because they think they have Salvation regardless of their actions.

It's like planting a garden using seeds. That gardener's energy and enthusiasm are there after they have hoed the rows, preparing them for the seeds to be planted. He carefully plants the seeds and waters them regularly, just as a person who starts a relationship with God has energy and enthusiasm for their new-found faith.

If that gardener were to go on vacation right after planting his garden and expected to find fully grown plants when he returns, he would be greatly surprised! The garden would be overgrown and the vegetables would be strangled by the weeds while the remnants of the garden would still be there. This is similar to what happens to the Christian who doesn't tend to their faith regularly by making it a DAILY part of their life.

That Christian's faith will wither away, strangled by the weeds of worldly living while the remnants of that faith will still be there. Our faith needs constant cultivation and care just as the garden does in order to grow and flourish.

And He said unto His disciples, Therefore I say unto you, Take no thought for your life, what ye shall eat; neither for the body, what ye shall put on. The life is more than meat, and the body is more than raiment. Consider the ravens: for they neither sow nor reap; which neither have storehouse nor barn; and God feedeth them: how much more are ye better than the fowls? And which of you with taking thought can add to his stature one cubit? If ye then be not able to do that thing which is least, why take ye thought for the rest? Consider the lilies how they grow: they toil not, they spin not; and yet I say unto you, that Solomon in all his glory was not arrayed like one of these. If then God so clothe the grass, which is today in the field, and tomorrow is cast into the oven; how much more will He clothe you, O ye of little faith? And seek not ye what ye shall eat, or what ye shall drink, neither be ye of doubtful mind. For all these things do the nations of the world seek after: and your Father knoweth that ye have need of these things. But rather seek ye the kingdom of God; and all these things shall be added unto you. Fear not, little flock, for it is your Father's good pleasure to give you the kingdom. Luke, Chapter 12, verses 22-32.

  This is one of my favorite passages in the whole Bible. It has personal significance to me because of my experience with it. Years ago, I was on a very tight budget. It was so tight that I had to buy powdered milk in case I didn't have enough money to have milk for my children's breakfast. Now, I know our situation wasn't as bad as some, but I just want you to know that things were tight and I had to be very careful about my spending. Now, one of my biggest vices, as I've shared, is the need to be in control of my life.

  Since things were so tight, I would spend hours making a budget or revising it every time there appeared to be a need. I lived my life by this budget and tried very hard to not deviate from it. I spent most of my waking hours trying to plan, scheme and figure out ways to get by through the month. Then one day, God had me read this particular passage and it totally turned my life and my relationship with God around!

  I found out that God didn't want me spending the vast majority of my time fretting over bills and figuring out ways to make ends meet. When I was doing that, I was showing that I didn't trust God to provide for my family's needs. I was also wasting a lot of time planning when I could have spent that time reading the Bible, praying or spending time with my family.

It was like I was saying, "God, you know I love you and I think you're wonderful, but I just don't think you are going to take good enough care of my family. I'm going to devise a plan to take care of them, just in case you fail us." Well, that isn't the message I want to be giving God.

I can't say I don't ever get caught up in worrying about finances anymore, but quite often God will put the thought of this passage in my mind which helps me refocus. I need to trust God to take care of my family's needs and I need to be an example of how God works in my life.

This is a disclaimer of sorts. This doesn't mean a person should go out and spend their family's money on gambling, alcohol, Bingo, possessions, etc. and God will make sure that all their needs are met. I don't think He wants us to ever take advantage of Him.

It would be like telling an unemployed relative that he could stay with you for a month or two while he gets back on his feet. While your relative goes out to look for work every day you tell him, "Don't worry about cleaning up your room. I have a little extra time and I'll take care of it." This is a genuine offer and you don't mind cleaning up the minor things the relative leaves around.

Then the relative starts taking advantage of the fact that he has someone taking care of him. The relative starts leaving all his clothes on the floor. He leaves his dirty towels lying around instead of putting them in the hamper. He leaves his dirty dishes lying on the table. It's bad enough that you have to take his dirty dishes to the sink and wash them, but they are hard, crusty and difficult to wash.

To top this all off, the relative is getting used to having someone pay all the bills, cook the meals and clean up after him. Having a job, getting up early and going to work is looking less and less attractive to him.

Your relative isn't getting up early in the morning anymore to look for work. In fact, he seems to be staying in bed later and later every day. You bring the paper to your relative with some potential jobs circled and find that he has tossed it on the floor with the rest of his dirty clothes, making no attempt to look for work or even call any of the ads you carefully circled.

You aren't empowering your relative by helping him become the best he can be. Instead, you realize that you are enabling him and making him dependent on you. Finally, you recognize that enough is enough and you tell your relative that you aren't going to be doing things for him anymore. You notify him that he has to be responsible for himself and if he doesn't get a job in a certain amount of time or at least make a decent effort; he will be out on his ear.

Well, don't you think that if we could feel this way, maybe God would get a little upset if we took advantage of Him? I don't think He would like it if we spent our money carelessly so that we didn't have enough for our bills, but relied on Him to pick up all the pieces and work everything out. So, although I'm saying God will take care of our every need (and He really does, even better than I ever did when I was budgeting so tightly), we still need to be responsible about our finances and choices by not taking advantage of God's forgiving nature.

....

Surely Thou wilt slay the wicked, O God; depart from me therefore, ye bloody men, For they speak against Thee wickedly, and Thine enemies take Thy Name in vain. Psalm, Chapter 139, verses 19-20.

It doesn't sound to me that God takes it lightly when people curse Him or use His Name inappropriately. That's why I am very concerned about people casually using "God" and "Jesus" in their everyday speech. I don't think people realize how strongly God feels about it.

All the passages that say we aren't to profane God's Name or to use His Name in vain really made me stop and think. It has become very common these days for people to say "God" or "Jesus," without really any thought. You hear people say things like, "God that was a great game!" "Jesus Christ! I ran out of bread again!" "Oh, good God, get off your high horse and give me a hand around here."

Of course, I can't mention all the possible ways I've heard people use God's Name inappropriately. The point of great concern is that these people really aren't focusing on God when they say these things. They aren't praying or genuinely telling other people about God or glorifying Him either. God states very clearly throughout the Bible that we aren't supposed to use His Name in vain.

Reading many passages about this in the Bible has caused me to become alarmed about this issue. I don't think people realize how often they're saying "God" or "Jesus," in their everyday language. It's on TV and it's in the movies. Almost everyone seems to be doing it, even the little kids and people we respect. Some people who are doing this consider themselves to be good Christians. I don't think these people even know they are using God's Name in vain or that they are being a poor example of their faith in Jesus.

I realize that some people may not like hearing this. Most of us like thinking we are pretty good people. This may hurt our self-perception of the type of Christian we think we are. I'm hoping that we will get beyond this and become much more aware of the words we choose to use.

Using God's Name in vain has become just casual slang, like, "Shucks" used to be when I was a kid. I hope one of the things that you get out of this book is a deeper awareness of this issue. Listen to people talk. What if each and every person who used God's Name in vain as slang was to lose their Salvation? That would be a pitiful thing.

Maybe that's what my job is. Maybe I'm supposed to make people aware that they are doing this. Maybe I'm supposed to draw their attention to the possible repercussions of using God's Name in vain. I have no idea. I just know I felt led to write this book and God will take care of the rest!

Fortunately, God is very merciful and will forgive us if we ask Him to, provided we make the necessary changes to only use His Name in ways that glorify Him.

Here are some related passages:

*Thou shalt not take the Name of the LORD thy God in vain; for the LORD will not hold him guiltless that taketh His Name in vain. Exodus, Chapter 20, verse 7.

*And ye shall not swear by My Name falsely, neither shalt thou profane the Name of thy God: I am the LORD. Leviticus, Chapter 19, verse 12.

*And thou shalt speak unto the children of Israel saying, Whosoever curseth his God shall bear his sin. And he that blasphemeth the Name of the LORD, he shall surely be put to death, and all the congregation shall certainly stone him: as well the stranger, as he that is born in the land, when he blasphemeth the Name of the LORD, shall be put to death. Leviticus, Chapter 24, verses 15-16.

*And thou shalt not let any of thy seed pass through the fire to Molech, neither shalt thou profane the Name of thy God: I am the LORD. Leviticus, Chapter 18, verse 21.

*Thou shalt not take the Name of the LORD thy God in vain: for the LORD will not hold him guiltless that taketh His Name in vain. Keep the Sabbath day to sanctify it, as the LORD thy God hath commanded thee. Six days thou shalt labour, and do all thy work: But the seventh day is the Sabbath of the LORD *thy God: in it thou shalt not do any work, thou, nor thy son, nor thy daughter, nor thy manservant, nor thy maidservant, nor thine ox, nor thine ass, nor any of thy cattle, nor thy stranger that is within thy gates; that thy manservant and thy maidservant may rest as well as thou. And remember that thou wast a servant in the land of Egypt, and that the LORD thy God brought thee out thence through a mighty hand and by a stretched out Arm: therefore the LORD thy God commanded thee to keep the Sabbath day. Deuteronomy, Chapter 5, verses 11-15.*

*I said, I will take heed to my ways, that I sin not with my tongue: I will keep my mouth with a bridle, while the wicked is before me. Psalm, Chapter 39, verse 1.

*He that keepeth his mouth keepeth his life: but he that openeth wide his lips shall have destruction. Proverbs, Chapter 13, verse 3.

*Be not deceived: evil communications corrupt good manners.   1 Corinthians, Chapter 15, verse 33.

....

He spake also this parable; A certain man had a fig tree planted in his vineyard and he came and sought fruit thereon, and found none. Then said he unto the dresser of his vineyard, Behold, these three years I come seeking fruit on this fig tree, and find none: cut it down, why cumbereth it the ground? And he answering said unto him, Lord, let it alone this year also, till I shall dig about it, and dung it: And if it bear fruit, well: and if not, then after that thou shalt cut it down. Luke, Chapter 13, verses 6-9.

If a person stole from stores and then said to God, "I'm sorry I am not the Christian You want me to be; please forgive me," but neglected to try to change anything, God would be patient with him up to a point. This passage makes me think that there comes a time when God says that He's given enough chances for the person to change their actions and if they haven't, then He cuts His losses.

Fortunately for us, God is very forgiving. If that person finally turns his life around to be the Christian that God wants; all will be forgiven. God doesn't want us to put off our faith until the last minute.

Here are some related passages:

And now also the axe is laid unto the root of the trees: therefore every tree which bringeth not forth good fruit is hewn down, and cast into the fire. Matthew, Chapter 3, verse 10.

Whose fan is in His hand, and He will thoroughly purge His floor, and gather His wheat into the garner; but He will burn up the chaff with unquenchable fire. Matthew, Chapter 3, verse 12.

Ye are the salt of the earth: but if the salt have lost his savour, wherewith shall it be salted? It is thenceforth good for nothing, but to be cast out, and to be trodden under foot of men. Matthew, Chapter 5, verse 13.

Ye shall know them by their fruits. Do men gather grapes of thorns, or figs of thistles? Even so every good tree bringeth forth good fruit; but a corrupt tree bringeth forth evil fruit. A good tree cannot bring forth evil fruit, neither can a corrupt tree bring forth good fruit. Every tree that bringeth not forth good fruit is hewn down, and cast into the fire. Wherefore by their fruits ye shall know them. Not every one that saith unto Me, Lord, Lord, shall enter into the kingdom of heaven; but he that doth the will of My Father which is in heaven. Many will say to Me in that day, Lord, Lord, have we not prophesied in Thy Name? and in Thy Name have cast out devils? And in Thy Name done many wonderful works? And then will I profess unto them, I never knew you: depart from Me, ye that work iniquity. Matthew, Chapter 7, verses 16-23.

But He answered and said, Every plant, which My heavenly Father hath not planted, shall be rooted up. Matthew, Chapter 15, verse 13.

....

Then said He, Unto what is the kingdom of God like? and whereunto shall I resemble it? It is like a grain of mustard seed, which a man took, and cast into his garden; and it grew, and waxed a great tree; and the fowls of the air lodged in the branches of it. Luke, Chapter 13, verses 18-19.

This reminds me of when I mention to someone else about how God looked after me in a particular situation. It's like planting a seed that has the potential to grow and to continue to grow into a full-fledged belief in God. It's just like the mustard tree that grows from that tiny seed that is planted.

It makes me think that we never know how the little things we share might make a difference in someone else's life. My being fearful of sharing my relationship with God may not be giving that person the opportunity to come to have a relationship with God.

Here are some related passages:

*Another parable put He forth unto them, saying, The kingdom of heaven is like to a grain of mustard seed, which a man took, and sowed in his field: Which indeed is the least of all seeds: but when it is grown, it is the greatest among herbs, and becometh a tree, so that the birds of the air come and lodge in the branches thereof. Matthew, Chapter 13, verses 31-32.

*And He said, Whereunto shall we liken the kingdom of God? or with what comparison shall we compare it? It is like a grain of mustard seed, which, when it is sown in the earth, is less than all the seeds that be in the earth: But when it is sown, it groweth up, and becometh greater than all herbs, and shooteth out great branches; so that the fowls of the air may lodge under the shadow of it. Mark, Chapter 4, verses 30-32.

....

Then said one unto Him, Lord, are there few that be saved? And He said unto them, Strive to enter in at the strait gate: for many, I say unto you, will seek to enter in, and shall not be able. When once the Master of the house is risen up, and hath shut to the door, and ye begin to stand without, and to knock at the door, saying, Lord, Lord, open unto us; and He shall answer and say unto you, I know you not whence ye are: Then shall ye begin to say, We have eaten and drunk in thy presence, and thou hast taught in our streets. But He shall say, I tell you, I know you not whence ye are; depart from me, all ye workers of iniquity. Luke, Chapter 13, verses 23-27.

This reminds me of when I was heavy and there were people that weren't really friendly to me. When I lost the weight, all of a sudden these same people were much friendlier. I didn't really want to be close friends with them at that point. They had an opportunity to be friendly with me before when I was heavy, and they hadn't chosen to.

Jesus may be telling us something very similar about putting off our decision to become active Christians. If we don't acknowledge Him when He calls us, maybe He won't remember us when we get around to asking Him for help.

Something unexpected like an accident might happen where we don't ever get another chance. If I'm a "Bird in the Hand Christian," I need to develop my relationship with God now, while I have the chance.

Here is a related passage:

> *Enter ye in at the strait gate: for wide is the gate, and broad is the way, that leadeth to destruction, and many there be which go in thereat: Because strait is the gate, and narrow is the way, which leadeth unto Life, and few there be that find it. Matthew, Chapter 7, verses 13-14.

....

> O Jerusalem, Jerusalem, which killest the prophets, and stonest them that are sent unto thee; how often would I have gathered thy children together, as a hen doth gather her brood under her wings, and ye would not! Behold, your house is left unto you desolate: and verily I say unto you, Ye shall not see Me, until the time come when ye shall say, Blessed is He that cometh in the Name of the Lord. Luke, Chapter 13, verses 34-35.

When I was reading my Bible this morning, I was thinking about how God uses picturesque language throughout the Bible to give us a mental picture of what He is trying to convey to us. This passage is a good example of that.

I can picture a mother hen spreading her wings trying to focus her children to go in the correct direction, just as Jesus does for us. Do we listen? No, just like kids we say we want to do things our own way and tend to wander off, losing our focus. Now, when something traumatic happens in our lives or the lives of our loved ones, BAM, we are right back on target, asking God to help with this situation.

On Judgment Day, do you think Jesus will have pity on us who decide at that moment that we are finally ready to become Christian when our lives haven't reflected that dedication all along????

Here is a related passage:

> *O Jerusalem, Jerusalem, thou that killest the prophets, and stonest them which are sent unto thee, how often would I have gathered thy children together, even as a hen gathereth her chickens under her wings, and ye would not! Behold, your house is left unto you desolate. For I say unto you, Ye shall not see Me henceforth, till ye shall say, Blessed is He that cometh in the Name of the Lord. Matthew, Chapter 23, verses 37-39.

....

Bible Passages That Can Influence Your Life

For whosoever exalteth himself shall be abased; and he that humbleth himself shall be exalted. Luke, Chapter 14, verse 11.

In the previous three verses in the Bible, Jesus was talking about a wedding to teach us to have humility. Rather than go to a wedding and sit in a seat of honor, only to be embarrassed when asked to sit in a position of lower status, it was better to be humble and sit in the lower status seats. and then, to be asked to sit in the position of honor. I think He was trying to convey that He doesn't want us getting so self-righteous and big-headed that we lose our focus and humility.

Here are some related passages:

*But many that are first shall be last; and the last shall be first. Matthew, Chapter 19, verse 30.

*But Jesus called them unto Him, and said, Ye know that the princes of the Gentiles exercise dominion over them, and they that are great exercise authority upon them. But it shall not be so among you: but whosoever will be great among you, let him be your minister; And whosoever will be chief among you, let him be your servant: Even as the Son of Man came not to be ministered unto, but to minister, and to give His life a ransom for many. Matthew, Chapter 20, verses 25-28.

*And there was also a strife among them, which of them should be accounted the greatest. And He said unto them, The kings of the Gentiles exercise lordship over them; and they that exercise authority upon them are called benefactors. But ye shall not be so: but he that is greatest among you, let him be as the younger; and he that is chief, as he that doth serve. For whether is greater, he that sitteth at meat, or he that serveth? Is not he that sitteth at meat? but I am among you as He that serveth. Luke, Chapter 22, verses 24-27.

. . . .

Then said He also to him that bade Him, When thou makest a dinner or a supper, call not thy friends, nor thy brethren, neither thy kinsmen, nor thy rich neighbors; lest they also bid thee again, and a recompense be made thee. But when thou makest a feast, call the poor, the maimed, the lame, the blind: And thou shalt be blessed; for they cannot recompense thee: for thou shalt be recompensed at the resurrection of the just. Luke, Chapter 14, verses 12-14.

This passage lets me know that when I do nice things for others I need to make sure that I'm doing them for people who really need it and not to do it to gain some sort of personal recognition for my actions.

It's sometimes a hard one to live by because it makes me look at my motives for doing favors. Yes, I have found there have been times when I was choosing to do things for someone to draw attention to myself. Now, I'm trying to be more discreet in my favors to avoid this self-focus.

....

So likewise, whosoever he be of you that forsaketh not all that he hath, he cannot be My disciple. Luke, Chapter 14, verse 33.

I spent all day yesterday packing up my classroom. My husband has taken a job in a state that we had previously lived in. I thought it would only take a few hours to finish packing, but it was 7:00 p.m. when my husband and I finally pulled away from the school.

I was amazed because I had given so many teaching resources away during the year and still had so much stuff. One of the teachers came by and made a comment about how I should get rid of all the stuff. I was appalled with the idea. I couldn't get rid of all my stuff. It was important to me!

The stuff in my life becomes too important and gets in the way of my relationship with God. I would hate for Jesus to tell me that I couldn't come to heaven to be with Him because my stuff had become more important than He was.

I had to come back and add this to what I had written this morning. My husband came home and I was preparing to paint the bathroom before we put our house on the market. I said something about taking all my paint to our new house so I can try my hand at sponge painting the next house we buy. He said it would take too much room and we can get more paint after we move. I got upset with him for even thinking of getting rid of it. Then I realized that I hadn't learned very much from writing about this earlier. I was still having a hard time letting go of stuff!

God had perfect timing by having me deal with this particular passage right now. It wasn't one week earlier or a month later. It was the exact same day that I am having stuff withdrawal issues. Isn't it wonderful that God could time this so precisely? He knows as well as I do, I really need to continue to work on this one!!!!!

Here are some related passages:

*In that day, he which shall be upon the housetop, and his stuff in the house, let him not come down to take it away: and he that is in the field, let him likewise not return back. Remember Lot's wife. Whosoever shall seek to save his life shall lose it; and whosoever shall lose his life shall preserve it. Luke, Chapter 17, verses 31-33.

*Let him which is on the housetop not come down to take any thing out of his house: Neither let him which is in the field return back to take his clothes. Matthew, Chapter 24, verses 17-18.

. . . .

And He said, A certain man had two sons: And the younger of them said to his father, Father, give me the portion of goods that falleth to me. And he divided unto them his living. And not many days after the younger son gathered all together, and took his journey into a far country, and there wasted his substance with riotous living. And when he had spent all, there arose a mighty famine in that land; and he began to be in want. And he went and joined himself to a citizen of that country; and he sent him into his fields to feed swine, And he would fain have filled his belly with the husks that the swine did eat: and no man gave unto him. And when he came to himself, he said, How many hired servants of my father's have bread enough and to spare, and I perish with hunger! I will arise and go to my father, and will say unto him, Father, I have sinned against heaven, and before thee, And am no more worthy to be called thy son: make me as one of thy hired servants. And he arose, and came to his father. But when he was yet a great way off, his father saw him, and had compassion, and ran, and fell on his neck, and kissed him. And the son said unto him, Father, I have sinned against heaven, and in thy sight, and am no more worthy to be called thy son. But the father said to his servants, Bring forth the best robe, and put it on him; and put a ring on his hand, and shoes on his feet: and bring hither the fatted calf, and kill it; and let us eat, and be merry: For this my son was dead, and is alive again; he was lost, and is found. And they began to be merry. Now his elder son was in the field: and as he came and drew nigh to the house, he heard music and dancing. And he called one of the servants, and asked what these things meant. And he said unto him, thy brother is come; and thy father hath killed the fatted

> *calf, because he hath received him safe and sound. And he was angry, and would not go in: therefore came his father out, and entreated him. And he answering said to his father, Lo, these many years do I serve thee, neither transgressed I at any time thy Commandment: and yet thou never gavest me a kid, that I might make merry with my friends: But as soon as this thy son was come, which hath devoured thy living with harlots, thou hast killed for him the fatted calf. And he said unto him, Son, thou art ever with me, and all that I have is thine. It was meet that we should make merry, and be glad: for this thy brother was dead, and is alive again, and was lost, and is found. Luke, Chapter 15, verses 11-32.*

I could get my Christian nose out of joint from this passage, but I do the same thing in the classroom. I love teaching kids, but where I get the most personal reward isn't from the gifted kids who could be successful on their own; it's from helping students who thought they weren't competent. I try to help them find out how capable they really are. I guess God likes seeing people turn their lives and their focus around, in somewhat a similar manner.

Here are some related passages:

> **And the Pharisees and scribes murmured, saying, This Man receiveth sinners, and eateth with them. And He spake this parable unto them, saying, What man of you, having an hundred sheep, if he lose one of them, doth not leave the ninety and nine in the wilderness, and go after that which is lost, until he find it? And when he hath found it, he layeth it on his shoulders rejoicing. And when he cometh home, he calleth together his friends and neighbours, saying unto them, Rejoice with me; for I have found my sheep which was lost. I say unto you, that likewise joy shall be in heaven over one sinner that repenteth, more than over ninety and nine just persons, which need no repentance. Luke, Chapter 15, verses 2-7.*

> **Either what woman having ten pieces of silver, if she lose one piece, doth not light a candle, and sweep the house, and seek diligently till she find it? And when she hath found it, she calleth her friends and her neighbours together, saying, Rejoice with me; for I have found the piece which I had lost. Likewise, I say unto you, there is joy in the presence of the angels of God over one sinner that repenteth. Luke, Chapter 15, verses 8-10.*

For the Son of Man is come to save that which was lost. How think ye? If a man have an hundred sheep, and one of them be gone astray, doth he not leave the ninety and nine, and goeth into the mountains, and seeketh that which is gone astray? And if so be that he find it, verily I say unto you, he rejoiceth more of that sheep, than of the ninety and nine which went not astray. Even so it is not the will of your Father which is in heaven, that one of these little ones should perish. Matthew, Chapter 18, verses 11-14.

....

For the kingdom of heaven is like unto a man that is an householder, which went out early in the morning to hire labourers into his vineyard. And when he had agreed with the labourers for a penny a day, he sent them into his vineyard. And he went out about the third hour, and saw others standing idle in the marketplace, And said unto them, Go ye also into the vineyard, and whatsoever is right I will give you. And they went their way. Again he went out about the sixth and ninth hour, and did likewise. And about the eleventh hour he went out, and found others standing idle, and saith unto them, Why stand ye here all day idle? They say unto him, Because no man hath hired us. He saith unto them, Go ye also into the vineyard; and whatsoever is right, that shall ye receive. So when even was come, the lord of the vineyard saith unto his steward, Call the labourers, and give them their hire, beginning from the last unto the first. And when they came that were hired about the eleventh hour, they received every man a penny. But when the first came, they supposed that they should have received more: and they likewise received every man a penny. And when they had received it, they murmured against the goodman of the house, Saying These last have wrought but one hour, and thou hast made them equal unto us, which have borne the burden and heat of the day. But he answered one of them, and said, Friend, I do thee no wrong: didst not thou agree with me for a penny? Take that thine is, and go thy way: I will give unto this last, even as unto thee. Is it not lawful for me to do what I will with mine own? Is thine eye evil, because I am good? So the last shall be first, and the first last: for many be called, but few chosen. Matthew, Chapter 20, verses 1-16.

I'm ashamed to say that I relate all too well with the first laborers who wanted more than what was promised for their extra time and effort. If I'm truly being honest, there have been times where I expected preferential treatment because I tried to be good and follow all the rules. I have deliberately flaunted the good choices I have made in hopes that teachers, employers and family members would like me better than others.

Well, it may have possibly worked since the people mentioned are human beings who could not see my ulterior motives, but God doesn't get suckered into struggles for attention. He loves us all the way we are. So the prostitute, the rock star, the janitor, the prisoner, the president, the former drug addict, the school teacher and anyone else who loves Jesus as their Savior can go to heaven. There is no preferential treatment there!

....

And the Pharisees also, who were covetous, heard all these things: and they derided Him. And He said unto them, Ye are they which justify yourselves before men; but God knoweth your hearts: for that which is highly esteemed among men is abomination in the sight of God. Luke, Chapter 16, verses 14-15.

People tend to look up to people who are rich, famous or have climbed their way up the corporate ladder. I like to watch the channel that shows the lives of famous T.V. and movie stars, past and present. Some, but not all of these, have been involved in lifestyles that included drugs, excessive drinking and some heavy-duty partying.

Even though people admire these stars, I think God would consider that type of lifestyle an abomination. Fortunately, some of these stars have had the opportunity to turn their lives around as they tell how they've gone from their party-hardy lifestyles to making God a priority in their lives.

....

There was a certain rich man, which was clothed in purple and fine linen, and fared sumptuously every day: And there was a certain beggar named Lazarus, which was laid at his gate, full of sores, And desiring to be fed with the crumbs which fell from the rich man's table: moreover the dogs came and licked his sores. And it came to pass, that the beggar died, and was carried by the angels into Abraham's bosom: the rich man also died, and was buried; And in hell he lift up his eyes, being in torments, and seeth Abraham afar off, and Lazarus in his bosom. And he cried and said, Father Abraham have mercy on me, and send Lazarus, that he may dip the tip of his finger in water, and cool my tongue; for I am tormented in this flame. But Abraham said, Son remember that thou in thy lifetime receivest thy good things, and likewise Lazarus evil things: but now he is comforted, and thou art tormented. Luke, Chapter 16, verses 19-25.

Do I want all the notoriety of the rich, famous and those who have climbed up the corporate ladder or would I prefer to focus on leading a lifestyle that allows me to go to heaven?

In order to get to heaven, I have to make sure I'm focused on Jesus, living as an example of how He works in my life on a daily basis. It's not always easy because I'm human and let greed and jealousy sneak into my life. I keep praying that God gives me the willingness to be the example He wants me to be, despite my very human nature.

....

Take heed to yourselves: If thy brother trespass against thee, rebuke him; and if he repent, forgive him. And if he trespass against thee seven times in a day, and seven times in a day turn again to thee, saying, I repent; thou shalt forgive him. Luke, Chapter 17, verses 3-4.

I'm sitting at the computer thinking about getting a job when we move instead of focusing on this. I said a little prayer and asked God to forgive me for being so distracted, and then it all came to me! God forgives me ninety billion times a day. He forgives all my distractions, angry, jealous and other human thoughts on a regular basis. When I ask God to forgive me, He never says, "No way! You've already long passed your quota of times to be forgiven."

If God forgives me an unlimited number of times, then He wants me to be more forgiving and tolerant of others. I shouldn't be there with my little mental clipboard saying, "Well, you've done this three times and that's it. I will no longer forgive you or be your friend!" If God treated me like that, I would have been "a gonner" a long time ago!

....

And the apostles said unto the Lord, Increase our faith. And the Lord said, If ye had faith as a grain of mustard seed, ye might say unto this sycamine tree, Be thou plucked up by the root, and be thou planted in the sea; and it should obey you. Luke, Chapter 17, verses 5-6.

This passage seems especially appropriate since I'm a "Focused on Other Things Christian," thinking about selling my house, finding a job and buying another house. If I were really paying attention to what I'm writing, I would realize my faith is weak, because I am worrying and having sleepless nights.

I need to focus on God and things will fall into place. He works everything out so beautifully in timing, if I have the patience to let Him.

Here are some related passages:

> *Are not five sparrows sold for two farthings, and not one of them is forgotten before God? But even the very hairs of your head are all numbered. Fear not therefore: ye are of more value than many sparrows. Luke, Chapter 12, verses 6-7.*

> **Are not two sparrows sold for a farthing? And one of them shall not fall on the ground without your Father. But the very hairs of your head are all numbered. Fear ye not therefore, ye are of more value than many sparrows. Matthew, Chapter 10, verses 29-31.*

....

> *And it came to pass, as He went to Jerusalem that He passed through the midst of Samaria and Galilee. And as He entered into a certain village, there met Him ten men that were lepers, which stood afar off: And they lifted up their voices, and said, Jesus, Master, have mercy on us. And when He saw them, He said unto them, Go show yourselves unto the priests. And it came to pass, that, as they went, they were cleansed. And one of them, when he saw that he was healed, turned back, and with a loud voice glorified God, And fell down on his face at His feet, giving Him thanks: and he was a Samaritan. And Jesus answering said, Were there not ten cleansed? but where are the nine? There are not found that returned to give glory to God, save this stranger. And He said unto him, Arise, go thy way: thy faith hath made thee whole. Luke, Chapter 17, verses 11-19.*

I pray to God about things that concern me in my everyday life. Do I stop and thank Him for resolving all these issues? Not for the most part! My life runs smoothly because the problem has been resolved and I go on with my life, putting Jesus back on the shelf until I need him again.

After I read this passage, I thought about how ungrateful the nine healed lepers were. Isn't that exactly what I'm doing when I don't take the time to thank God for resolving the issues in my life?

....

Luke, Chapter 17, verses 34-37, is very controversial. I have heard many different opinions from supposed authorities on these passages. I decided years ago that it's more important for me to continue to focus on my relationship with God. Spending my time arguing over how and when I am going to heaven is time wasted, in my opinion, when I could have spent the time being a better example of Jesus' influence on my life.

I don't have to spend years trying to figure out whose interpretation of this Bible passage is correct. My Salvation is guaranteed through Jesus' death and Resurrection as long as I continue to love Him as my Lord and Savior and try to lead a life that reflects my faith in Him. If I do these, I will have Salvation at the time and in the manner that God deems is best. I think God has other things He would like me to focus on, like reading the Bible rather than worrying about the details of how and when this is all going to happen.

....

And He spake this parable unto certain which trusted in themselves that they were righteous, and despised others: Two men went up into the temple to pray; the one a Pharisee, and the other a publican. The Pharisee stood and prayed thus with himself, God, I thank thee, that I am not as other men are, extortioners, unjust, adulterers, or even as this publican. I fast twice in the week, I give tithes of all that I possess. And the publican, standing afar off, would not lift up so much as his eyes unto heaven, but smote upon his breast, saying, God be merciful to me a sinner. I tell you, this man went down to his house justified rather than the other: for every one that exalteth himself shall be abased; and he that humbleth himself shall be exalted. Luke, Chapter 18, verses 9-14.

This passage is kind of like Biblical irony. The Pharisee with the higher status, self-righteous attitude and brags about all the wonderful things he has done for others, isn't justified. The humble man with the low status, who states how unworthy he is, is justified.

It really opens my eyes. Sometimes I become very self-righteous like the Pharisee, boasting to myself about all the good things I've done. (Actually it wasn't me doing them in the first place. God gave me the instincts to do those things, but I was taking credit for them while boasting.) I need to be much more humble and not get so caught up in the egotistical part. That's how Satan sneaks in and leads Christians astray!

....

> *And they brought unto Him also infants, that He would touch them: but when His disciples saw it, they rebuked them. But Jesus called them unto Him, and said, Suffer little children to come unto Me, and forbid them not: for of such is the kingdom of God. Verily I say unto you, Whosoever shall not receive the kingdom of God as a little child shall in no wise enter therein.* Luke, Chapter 18, verses 15-17.

As an elementary school teacher, it never ceases to amaze me how sweet, trusting and honest little children are. It seems some get corrupted as they grow up and become cynical by the ways of the world, media and life, in general.

In the early grades the children would play with almost any other person that was willing to play with them. They generally got along well with everyone except for little squabbles, regardless of ethnicity or any other factor. Nearing the intermediate grades, these same groups of children would no longer associate with some of the children that they used to consider their best friends. They seemed to group themselves by ethnicity and other factors like income. I think Jesus wants us to be "Uncorrupted Christians" who generally get along well with others, regardless of ethnicity or any other factor.

Here is a related passage:

> **Then were there brought unto Him little children, that He should put His hands on them, and pray: and the disciples rebuked them, But Jesus said, Suffer little children, and forbid them not, to come unto Me: for of such is the kingdom of heaven. And He laid His hands on them and departed thence.* Matthew, Chapter 19, verses 13-15.

....

> *Then He took unto Him the twelve, and said unto them, Behold, we go up to Jerusalem, and all things that are written by the prophets concerning the Son of Man shall be accomplished. For He shall be delivered unto the Gentiles, and shall be mocked, and spitefully entreated, and spitted on: And they shall scourge Him, and put Him to death: and the third day He shall rise again.* Luke, Chapter 18, verses 31-33.

This passage is soooooo amazing! Jesus knows how terribly they are going to treat Him, how they are going to mock Him, spit on Him and crucify Him. Yet Jesus is still willing to go through all that utter humiliation to save us from our sins. Now a parent might possibly be willing to go through all of that to save the life of their child, but would they be willing to go through all of that for complete strangers, for people who are hateful and rude to them? No way!!! Jesus gave His life for us knowing in advance how terribly humiliating it would be, because He loves us that much!

Jesus told the disciples about what was going to happen to Him in advance. He wanted them to remember what He had told them as another proof that Jesus is the One True Savior of all. It's sad that Jesus can be willing to give His life for us, and we need ALL this proof first before we are willing to believe in Him.

Here are some related passages:

From that time forth began Jesus to show unto His disciples, how that He must go unto Jerusalem, and suffer many things of the elders and chief priests and scribes, and be killed, and be raised again the third day. Then Peter took Him, and began to rebuke Him, saying, Be it far from Thee, Lord: this shall not be unto Thee. But He turned and said unto Peter, Get thee behind Me, Satan, thou art an offence unto Me: for thou savourest not the things that be of God, but those that be of men. Matthew, Chapter 16, verses 21-23.

And they came down from the mountain, Jesus charged them, saying, Tell the vision to no man, until the Son of Man be risen again from the dead. Matthew, Chapter 17, verse 9.

And while they abode in Galilee, Jesus said unto them, The Son of Man shall be betrayed into the hands of men: And they shall kill Him, and the third day He shall be raised again. And they were exceeding sorry. Matthew, Chapter 17, verses 22-23.

And Jesus going up to Jerusalem took the twelve disciples apart in the way, and said unto them, Behold, we go up to Jerusalem; and the Son of Man shall be betrayed unto the chief priests and unto the scribes, and they shall condemn Him to death, And shall deliver Him to the Gentiles to mock, and to scourge, and to crucify Him: and the third day He shall rise again. Matthew, Chapter 20, verses 17-19.

What think ye? They answered and said, He is guilty of death. Then did they spit on His face, and buffeted Him; and others smote Him with the palms of their hands. Saying, Prophesy unto us, Thou Christ, Who is he that smote Thee? Matthew, Chapter 26, verses 66-68.

For scarcely for a righteous man will one die: yet peradventure for a good man some would even dare to die. But God commendeth His love toward us, in that, while we were yet sinners, Christ died for us. Much more then, being now justified by His blood, we shall be saved from wrath through Him. For if, when we were enemies we were reconciled to God by the death of His Son, much more, being reconciled, we shall be saved by His life. And not only so, but we also joy in God through our Lord Jesus Christ, by whom we have now received the atonement. Romans, Chapter 5, verses 7-11.

Grace be to you and peace from God the Father, and from our Lord Jesus Christ, Who gave Himself for our sins, that He might deliver us from this present evil world, according to the Will of God and our Father: To whom be glory for ever and ever. Amen. Galatians, Chapter 1, verses 3-5.

....

And it came to pass, that as He was come nigh unto Jericho, a certain blind man sat by the way side begging: and hearing the multitude pass by, he asked what it meant. And they told him, that Jesus of Nazareth passeth by. And he cried, saying, Jesus, Thou Son of David, have mercy on me. And they which went before rebuked him, that he should hold his peace: but he cried so much the more, Thou Son of David, have mercy on me. And Jesus stood, and commanded him to be brought unto Him: and when he was come near, He asked him, Saying, What wilt thou that I shall do unto thee? And he said, Lord, that I may receive my sight. And Jesus said unto him, Receive thy sight: thy faith hath saved thee. And immediately he received his sight, and followed Him, glorifying God: and all the people when they saw it, gave praise unto God. Luke, Chapter 18, verses 35-43.

Jesus is on His way to His crucifixion knowing full well what terrible things are going to happen to Him, but Jesus still takes time out to heal this blind man despite all He is about to go through. It reinforces how Jesus takes time to be there for me and my very trivial concerns. I'm so fortunate to have Jesus as my Savior!!!

Here is a related passage:

And the blind and the lame came to Him in the temple: and He healed them. And when the chief priest and scribes saw the wonderful things that He did, and the children crying in the temple, and saying, Hosanna to the Son of David; they were sore displeased. And said unto Him, Hearest thou what these say? And Jesus saith unto them, Yea; have ye never read, Out of the mouth of babes and sucklings thou hast perfected praise. Matthew, Chapter 21, verses 14-16.

....

And Jesus entered and passed through Jericho. And, behold, there was a man named Zacchaeus, which was the chief among the publicans, and he was rich. And he sought to see Jesus who He was; and could not for the press, because he was little of stature. And he ran before, and climbed up into a sycamore tree to see Him: for He was to pass that way. And when Jesus came to the place, He looked up, and saw him, and said unto him, Zacchaeus, make haste, and come down; for today I must abide at thy house. And he made haste, and came down, and received Him joyfully. And when they saw it, they all murmured, saying, That He was gone to be guest with a man that is a sinner. And Zacchaeus stood and said unto the Lord; Behold, Lord, the half of my goods I give to the poor; and if I have taken any thing from any man by false accusation, I restore him fourfold. And Jesus said unto him, This day is Salvation come to this house, forsomuch as he also is a son of Abraham. For the Son of Man is come to seek and to save that which was lost. Luke, Chapter 19, verses 1-10.

I remember hearing a group of people talking amongst themselves saying something about not associating with sinners. That rushed through my mind when I saw a display outside a church that said, "Sinners Welcome!" Jesus didn't give His life to save those who are perfect. (That would mean He had given His life to save Himself since Jesus is the only perfect person. Now that doesn't even make sense!)

Jesus died and rose to save sinners like you and me. He gave His life for those people who were judgmental of others and the people they thought were unworthy of their association. If Jesus can turn the life of Zacchaeus around who was a self-serving tax collector, then who is to say that He can't turn around the lives of those people deemed unfit?

If no one invites or welcomes these people into church, how will they be saved? Do you want it on your shoulders that you had the opportunity to befriend one of these "undesirable" people by being an example of how God works in your life, but you ignored that responsibility because you decided that those people didn't deserve it? Something I wouldn't want to have to explain to God on Judgment Day!

Here is a related passage:

*And when the Pharisees saw it, they said unto His disciples, Why eateth your Master with publicans and sinners? But when Jesus heard that, He said unto them, They that be whole need not a physician, but they that are sick. But go ye and learn what that meaneth, I will have mercy, and not sacrifice: for I am not come to call the righteous, but sinners to repentance. Matthew, Chapter 9, verses 11-13.

....

And as they heard these things, He added and spake a parable, because He was nigh to Jerusalem, and because they thought that the kingdom of God should immediately appear. He said therefore, A certain nobleman went into a far country to receive for himself a kingdom, and to return. And he called his ten servants, and delivered them ten pounds, and said unto them, Occupy till I come. But his citizens hated him, and sent a message after him, saying, we will not have this man to reign over us. And it came to pass, that when he was returned, having received the kingdom, then he commanded these servants to be called unto him, to whom he had given the money, that he might know how much every man had gained by trading. Then came the first, saying, Lord, thy pound hath gained ten pounds. And he said unto him, Well, thou good servant: because thou hast been faithful in a very little, have thou authority over ten cities. And the second came, saying, Lord, thy pound hath gained five pounds. And he said likewise to him, Be thou also over five cities. And another came, saying, Lord, behold, here is thy pound, which I have kept laid up in a napkin: For I feared thee, because thou art an austere man: thou takest up that thou layedst not down, and reapest that thou did not sow. And he saith unto him, Out of thine own mouth will I judge thee, thou wicked servant. Thou knewest that I was an austere man, taking up that I laid not down, and reaping that I did not sow: Wherefore then gavest not thou my money unto the bank, that at my coming I might have required mine own with usury? And he said unto them that stood by, Take from him the pound, and give it to him that hath ten pounds. (And they said unto him, Lord, he hath ten pounds.) For I say unto you, That unto every one which hath *shall be given; and from him that hath not, even that he hath shall be taken away from him. But those mine enemies, which would not that I should reign over them, bring hither, and slay them before me. Luke, Chapter 19, verses 11-27.*

Jesus may say on the Last Day, "You were all given the same task to be examples of how I work in your lives and to share your love of Me with others. Did you do it? When you had problems you turned to Me but when I solved those problems for you, you didn't even take the time to thank Me. You just turned back to your life like I didn't exist until the next problem or religious holiday came around. Then, you were so focused on showing off your new clothes at church that you didn't even pay attention to Me and the real reason for the season. Sorry, Charlie, you're not making it to heaven!"

Here is a related passage:

*For the kingdom of heaven is as a man traveling into a far country, who called his own servants, and delivered unto them his goods. And unto one he gave five talents, to another two, and to another one; to every man according to his several ability; and straightway took his journey. Then he that had received the five talents went and traded with the same, and made them other five talents. And likewise he that had received two, he also gained other two. But he that had received one went and digged in the earth, and hid his lord's money. After a long time the lord of those servants cometh, and reckoneth with them. And so he that had received five talents came and brought other five talents, saying, Lord, thou deliveredst unto me five talents: behold, I have gained beside them five talents more. His lord said unto him, Well done, thou good and faithful servant: thou hast been faithful over a few things, I will make thee ruler over many things: enter thou into the joy of thy lord. He also that had received two talents came and said, Lord, thou deliveredst unto me two talents: behold, I have gained two other talents beside them. His lord said unto him, Well done, good and faithful servant; thou hast been faithful over a few things, I will make thee ruler over many things: enter thou into the joy of thy lord. Then he which had received the one talent came and said, Lord, I knew thee that thou art an hard man, reaping where thou hast not sowed, and gathering where thou hast not strawed: And I was afraid, and went and hid thy talent in the earth: lo there thou hast that is thine. His lord answered and said unto him, Thou

wicked and slothful servant, thou knewest that I reap where I sowed not, and gather where I have not strawed: Thou oughtest therefore to have put my money to the exchangers, and then at my coming I should have received mine own with usury. Take therefore the talent from him, and give it unto him which hath ten talents. For unto every one that hath shall be given, and he shall have abundance: but from him that hath not shall be taken away even that which he hath. And cast ye the unprofitable servant into outer darkness: there shall be weeping and gnashing of teeth. When the Son of Man shall come in His glory, and all the holy angels with Him, then shall He sit upon the throne of His glory. And before Him shall be gathered all nations: and He shall separate them one from another, as a Shepherd divideth His sheep from the goats. And He shall set the sheep on His right hand, but the goats on the left. Matthew, Chapter 25, verses 14-33.

....

Then began He to speak to the people this parable: A certain man planted a vineyard, and let it forth to husbandmen, and went into a far country for a long time. And at the season he sent a servant to the husbandmen, that they should give him of the fruit of the vineyard: but the husbandmen beat him, and sent him away empty. And again he sent another servant; and they beat him also, and entreated him shamefully, and sent him away empty. And again he sent a third: and they wounded him also, and cast him out. Then said the lord of the vineyard, What shall I do? I will send my beloved son: it may be they will reverence him when they see him. But when the husbandmen saw him they reasoned among themselves, saying, This is the heir: come, let us kill him, that the inheritance may be ours. So they cast him out of the vineyard, and killed him. What therefore shall the lord of the vineyard do unto them? He shall come and destroy these husbandmen, and shall give the vineyard to others. And when they heard it, they said, God forbid. Luke, Chapter 20, verses 9-16.

After reading the parable, this is my opinion of what God might say. "I protected My people and promised them a Savior (Jesus). Then I sent them prophets to tell of Jesus' coming and they ignored them. I thought that they just didn't understand that I'm trying to help them turn their lives around so that they can have Salvation with Me. So, I decided to send John the Baptist and they ignored and killed him. I figured surely they will acknowledge My only begotten Son, Jesus, so I sent Jesus to them.

"They totally ignored the fact that Jesus is the Son of God, and then they had the audacity to kill Him. That way they didn't have to feel guilty anymore for living their worldly lives not focused on My teachings. They didn't have any idea about who they were dealing with, because Jesus arose from the grave on the third day to fulfill the Scriptures. He conquered death so that all who truly believe in Him will have eternal life in heaven.

"You ungrateful people! You killed My only begotten Son and don't deserve the gift of Salvation that Jesus has provided for you. I'm going to give that gift to anyone who believes that Jesus is their Savior, because you aren't worthy of it!"

Here are some related passages:

Hear another parable: There was a certain householder, which planted a vineyard, and hedged it round about, and digged a winepress in it, and built a tower, and let it out to husbandmen, and went into a far country: And when the time of the fruit drew near, he sent his servants to the husbandmen, that they might receive the fruits of it. And the husbandmen took his servants, and beat one, and killed another, and stoned another. Again, he sent other servants more than the first: and they did unto them likewise. But last of all he sent unto them his son, saying They will reverence my son. But when the husbandmen saw the son, they said among themselves, This is the heir, come, let us kill him, and let us seize on his inheritance. And they caught him, and cast him out of the vineyard, and slew him. When the lord therefore of the vineyard cometh, what will he do unto those husbandmen? They say unto Him, he will miserably destroy those wicked men, and will let out his vineyard unto other husbandmen, which shall render him the fruits in their seasons. Jesus saith unto them, Did ye never read in the Scriptures, The stone which the builders rejected the same is become the head of the corner: this is the Lord's doing and it is marvelous in our eyes? Therefore say I unto you, The kingdom of God shall be taken from you and given to a nation bringing forth the fruits thereof. And whomsoever shall fall on this stone shall be broken: but on whosoever it shall fall, it will grind him to powder. Matthew, Chapter 21, verses 33-44.

And He began to speak unto them by parables. A certain man planted a vineyard, and set an hedge about it, and digged a place for the winevat, and built a tower, and let it out to husbandmen, and went into a far country. And at the season he sent to the husbandmen a servant that he might receive from the husbandmen of the fruit of the vineyard. And they caught him, and beat him, and sent him away empty. And again he sent unto them another servant; and at him they cast stones, and wounded him in the head, and sent him away shamefully handled. And again he sent another; and him they killed, and many others; beating some and killing some. Having yet therefore one son, his well beloved, he sent him also last unto them, saying, They will reverence my son. But those husbandmen said among themselves, This is the heir; come let us kill him, and the inheritance shall be ours. And they took him, and killed him, and cast him out of the vineyard. What shall therefore the lord of the vineyard do? he will come and destroy the husbandmen, and will give the vineyard unto others. Mark, Chapter 12, verses 1-9.

....

And they watched Him, and sent forth spies, which should feign themselves just men, that they might take hold of His Words, that so they might deliver Him unto the power and authority of the governor. And they asked Him, saying, Master, we know that Thou sayest and teachest rightly, neither acceptest thou the person of any, but teachest the way of God truly: Is it lawful for us to give tribute unto Caesar, or no? But He perceived their craftiness, and said unto them, Why tempt ye Me? Show Me a penny. Whose image and superscription hath it? And He said unto them, Render therefore unto Caesar the things which be Caesar's, and unto God the things which be God's. And they could not take hold of His Words before the people: and they marvelled at His answer, and held their peace. Luke, Chapter 20, verses 20-26.

I keep having problems with this one. I've sold several different products in side-line businesses for the sole purpose of trying to give Caesar a little less of what seems mine. (Now there is nothing wrong with having a side-line business or selling things to gain a profit. My goal was distinctly motivated toward being able to legally keep more of my money, although I did everything in my power to do it legally.)

Writing this book has made me more aware of my motives. I have given up the side-line businesses, since my motives weren't in-line with what God would want me to do. I keep letting worldly things sneak in and put a wedge in my relationship with God.

I guess I have two options when God makes me aware of these things. I can try to ignore them and pretend that I have blinders on and don't really understand what He is showing me, or I can make the changes necessary to be in-line with what God wants. In order to do that, I am donating the profits I get from this book to a non-profit organization or a charitable cause. Money wasn't the reason I wrote this. I felt strongly led to share these insights with you, with the desire that you would better understand the positive influence the Bible can have in your daily life.

Here are some related passages:

And they send unto Him certain of the Pharisees and of the Herodians, to catch Him in His Words. And when they were come, they say unto Him, Master, we know that Thou art True, and carest for no man, for Thou regardest not the person of men, but teachest the way of God in Truth: Is it lawful to give tribute to Caesar, or not? Shall we give, or shall we not give? But He, knowing their hypocrisy, said unto them, Why tempt ye Me? bring Me a penny, that I may see it. And they brought it. And He saith unto them, Whose is this image and superscription? And they said unto Him, Caesar's. And Jesus answering said unto them, Render to Caesar the things that are Caesar's, and to God the things that are God's. And they marvelled at Him. Mark, Chapter 12, verses 13-17.

And when they were come to Capernaum, they that received tribute money came to Peter, and said, Doth not your Master pay tribute? He saith, Yes. And when he was come into the house, Jesus prevented him, saying, What thinkest thou, Simon? Of whom do the kings of the earth take custom or tribute? Of their own children, or of strangers? Peter saith unto Him, Of strangers. Jesus saith unto him, Then are the children free. Notwithstanding, lest we should offend them, go thou to the sea, and cast an hook, and take up the fish that first cometh up; and when thou hast opened his mouth, thou shalt find a piece of money: that take, and give unto them for Me and thee. Matthew, Chapter 17, verses 24-27.

*Tell us therefore, What thinkest Thou? Is it lawful to give tribute unto Caesar, or not? But Jesus perceived their wickedness, and said, Why tempt ye Me, ye hypocrites? Show Me the tribute money. And they brought unto Him a penny. And He saith unto them, Whose is this image and superscription? They say unto Him, Caesar's. Then saith He unto them, Render therefore unto Caesar the things which are Caesar's; and unto God the things that are God's. When they had heard these Words, they marveled, and left Him, and went their way. Matthew, Chapter 22, verses 17-22.

....

Then in the audience of all the people He said unto His disciples, Beware of the scribes, which desire to walk in long robes, and love greetings in the markets, and the highest seats in the synagogues, and the chief rooms at feasts; Which devour widows' houses, and for a show make long prayers: the same shall receive greater damnation. Luke, Chapter 20, verses 45-47.

This reminds me of old westerns I used to watch on TV. It would show the banker (not to imply this is the way bankers are or this behavior is limited only to bankers.) He would appear nice enough, saying hi to the husband, tip his hat to the wife and did "coochie coos" to her baby. This banker is a good upstanding churchgoer. He appears to be the pillar of society, a role model to others.

Then as the plot thickens, the banker and his cohorts try to squeeze the farmer and his family off their land. He secretly knows there is a lot of profit to be gained by that particular piece of property. The husband dies in a freak accident which is highly suspicious. Then the banker comes to give the grieving wife his condolences and tell her how sorry he is about her loss. He says that out of the goodness of his heart, he will give the wife an extra month's extension on paying what is owed on the property before he forecloses on their mortgage.

The rest of the movie is dedicated to showing how the banker and his cohorts try to make it difficult for her, and those that befriend her, to pay the money owed. Of course, in the movie, good wins out over evil and the lady and her baby get to stay in their home. But, in real life; that doesn't always happen.

There are some who are very cunning and would have no remorse for evicting the widow and her child from their home, because they are within their rights as far as the law goes. These people would continue to go to church without a guilty conscience, because they have rationalized their actions. The thing is...God knows what they do and no amount of rationalization is going to cut it with God for those who take advantage of widows and orphans!

Here are some related passages:

**Woe unto you, scribes and Pharisees, hypocrites! For ye devour widows' houses, and for a pretence make long prayer: therefore ye shall receive the greater damnation. Matthew, Chapter 23, verse 14.*

*Woe unto them that decree unrighteous decrees, and that write grievousness which they have prescribed; To turn aside the needy from judgment, and to take away the right from the poor of My people, that widows may be their prey, and that they may rob the fatherless! And what will ye do in the day of visitation, and in the desolation which shall come from far? to whom will ye flee for help? And where will ye leave your glory? Without Me they shall bow down under the prisoners, and they shall fall under the slain. For all this His anger is not turned away, but His Hand is stretched out still. Isaiah, Chapter 10, verses 1-4.

*And her prophets have daubed them with untempered mortar, seeing vanity, and divining lies unto them saying, Thus saith the Lord God, when the Lord hath not spoken. The people of the land have used oppression, and exercised robbery, and have vexed the poor and needy: yea, they have oppressed the stranger wrongfully. Ezekiel, Chapter 22, verses 28-29.

....

And when the hour was come, He sat down, and the twelve apostles with Him. And He said unto them, With desire I have desired to eat this passover with you before I suffer: For I say unto you, I will not any more eat thereof, until it be fulfilled in the kingdom of God. And He took the cup, and gave thanks, and said, Take this, and divide it among yourselves: For I say unto you, I will not drink of the fruit of the vine, until the kingdom of God shall come. And He took Bread, and gave thanks, and brake it, and gave unto them, saying, This is My Body which is given for you: this do in remembrance of Me. Likewise also the Cup after supper, saying, This Cup is the New Testament in My Blood which is shed for you. Luke, Chapter 22, verses 14-20.

These words are very significant to me each time I prepare to have Communion. They remind me of how Jesus knew what was going to happen to Him and He still went through it anyway...for me. He gave His life for me, even though I get self-righteous at times and puff up my ego...For me, even though I can get cranky with my family, especially when my blood sugar is low...For me, even though I look at the angles to see how I can keep more of the money I think I deserve rather than giving it to Uncle Sam...For me, even though I have a difficult time giving up control and trusting God to take care of me...For me, even though I have some hateful, jealous thoughts in my mind, at times. I could go on, but you get the picture. I'm a very sinful human being and Jesus gave His life for me...and He gave it for you, too!

Here is a related passage:

> *And as they were eating, Jesus took Bread, and blessed it, and brake it, and gave it to the disciples, and said, Take, eat; this is My Body. And He took the Cup, and gave thanks, and gave it to them, saying Drink ye all of it. For this is My Blood of the New Testament, which is shed for many for the remission of sins. But I say unto you, I will not drink henceforth of this fruit of the vine, until that day when I drink it new with you in My Father's kingdom. Matthew, Chapter 26, verses 26-29.*

....

> *But, behold, the hand of him that betrayeth Me is with Me on the table. And truly the Son of Man goeth, as it was determined: but woe unto that man by whom He is betrayed! Luke, Chapter 22, verses 21-22.*

I remember times in high school when I thought people were talking about me when they looked in my general direction. They might not have been doing anything at all. I was just very self-conscious, as are many teenagers at that age. I had a difficult time associating with those people that I thought were disloyal to me, whether it was real or just perceived. It amazes me how Jesus didn't just think someone was going to betray Him, He knew it! He didn't avoid the whole situation, as I would have. He continued to associate with the person that was going to betray Him.

What love He had to have for us to bear these interactions, even when He knew the very people He loved were going to be disloyal to Him. It's difficult for me to comprehend such a truly selfless love for others. I'm so very fortunate Jesus is my Lord and Savior!

....

> *And the Lord said, Simon, Simon, behold, Satan hath desired to have you, that he may sift you as wheat: But I have prayed for thee, that thy faith fail not: and when thou art converted, strengthen thy brethren. And he said unto Him, Lord, I am ready to go with Thee, both into prison, and to death. And He said, I tell thee, Peter, the cock shall not crow this day, before that thou shalt thrice deny that thou knowest Me. Luke, Chapter 22, verses 31-34.*

(I've skipped some verses that I will come back to after this, so you can have the rest of Simon Peter's interactions.)

> *Then took they Him, and led Him, and brought Him into the high priest's house. And Peter followed afar off. And when they had kindled a fire in the midst of the hall, and were set down together, Peter sat down among them. But a certain maid beheld him as he sat by the fire, and earnestly looked upon him, and said, This man was also with Him. And he denied Him, saying, Woman, I know Him not. And after a little while another saw him, and said, Thou art also of them. And Peter said, Man, I am not. And about the space of one hour after another confidently affirmed, saying, Of a truth this fellow also was with Him, for he is a Galilean. And Peter said, Man, I know not what thou sayest. And immediately, while he yet spake, the cock crew. And the Lord turned, and looked upon Peter. And Peter remembered the Word of the Lord, how He had said unto him, Before the cock crow, thou shalt deny Me thrice. And Peter went out, and wept bitterly. Luke, Chapter 22, verses 54-62.*

When I read this Bible passage, I reflect on how I sometimes think I am very dedicated to God, but really I'm a "Luke-warm Christian!" In my mind, I feel like God is the most important part of my life, but when a situation arises where I could share my faith with others, I avoid it. I say to myself, "Well, this isn't the right timing for me to discuss Jesus and all He's done for me. Another time would be more beneficial and the person would probably be more open to it then."

Baloney!!! Who am I trying to fool? I guess the only one I'm trying to fool is myself, because God knows when I avoid situations where I could have shared my relationship with Him. Although I don't deny God openly as Simon Peter did, I'm denying Him in my heart through my choice not to share my love for Jesus with others. Sometimes, the truth hurts!

Here are some related passages:

And Peter remembered the Word of Jesus, which said unto him, Before the cock crow, thou shalt deny me thrice. And he went out and wept bitterly. Matthew, Chapter 26, verse 75.

Simon Peter said unto Him, Lord, whither goest Thou? Jesus answered him, Whither I go, thou canst not follow Me now; but thou shalt follow Me afterwards. Peter said unto Him, Lord, why cannot I follow Thee now? I will lay down my life for Thy sake. Jesus answered him, Wilt thou lay down thy life for My sake? Verily, verily, I say unto thee, The cock shall not crow, till thou hast denied Me thrice. John, Chapter 13, verses 36-38.

And Simon Peter followed Jesus, and so did another disciple: that disciple was known unto the high priest, and went in with Jesus into the palace of the high priest. But Peter stood at the door without. Then went out that other disciple, which was known unto the high priest, and spake unto her that kept the door, and brought in Peter. Then saith the damsel that kept the door unto Peter, Art not thou also one of this Man's disciples? He saith, I am not. And the servants and officers stood there, who had made a fire of coals; for it was cold: and they warmed themselves: and Peter stood with them, and warmed himself. John, Chapter 18, verses 15-18. [I'm skipping to the rest.] And Simon Peter stood and warmed himself. They said therefore unto him, Art thou also one of His disciples? He denied it, and said, I am not. One of the servants of the high priest, being his kinsman whose ear Peter cut off, saith, Did not I see thee in the garden with Him? Peter then denied again: and immediately the cock crew. John, Chapter 18, verses 25-27.

....

(This is the part I left out earlier.)

And He came out, and went, as He was wont, to the mount of Olives: and His disciples also followed Him. And when He was at the place, He said unto them, Pray that ye enter not into temptation. And He was withdrawn from them about a stone's cast, and kneeled down, and prayed, Saying, Father, if Thou be willing, remove this cup from Me: nevertheless not My will, but Thine, be done. And there appeared an angel unto Him from heaven, strengthening Him. And being in an agony He prayed more earnestly: and His sweat was as it were great drops of blood falling down to the ground. And when He rose up from prayer, and was come to His disciples, He found them sleeping for sorrow. And said unto them, Why sleep ye? rise and pray, lest ye enter into temptation. Luke, Chapter 22, verses 39-46.

As a Christian, it's easy for me to say, "Oh, no problem. I love You so much, Jesus; that there's no way I will slip into temptation." Well, if the disciples who loved Jesus very much could slip into temptation, then we need to learn from their actions and realize the importance of praying for God to keep us from temptation.

I recognize that sometimes when I say the Lord's Prayer each night, I tend to ramble through it even though I know I shouldn't. I'm not sure that God acknowledges prayers when we just ramble through them in a repetitive manner. When I say my prayers in the morning, I ask God to take care of all sorts of things: my family, the world, and me; but I don't ask Him to protect us from temptation. This has made me extremely aware of my need to add that to my daily prayers and to slow down and focus on what I'm praying.

Here are some related passages:

*Watch and pray, that ye enter not into temptation: the spirit indeed is willing, but the flesh is weak. Matthew, Chapter 26, verse 41.

*For it had been better for them not to have known the way of righteousness, than, after they have known it, to turn from the Holy Commandment delivered unto them. 2 Peter, Chapter 2, verse 21.

....

And while He yet spake, behold a multitude, and he that was called Judas, one of the twelve, went before them, and drew near unto Jesus to kiss Him. But Jesus said unto him, Judas, betrayest thou the Son of Man with a kiss? When they which were about Him saw what would follow, they said unto Him, Lord, shall we smite with the sword? And one of them smote the servant of the high priest, and cut off his right ear. And Jesus answered and said, Suffer ye thus far. And He touched his ear, and healed him. Luke, Chapter 22, verses 47-51.

I don't know if I could do something nice like heal a person who was part of a plot to kill me. I've been known to remember situations for over twenty years where someone has been rude or hurtful to me, yet I am dependent on Jesus' forgiving nature. If He remembered all my sins the same way I have harbored resentments toward others, there's no way I would ever make it to heaven. He forgives me over and over, even when I don't deserve His forgiveness. He is there loving me when I find it difficult to love myself. I'm so fortunate to have Jesus as my Savior and Redeemer.

I write these things and find I'm very two-faced. I say things like Savior and Redeemer in my writing and realize that I would never be caught dead saying these things in public. I think that's because I don't want to sound like a religious fanatic to others. I might say that I love Jesus, but that's usually as far as my profession of faith goes. I need to pay attention because I could be faced with Jesus saying, "I love Dorothy, but I can't allow her to have Salvation because she is afraid to risk the condemnation of others. She is afraid that if she says I'm her Savior and Redeemer, others will think she is a religious fanatic! What a shame. She had such potential, but if she can't acknowledge Me, I don't feel obliged to acknowledge her. Such a shame!"

Actually, this reminds me about the passage I had just written where Simon Peter denied Jesus three times. Well, Simon Peter still received Salvation, because he learned from his mistakes and realized how terrible it was that he had denied Jesus. Simon Peter turned his life around where he became someone who readily proclaimed his love for Jesus. Now I need to be able to do the same. I need to turn my life around and not hide behind my fear of what people will think of me. I'm still very weak in this area and need to ask that God gives me the willingness to let Him guide my actions and my words, now and always, not just when it's comfortable.

Here are some related passages:

And, behold, one of them which were with Jesus stretched out his hand, and drew his sword, and struck a servant of the high priest's, and smote off his ear. Then said Jesus unto him, Put up again thy sword into his place: for all they that take the sword shall perish with the sword. Thinkest thou that I cannot now pray to My Father, and He shall presently give Me more than twelve legions of angels? But how then shall the Scriptures be fulfilled, that thus it must be? Matthew, Chapter 26, 51-54.

O my God, I trust in Thee: let me not be ashamed, let not mine enemies triumph over me. Psalm, Chapter 25, verse 2.

As for our Redeemer, the LORD of Hosts is His Name, the Holy One of Israel. Isaiah, Chapter 47, verse 4.

And they asked him, and said unto him, Why baptized thou then, if thou be not that Christ, nor Elias, neither that prophet? John answered them, saying, I baptize with water: but there standeth One among you, Whom ye know not; He it is, who coming after me is preferred before me, Whose shoe's latchet I am not worthy to unloose. These things were done in Bethabara beyond Jordan, where John was baptizing. The next day John seeth Jesus coming unto him and saith, Behold the Lamb of God, which taketh away the sin of the world. This is He of whom I said, After me cometh a Man which is preferred before me: for He was before me. And I knew Him not: but that He should be made manifest to Israel, therefore am I come baptizing with water. And John bare record, saying, I saw the Spirit descending from heaven like a dove, and it abode upon Him. And I knew Him not: but He that sent me to baptize with water, the same said unto me, Upon whom thou shalt see the Spirit descending, and remaining on Him, the same is He which baptizeth with the Holy Ghost. And I saw, and bare record that this is the Son of God. Again the next day after John stood, and the two of His disciples: and looking upon Jesus as He walked, he saith, Behold the Lamb of God! And the two disciples heard Him speak, and they followed Jesus. Then Jesus turned, and saw them following, and saith unto them, What seek ye? They said unto Him, Rabbi, (which is to say, being interpreted, Master,) where dwellest Thou? He saith unto them, Come and see. They came and saw where He dwelt, and abode with Him that day: for it was about the tenth hour. One of the two which heard John speak, and followed him, was Andrew, Simon Peter's brother. He first findeth his own brother Simon, and saith unto him, We have found the Messias, which is being interpreted, the Christ. And he brought him to Jesus. And when Jesus beheld him, He said, Thou art Simon the son of Jona: thou shalt be called Cephas, which is by interpretation, A stone. The day following Jesus would go forth into Galilee, and findeth Philip, and saith unto him, Follow Me. Now Philip was of Bethsaida, the city of Andrew and Peter. Philip findeth Nathanael, and saith unto him, We have found Him, of whom Moses in the Law, and the prophets, did write, Jesus of Nazareth, the son of Joseph. John, Chapter 1, verses 25-45.

I think this passage is very moving. It shows the dedication of the followers of Jesus. John the Baptist spent his adult life not earning a good living, gaining status or climbing the ladder of success; but instead, he told people of the coming of Jesus. John the Baptist had a very humble, but magnificent job! Jesus' disciples gave up their previous jobs and lifestyles to join Him. They didn't ask Jesus if there would be good benefits, what the stock options were or what was in it for them. They just followed Jesus.

It's sad that it would be difficult in this day and age for most of us, including me, to totally give up everything and follow Jesus. I want to go in the direction where Jesus needs me just like the disciples who were willing to do as Jesus asked.

Here are some related passages:

**I indeed baptize you with water unto repentance: but He that cometh after me is mightier than I, whose shoes I am not worthy to bear: He shall baptize you with the Holy Ghost, and with Fire. Matthew, Chapter 3, verse 11.*

*And His disciples asked Him, saying, Why then say the scribes that Elias must first come? And Jesus answered and said unto them, Elias truly shall first come, and restore all things. But I say unto you, That Elias is come already, and they knew him not, but have done unto him whatsoever they listed. Likewise also the Son of Man suffer of them. Then the disciples understood that He spake unto them of John the Baptist. Matthew, Chapter 17, verses 10-13.

....

Then answered the Jews and said unto Him, What sign showest Thou unto us, seeing that Thou doest these things? Jesus answered and said unto them, Destroy this temple, and in three days I will raise it up. Then said the Jews, Forty and six years was this temple in building, and wilt Thou rear it up in three days? But He spake of the Temple of His Body. When therefore He was risen from the dead, His disciples remembered that He had said this unto them; and they believed the Scripture, and the Word which Jesus had said, Now when He was in Jerusalem at the passover, in the feast day, many believed in His Name, when they saw the miracles which He did. John, Chapter 2, verses 18-23.

This reminds me of Missouri, the Show Me State. It's kind of like we say to God, "I'll believe that Jesus is our Savior if You show me the proof, if You show me a sign, if You show me..."

I think that's how many Christians get led astray to metaphysical and cult types of churches. They are looking for valid proof of Jesus' existence and a concrete explanation for the creation of the world. These metaphysical churches seem to appeal to them because they combine religion with science in a way that makes some kind of sense to them.

Jesus' telling us that His body is going to be raised up on the third day defies any explanation, real or metaphysical. It's in the Bible and enough different disciples wrote about it from their perspective, so we know that no one made this up. This allows us to compare what was foretold in the Bible years before Jesus' birth with what the different disciples wrote. That's why reading the Bible is beneficial, especially for those that have doubts.

Even Thomas told the other disciples that he didn't believe that Jesus had risen from the grave. Knowing this, Jesus appeared to Thomas and told him to touch the nail prints in His hands and thrust his hand into His side in order for him to believe. It really did happen! Although it defies our human logic, Jesus arose from the grave to save us all from our sins.

I see Jesus' work in my life each and every day in ways that defy all explanation, but I do. I try to turn my life over to God and turn to Him to take care of my daily issues and concerns. He gives me the Peace Which Passes All Understanding to get through the tough times. He is always there taking care of me.

We talk about signs. What sign do I have that Jesus is there? Well, I'm usually pretty private about this one, but it's the biggest sign I can think of. I guess if it lets one of you turn to God, then it was worth sharing with you. My previous marriage was unhealthy and I stayed in it longer than I should have. I thought that's what God would want me to do. Boy, was I ever wrong!

One day while I was driving, I prayed for God to give me a sign so that I would know whether I should stay in the marriage or leave. I was confused and had gone back and forth and needed guidance to know God's Will. A little later in the day when I looked down at my wedding rings, I noticed the diamond was missing! Now, I didn't lose the diamond from my rings the day before I prayed for a sign or five days later, but on the very same day that I had asked for a sign.

Fortunately for me, I listened to the sign that God gave me and got out of that unhealthy marriage. Later, I found out about the impact that living in an unhealthy relationship all those years can have on a family. I'm so glad I listened when God gave me the sign that defies all explanation, the same way that Jesus' rising from the grave to save us from our sins defies all explanation…but it's true!!!!

Here is a related passage:

> *But He answered and said unto them, An evil and adulterous generation seeketh after a sign: and there shall no sign be given to it, but the sign of the prophet Jonas: For as Jonas was three days and three nights in the whale's belly; so shall the Son of Man be three days and three nights in the heart of the earth. The men of Nineveh shall rise in judgment with this generation, and shall condemn it: because they repented at the preaching of Jonas; and, behold, a greater than Jonas is here [Jesus]. Matthew, Chapter 12, verses 39-41.*

....

> *Jesus answered and said unto him, Verily, verily, I say unto thee, Except a man be born again, he cannot see the kingdom of God. Nicodemus saith unto Him, How can a man be born when he is old? can he enter the second time into his mother's womb, and be born? Jesus answered, Verily, verily, I say unto thee, Except a man be born of water and of the Spirit, he cannot enter into the kingdom of God. That which is born of the flesh is flesh; and that which is born of the Spirit is Spirit. Marvel not that I said unto thee, Ye must be born again. The wind bloweth where it listeth, and thou hearest the sound thereof, but canst not tell whence it cometh, and whither it goeth: so is every one that is born of the Spirit. John, Chapter 3, verses 3-8.*

I tend to get distracted when I say my prayers for my family, myself and the world situation. When I find myself doing this, I pray for God to give me His Holy Spirit to guide me and to keep me focused. When God's Holy Spirit lives within me; my actions are more God-focused. Otherwise, it's very easy for me to get distracted by living a life with worldly values.

Well, it's the same for being a Christian. I can say that I believe in Jesus and live a worldly life not focused on Jesus at all. Will I go to heaven? Possibly not. If I love Jesus enough to commit to be baptized, will I go to heaven? Well, it's a start, but it's not enough. There are lots of people who were baptized years ago who spend their lives focused on drugs, alcohol, power, prestige and self instead of God. After you're baptized, you need to be an example of Jesus' positive influence on your life. What if I live a good life, but don't recognize Jesus as my Savior? Will I still go to heaven? There are lots of Bible passages that state a person doesn't have Salvation by good works alone. They have to believe in Jesus as their Savior and to try to live their lives as examples to others.

....

> *If I have told you earthly things, and ye believe not, how shall ye believe, if I tell you of heavenly things? And no man hath ascended up to heaven, but He that came down from heaven, even the Son of Man which is in heaven. And as Moses lifted up the serpent in the wilderness, even so must the Son of Man be lifted up: That whosoever believeth in Him should not perish, but have eternal life. For God so loved the world, that He gave His only begotten Son, that whosoever believeth in Him should not perish, but have everlasting life. For God sent not His Son into the world to condemn the world; but that the world through Him might be saved. He that believeth on Him is not condemned: but he that believeth not is condemned already, because he hath not believed in the Name of the only begotten Son of God. And this is the condemnation, that Light is come into the world, and men loved darkness rather than Light, because their deeds were evil. For every one that doeth evil hateth the Light, neither cometh to the Light, lest his deeds should be reproved. But he that doeth Truth cometh to the Light, that his deeds may be made manifest that they are wrought in God. John, Chapter 3, verses 12-21.*

This passage makes me think of Satan as lying within the shadows ready to pounce on unsuspecting people by tempting them. Satan entices them with worldly pleasures and lifestyle choices that lead them away from the Light and into the shadows. I think of Jesus as the Light that is turned on in the dark, to illuminate our way and to make our path clearly visible.

Jesus made the ultimate sacrifice for us and Lights the way to Salvation. As the children of Light, we need to lead our lives accordingly. Are we making the lifestyle choices and leading our lives as examples of the Light that Jesus provides for us? Or, do we fall prey to Satan sneaking up and dimming our focus through worldly choices and people who lead us astray? We need to be in prayerful consideration of these questions.

Here are some related passages:

Be Ye therefore followers of God, as dear children; And walk in love, as Christ also hath loved us, and hath given Himself for us an offering and a sacrifice to God for a sweet smelling savour. But fornication, and all uncleanness, or covetousness, let it not be once named among you, as becometh saints; Neither filthiness, nor foolish talking, nor jesting which are not convenient: but rather giving of thanks. For this ye know, that no whoremonger, nor unclean person, nor covetous man, who is an idolater, hath any inheritance in the kingdom of Christ and of God. Let no man deceive you with vain words: for because of these things cometh the wrath of God upon the children of disobedience. Be not ye partakers with them. For ye were sometimes darkness, but now are ye Light in the Lord: walk as children of Light. Ephesians, Chapter 5, verses 1-8.

The people which sat in darkness saw great Light; and to them which sat in the region and shadow of death Light is sprung up. From that time Jesus began to preach, and to say, Repent: for the kingdom of heaven is at hand. Matthew, Chapter 4, verses 16-17.

The people answered Him, We have heard out of the Law that Christ abideth for ever: and how sayest Thou, The Son of Man must be lifted up? Who is this Son of Man? Then Jesus said unto them, Yet a little while is the Light with you. Walk while ye have the Light, lest darkness come upon you: for he that walketh in darkness knoweth not whither he goeth. While ye have Light, believe in the Light, that ye may be the children of Light. These things spake Jesus, and departed, and did hide Himself from them. But though He had done so many miracles before them, yet they believed not on Him. John, Chapter 12, verses 34-37.

*Nevertheless among the chief rulers also many believed on Him; but because of the Pharisees they did not confess Him, lest they should be put out of the synagogue: For they loved the praise of men more than the praise of God. Jesus cried and said, He that believeth on Me, believeth not on Me, but on Him that sent Me. And he that seeth Me seeth Him that sent Me. I am come a Light into the world, that whosoever believeth on Me should not abide in darkness. And if any man hear My Words, and believe not, I judge him not: for I came not to judge the world, but to save the world. He that rejecteth Me, and receiveth not My Words, hath One that judgeth him: the Word that I have spoken, the same shall judge him in the Last Day. For I have not spoken of Myself; but the Father which sent Me, He gave Me a Commandment, what I should say, and what I should speak. And I know that His Commandment is life everlasting whatsoever I speak therefore, even as the Father said unto Me, so I speak. John, Chapter 12, verses 42-50.

*Therefore I will look unto the Lord; I will wait for the God of my Salvation: my God will hear me. Rejoice not against me, O mine enemy: when I fall, I shall arise; when I sit in darkness, the Lord shall be a Light unto me. Micah, Chapter 7, verses 7-8.

*The light of the body is the eye: if therefore thine eye be single, thy whole body shall be full of Light. But if thine eye be evil, thy whole body shall be full of darkness. If therefore the Light that is in thee be darkness, how great is that darkness! Matthew, Chapter 6, verses 22-23.

....

For He whom God hath sent speaketh the Words of God: for God giveth not the Spirit by measure unto Him. The Father loveth the Son, and hath given all things into His hand. He that believeth on the Son hath everlasting life: and he that believeth not the Son shall not see life; but the wrath of God abideth on him. John, Chapter 3, verses 34-36.

God tells us through the Bible in plain and simple Words: If we believe in Jesus, God's Son, we will have everlasting life in heaven; and if we don't, we will have God's wrath instead! I don't know about you, but I would much rather have everlasting life with God than to endure His wrath. What about you?

Here are some related passages:

*All things are delivered unto Me of My Father: and no man knoweth the Son, but the Father; neither knoweth any man the Father, save the Son and he to whomsoever the Son will reveal Him. Matthew, Chapter 11, verse 27.

*And now, Israel, what doth the LORD thy God require of thee, but to fear the LORD thy God, to walk in all His ways, and to love Him, and to serve the LORD thy God with all thy heart and with all thy soul. Deuteronomy, Chapter 10, verse 12.

....

Then cometh He to a city of Samaria, which is called Sychar, near to the parcel of ground that Jacob gave to his son Joseph. Now Jacob's well was there. Jesus therefore, being wearied with His journey, sat thus on the well: and it was about the sixth hour. There cometh a woman of Samaria to draw water: Jesus saith unto her, Give Me to drink. (For His disciples were gone away unto the city to buy meat.) Then saith the woman of Samaria unto Him, How is it that Thou, being a Jew, askest drink of me, which am a woman of Samaria? for the Jews have no dealings with the Samaritans. Jesus answered and said unto her, If thou knewest the gift of God, and Who It is that saith to thee, Give Me to drink; thou wouldest have asked of Him, and He would have given thee Living Water. The woman saith unto Him, Sir, Thou hast nothing to draw with, and the well is deep: from whence then hast Thou that Living Water? Art Thou greater than our father Jacob, which gave us the well, and drank thereof himself, and his children, and his cattle? Jesus answered and said unto her, Whosoever drinketh of this water shall thirst again: But whosoever drinketh of the Water that I shall give him shall never thirst; but the Water that I shall give him shall be in him a well of Water springing up into everlasting life. John, Chapter 4, verses 5-14.

I like the picture I get when I read this. I know that I get thirsty and get a glass of water; but in a little while, I might get thirsty again. Sometimes, it becomes annoying when I have to run downstairs to get another glass of water. Other times when I'm away from home and find myself without a place to get water, my thirst seems unquenchable.

I have never thought of being so satisfied that I'm never thirsty again. Of course, Jesus isn't talking about actual water, but we do have a thirst to have eternal life with Him. If we ignore that inner thirst and choose to lead a more worldly life, that thirst is still there, unquenched. If we satisfy our thirst, by finding out more about Jesus and His love for us and try to be examples of how He works in our lives, our thirst for a relationship with Jesus is quenched. We don't have to seek eternal life, because we will have it through our love of Jesus, who will quench all our needs, if we only ask Him.

....

> *God is a Spirit: and they that worship Him must worship Him in Spirit and in Truth. The woman saith unto Him, I know that Messias cometh, which is called Christ: when He is come, He will tell us all things. Jesus saith unto her, I that speak unto thee am He. John, Chapter 4, verses 24-26.*

Have you ever watched movies where men or women are looking for their true love, but have a good friend they overlook because they are looking for the ideal partner? The majority of the movie is focused on the main character pursuing people who are attractive, popular, etc., but never are satisfied. Later, in the movie, they find that the ideal person for them is their true-blue friend who has been there, all along.

It's like this lady who is desperately searching for Jesus, without realizing He is right in front of her. He isn't attractive, popular, etc., so He might go unnoticed. He is our true-blue friend and Savior who is there to save us, but do we notice Him? Like the song says, "Looking for love in all the wrong places," do we want to be a "Looking for Jesus in All the Wrong Places Christian" or should we stop to realize that He has been right here in front of us, all along?

....

> *So Jesus Himself came again into Cana of Galilee, where He made the water wine. And there was a certain nobleman whose son was sick at Capernaum. When he had heard that Jesus was come out of Judaea into Gaililee, he went unto Him, and besought Him that He would come down, and heal his son: for he was at the point of death. Then said Jesus unto him, Except ye see signs and wonders, ye will not believe. The nobleman saith unto Him, Sir, come down ere my child die. Jesus saith unto him, Go thy way; thy son liveth. And the man believed the Word that Jesus had spoken unto him, and he went his way. And as he was now going down, his servants met him, and told him, saying, Thy son liveth. Then inquired he of them the hour when he began to amend. And they said unto him, Yesterday at the seventh hour the fever left him. So the father knew that it was at the same hour, in the which Jesus said unto him, Thy son liveth: and himself believed, and his whole house. This is again the second miracle that Jesus did, when He was come out of Judaea into Galilee. John, Chapter 4, verses 46-54.*

The thing that made all the difference in the life of the young boy was what the father believed Jesus when He told him that his son liveth. Now if the father had doubted Jesus, his son would be dead and he would have always regretted not having had the faith necessary to trust Jesus.

The sad thing is that some can't believe that Jesus is going to take care of their needs. It's almost funny that they can believe things like the following:

It's funny, they can believe their concerns are going to be taken care of by sending money to someone on TV, but they don't trust in Jesus. It's funny, they can believe in someone who looks at some tea leaves, crystals or lines in their hands, but they don't trust in Jesus. It's funny, some can believe in chanting some positive affirmation, but they don't trust in Jesus. It's funny, some believe in looking at their horoscope, but they don't trust in Jesus. It's funny, some can believe in putting positive thoughts in their minds, but they don't trust in Jesus. People can believe in all these ridiculous things and all they had to do was to have faith in Jesus. It's almost so simple that it eludes them.

We have choices in our lives. We can believe God is going to take care of our concerns in whichever way is His will (because He sees the Big Picture). Or we can doubt and live to regret, not having the faith necessary to trust Jesus.

Here are some related passages:

And when Jesus was entered into Capernaum, there came unto Him a centurion, beseeching Him, And saying, Lord, my servant lieth at home sick of the palsy, grievously tormented. And Jesus saith unto him, I will come and heal him. The centurion answered and said, Lord, I am not worthy that Thou shouldest come under my roof: but speak the Word only, and my servant shall be healed. For I am a man under authority, having soldiers under me: and I say to this man, Go, and he goeth; and to another, Come, and he cometh; and to my servant, Do this, and he doeth it. When Jesus heard it, He marveled and said to them that followed, Verily I say unto you, I have not found so great faith, no, not in Israel. And I say unto you, That many shall come from the east and west, and shall sit down with Abraham, and Isaac, and Jacob, in the kingdom of heaven. But the children of the kingdom shall be cast out into outer darkness: there shall be weeping and gnashing of teeth. And Jesus said unto the centurion, Go thy way; and as thou hast believed, so be it done unto thee. And his servant was healed in the selfsame hour. Matthew, Chapter 8, verses 5-13.

And when He was come into the house, the blind men came to Him: and Jesus saith unto them, Believe ye that I am able to do this? They said unto Him, Yea, Lord. Then touched

He their eyes, saying, according to your faith be it unto you. And their eyes were opened; and Jesus straitly charged them, saying, See that no man know it. Matthew, Chapter 9, verses 28-30.

*And behold, a woman of Canaan came out of the same coasts, and cried unto Him, saying, Have mercy on me, O Lord, Thou Son of David; my daughter is grievously vexed with a devil. But He answered her not a Word. And His disciples came and besought Him, saying, Send her away, for she crieth after us. But He answered and said, I am not sent but unto the lost sheep of the house of Israel. Then came she and worshipped Him, saying, Lord, help me. But He answered and said, It is not meet to take the children's bread, and to cast it to dogs. And she said, Truth, Lord: yet the dogs eat of the crumbs which fall from their Masters' table. Then Jesus answered and said unto her, O woman, great is thy faith: be it unto thee even as thou wilt, And her daughter was made whole from that very hour. Matthew, Chapter 15, verses 22-28.

Thus saith the LORD; Cursed be the man that trusteth in man, and maketh flesh his arm, and whose heart departeth from the LORD. For he shall be like the heath in the desert, and shall not see when good cometh; but shall inhabit the parched places in the wilderness, in a salt land and not inhabited. Blessed is the man that trusteth in the LORD, and whose hope the LORD is. For he shall be as a tree planted by the waters, and that spreadeth out her roots by the river, and shall not see when heat cometh, but her leaf shall be green; and shall not be careful in the year of drought, neither shall cease from yielding fruit. Jeremiah, Chapter 17, verses 5-8.

・・・

In these lay a great multitude of impotent folk, of blind, halt, withered, waiting for the moving of the water. For an angel went down at a certain season into the pool, and troubled the water: whosoever then first after the troubling of the water stepped in was made whole of whatsoever disease he had. And a certain man was there, which had an infirmity thirty and eight years. When Jesus saw him lie, and knew that he had been now a long time in that case, He saith unto him, Wilt thou be made whole? The impotent man answered Him, Sir, I have no man, when the water is troubled, to put me into the pool: but while I am coming, another steppeth down before me. Jesus saith unto him, Rise, take up thy bed, and walk. And immediately the man was made whole, and took up his bed, and walked: and on the same day was the Sabbath. The Jews therefore said unto him that was cured, It is the Sabbath day: it is not lawful for thee to carry thy bed. He answered them, He that made me whole, the same said unto me, Take up thy bed, and walk. Then asked they him, What Man is that which said unto thee, Take up thy bed, and walk? And he that was healed wist not Who it was: for Jesus had conveyed Himself away, a multitude being in that place. Afterward Jesus findeth him in the temple, and said unto him, Behold, thou art made whole: sin no more, lest a worse thing come unto thee. John, Chapter 5, verses 3-14.

Something that impresses me about this passage is that Jesus asked the handicapped man, "Wilt thou be made whole?" Now, it would seem any handicapped person in their right mind would say, "Sure I will. I would do anything to be made whole!" But I don't think we always do that as Christians. When Jesus gave His life for us and rose again to gain us Salvation, He is asking all of us, "Wilt thou be made whole?" What would we reply?

Would it be, "Yes, as long as my friends don't know that I'm a Christian"? "Yes, as long as I can still cheat on my spouse every now and then. It really doesn't mean a thing!" "Yes, as long as I can still stab my co-workers in the back to get another wrung up the ladder of success." "Yes, just as long as I can party every now and then. You know it doesn't really hurt anything. Besides, I need to relax now and then." When Jesus asks us if we will be made whole, all we have to do is believe in Him as our Lord and Savior. The other part of being made whole is trying to live as examples of how He works in our lives. I don't think any of the responses above reflect that. What will you say to the question Jesus poses in our lives, "Wilt thou be made whole?"

Here are some related passages:

When the even was come, they brought unto Him many that were possessed with devils: and He cast out the spirits with His Word, and healed all that were sick: That it might be fulfilled which was spoken by Esaias the prophet, saying, Himself took our infirmities, and bare our sicknesses. Matthew, Chapter 8, verses 16-17.

The blind receive their sight, and the lame walk, the lepers are cleansed, and the deaf hear, the dead are raised up, and the poor have the Gospel preached to them. Matthew, Chapter 11, verse 5.

> *Verily, verily, I say unto you, he that heareth My Word, and believeth on Him that sent Me, hath everlasting life, and shall not come into condemnation; but is passed from death unto life. Verily, verily, I say unto you, the hour is coming, and now is, when the dead shall hear the Voice of the Son of God: and they that hear shall live. John, Chapter 5, verses 24-25.*

I had a hearing problem when I was growing up. My mother took me to a specialist to check my hearing to make sure that there weren't any major problems. The doctor told my mother that I had selective-listening. This meant I tuned out the things that I didn't want to hear and only listened to the things that I wanted to hear. Are we "Selective-listening Christians," listening only to what we want to hear when it comes to God? Are we only open to doing the Christian acts that are comfortable for us and don't really require us to make any changes to grow as Christians?

You will notice that it talks about he that heareth My Word and believeth on Him that sent Me, not he that heareth only what he wants to hear and only believes when it's convenient. Hopefully, we aren't using selective-listening in our Christian lives.

> *And when even was now come, His disciples went down unto the sea, And entered into a ship, and went over the sea toward Capernaum. And it was now dark, and Jesus was not come to them. And the sea arose by reason of a great wind that blew. So when they had rowed about five and twenty or thirty furlongs, they see Jesus walking on the sea, and drawing nigh unto the ship: and they were afraid. But He saith unto them, It is I; be not afraid. Then they willingly received Him into the ship: and immediately the ship was at land whither they went. John, Chapter 6, verses 16-21.*

I recently talked with my daughter and told her that I say the Lord's Prayer or sing *I Surrender All*, when I'm feeling scared, stressed or like Satan is trying to pervade my thoughts to lead me astray. She told me that she says: *Be Not Afraid* when she is experiencing similar things. So, this passage has special significance for me for that reason.

I was thinking about the influence we have on our children's lifestyle choices and their relationship with God, through the modeling we do. My daughter has picked up some similar strategies to connect with God when she is feeling stressed, concerned, etc. It's much better that she picks up positive strategies like this, than seeing me turn to alcohol or worse, as situations arise. You don't realize the impact you have on your children by the choices you make. Are you making choices you want your children to emulate? If not, it's not too late to change the way you turn to God in time of need, joy, etc. It may have a positive impact on your child's life, regardless of their age.

Here is a related passage:

> *And it shall come to pass, that whosoever shall call on the Name of the Lord shall be saved. Acts, Chapter 2, verse 21.*

....

> *And when they had found Him on the other side of the sea, they said unto Him, Rabbi, when camest Thou hither? Jesus answered them and said, Verily, verily, I say unto you, Ye seek Me, not because ye saw the miracles, but because ye did eat of the loaves, and were filled. Labour not for the meat which perisheth, but for that Meat which endureth unto everlasting life, which the Son of Man shall give unto you for Him hath God the Father sealed. Then said they unto Him, What shall we do, that we might work the works of God? Jesus answered and said unto them, This is the work of God, that ye believe on Him whom He hath sent. They said therefore unto Him, What sign showest Thou then, that we may see, and believe Thee? what dost Thou work? Our fathers did eat manna in the desert; as it is written, He gave them bread from heaven to eat. Then Jesus said unto them, Verily, verily, I say unto you, Moses gave you not that bread from heaven; but My Father giveth you the True Bread from heaven. For the Bread of God is He which cometh down from heaven, and giveth life unto the world. Then said they unto Him, Lord, evermore give us this Bread. And Jesus said unto them, I am The Bread of Life: he that cometh to Me shall never hunger; and he that believeth on Me shall never thirst. But I said unto you, That ye also have seen Me, and believe not. All that the Father giveth Me shall come to Me; and him that cometh to Me I will in no wise cast out. For I came down from heaven, not to do Mine Own will, but the will of Him that sent Me. And this is the Father's will which hath sent Me, that of all which He hath given Me I should lose nothing, but should raise it up again at the Last Day. And this is the will of Him that sent Me, that every one which seeth the Son, and believeth on Him, may have everlasting life: and I will raise him up at the Last Day. John, Chapter 6, verses 25-40.*

With having a focus on eating most of my life, this passage gives me a whole different perspective. I need to focus on, *"Labour not for the meat which perisheth, but for that Meat which endureth unto everlasting life."* It makes me realize how I tend to get sidetracked by worldly things, like eating, etc. when my focus should always be on Jesus who will really satisfy all my needs.

....

Verily, verily, I say unto you, If a man keep My saying, he shall never see death. John, Chapter 8, verse 51.

Isn't it amazing? If we try to live our lives in a manner that reflects the positive impact that Jesus has on us, we will have everlasting life with Him in heaven.

....

As long as I am in the world, I am the Light of the World. When He had thus spoken, He spat on the ground, and made clay of the spittle, and He anointed the eyes of the blind man with the clay, And said unto him, Go, wash in the pool of Siloam, (which is by interpretation, Sent.) He went his way therefore, and washed, and came seeing. The neighbours therefore, and they which before had seen him that he was blind, said, Is not this he that sat and begged? Some said, this is he: others said, he is like him: but he said, I am he. Therefore said they unto him, How were thine eyes opened? He answered and said, A Man that is called Jesus made clay, and anointed mine eyes, and said unto me, Go to the pool of Siloam, and wash: and I went and washed, and I received sight. Then said they unto him, Where is He? He said, I know not. They brought to the Pharisees him that aforetime was blind. And it was the Sabbath day when Jesus made the clay, and opened his eyes. Then again the Pharisees also asked him how he had received his sight. He said unto them, He put clay upon mine eyes, and I washed, and do see. Therefore said some of the Pharisees, This man is not of God, because He keepeth not the Sabbath day. Others said, How can a Man that is a sinner do such miracles? And there was a division among them. They say unto the blind man again, What sayest thou of Him, that He hath opened thine eyes? He said, He is a prophet. But the Jews did not believe concerning him, that he had been blind, and received his sight, until they called the parents of him that had received his sight. And they asked them, saying, Is this your son, who ye say was born blind? how then doth he now see? His parents answered them and said, We know that this is our son, and that he was born blind: But by what means he now seeth, we know not; or who hath opened his eyes, we know not: he is of age; ask him: he shall speak for himself. These words spake his parents, because they feared the Jews: for the Jews had agreed already, that if any man did confess that He was Christ, he should be put out of the synagogue. Therefore said his parents, He is of age; ask him. Then again called they the man that was blind, and said unto him, Give God the praise, we know that this Man is a sinner. He answered and said, Whether He be a sinner or no, I know not: one thing I know, that, whereas I was blind, now I see. Then said they to him again, What did He to thee? how opened He thine eyes? He answered them, I have told you already, and ye did not hear: wherefore would ye hear it again? will ye also be His disciples? Then they reviled him, and said, Thou art His disciple, but we are Moses' disciples. We know that God spake unto Moses: as for this Fellow, we know not from whence He is. The man answered and said unto them, Why herein is a marvellous thing, that ye know not from whence He is, and yet He hath opened mine eyes. Now we know that God heareth not sinners: but if any man be a worshipper of God, and doeth His will, him He heareth. Since the world began it was not heard that any man opened the eyes of one that was born blind. If this Man were not of God, He could do nothing. They answered and said unto him, Thou wast altogether born in sins, and dost thou teach us? And they cast him out. Jesus heard that they had cast him out; and when He had found him, He said unto him, Dost thou believe on the Son of God? He answered and said, Who is He, Lord, that I might believe on Him? And Jesus said unto him, Thou hast both seen Him, and it is He that talketh with thee. And he said, Lord, I believe. And he worshipped Him. John, Chapter 9, 5-38.

If you ask me, it wasn't the person who was healed that was blind. Those men investigating the miracle Jesus performed on this man seemed to be blind. They still could not acknowledge that Jesus is their Savior, even after the miracle. Hopefully, we aren't "Blind Christians" who ignore the things that Jesus shows us in our lives.

Bible Passages That Can Influence Your Life

Verily, Verily, I say unto you, He that entereth not by the Door into the sheepfold, but climbeth up some other way, the same is a thief and a robber. But he that entereth in by the Door is the Shepherd of the sheep. To Him the porter openeth: and the sheep hear His Voice: and He calleth His own sheep by name, and leadeth them out, And when He putteth forth His own sheep, He goeth before them, and the sheep follow Him: for they know His Voice. And a stranger will they not follow, but will flee from him: for they know not the voice of strangers. This parable spake Jesus unto them: but they understood not what things they were which He spake unto them. Then said Jesus unto them again, Verily, verily, I say unto you, I am the Door of the sheep. All that ever came before Me are thieves and robbers: but the sheep did not hear them. I am the Door: by Me if any man enter in, he shall be saved, and shall go in and out, and find pasture. The thief cometh not, but for to steal, and to kill, and to destroy: I am come that they might have life, and that they might have it more abundantly. I am the Good Shepherd: the Good Shepherd giveth His Life for the sheep. But he that is an hireling, and not the Shepherd, whose own the sheep are not, seeth the wolf coming, and leaveth the sheep, and fleeth: and the wolf catcheth them, and scattereth the sheep. The hireling fleeth, because he is an hireling, and careth not for the sheep. I am the Good Shepherd, and know My sheep, and am known of Mine. As the Father knoweth Me, even so know I the Father: and I lay down My Life for the sheep. And other sheep I have, which are not of this fold: them also I must bring, and they shall hear My Voice; and there shall be one fold, and One Shepherd. Therefore doth My Father love Me, because I lay down My Life, that I might take it again. No man taketh it from Me, but I lay it down of Myself. I have power to lay it down, and I have power to take it again. This Commandment have I received of My Father. John, Chapter 10, verses 1-18.

Jesus answered them, I told you, and ye believed not: the works that I do in My Father's Name, they bear witness of Me. But ye believe not, because ye are not of My sheep, as I said unto you. My sheep hear My Voice, and I know them, and they follow Me: And I give unto them eternal life; and they shall never perish, neither shall any man pluck them out of My hand. My Father, which gave them Me, is greater than all; and no man is able to pluck them out of My Father's Hand. I and My Father are One. John, Chapter 10, verses 25-30.

Wow! There are so many wonderful comparisons that Jesus makes in this passage that I'm afraid I might leave some out. If I do, please forgive me. This is what this passage means to me, although I realize others may interpret it differently.

Jesus is speaking of the sheep as Christians (His people.) People who want to lead Christians (His people) astray aren't going to do it in a forthright manner. They aren't going to come through the front door and say, "I'm here to deceive you and lead you astray. Follow me and you are bound to lose your Salvation." If the Christians would know better than to follow them, they would stay with the rest of the sheep knowing that Jesus, their Shepherd, would always protect them and lead them to Salvation.

Instead, people who want to lead Christians astray, do it in a more subtle manner like the robber who sneaks in to steal the sheep. They work slyly trying to deceive Christians by making them believe that they are doing the Will of God. So sad!

True Christians stay focused on Jesus and His will for us, as shown in the Bible. That way we will know Jesus' Voice and won't be led astray by others who profess to be followers of His, but aren't. God the Father gave us to Jesus to be His sheep, and Jesus and God the Father are One.

Jesus is dedicated to protecting us like a Shepard who protects His sheep from wolves. A Shepherd would give His life to save His sheep, just as Jesus gave His Life to save us from our sinful nature. Those who deceive Christians are going to run for the hills when they see the wolves coming or when we stop giving them the money or the things they want from us. As long as we listen to our Shepherd's Voice, Jesus will keep us from being misled.

Here are some related passages:

*For ye were as sheep going astray; but are now returned unto the Shepherd and Bishop of your souls. 1 Peter, Chapter 2, verse 25.

*Behold, the Lord God will come with strong hand, and His arm shall rule for Him: behold, His reward is with Him, and His work is before Him. He shall feed His flock like a Shepherd: He shall gather the lambs with His Arm, and carry them in His Bosom, and shall gently lead those that are with young. Isaiah, Chapter 40, verses 10-11.

And the glory of the LORD shall be revealed, and all flesh shall see it together: for the Mouth of the LORD hath spoken it. The Voice said, Cry. And He said, What shall I cry? All flesh is grass, and all the goodliness thereof is as the flower of the field: The grass withereth, the flower fadeth: because the Spirit of the LORD bloweth upon it: surely the people is grass. The grass withereth, the flower fadeth: but the Word of our God shall stand for ever. Isaiah, Chapter 40, verses 5-8.

Beware of false prophets, which come to you in sheep's clothing, but inwardly they are ravening wolves. Matthew, Chapter 7, verse 15.

But when He saw the multitudes, He was moved with compassion on them, because they fainted, and were scattered abroad, as sheep having no shepherd. Then saith He unto His disciples, The harvest truly is plenteous, but the labourers are few; Pray ye therefore the Lord of the harvest, that He will send forth labourers into His harvest. Matthew, Chapter 9, verses 36-38.

Behold, send you forth as sheep in the midst of wolves; be ye therefore wise as serpents, and harmless as doves. Matthew, Chapter 10, verse 16.

Then saith Jesus unto them, All ye shall be offended because of Me this night: for it is written, I will smite the Shepherd, and the sheep of the flock shall be scattered abroad. But after I am risen again, I will go before you into Galilee. Matthew, Chapter 26, verses 31-32.

I have gone astray like a lost sheep; seek thy servant; for I do not forget Thy Commandments. Psalm, Chapter 119, verse 176.

....

If I do not the works of My Father, believe Me not. But if I do, though ye believe not Me, believe the works: that ye may know, and believe, that the Father is in Me, and I in Him. John, Chapter 10, verses 37-38.

It amazes me. The Israelites were told for generations that there would be a Savior and they waited for Him all those years. When Jesus, the Savior, did come, they didn't believe Him. Now, you might be able to understand why they might not believe Him just because He tells them that He is the Savior. I guess I could have been a little skeptical at that point, as well. Jesus knows they are doubtful and does major miracles like making people see who had been blind from birth, making the lame walk, bringing the dead back to life, taking water and making it into wine and taking a little bread and a few fish and making it feed thousands.

He did major miracles so people would realize He isn't just any man who is saying that He is the Savior. He really IS the Savior!! His miracles and all His actions attested to this, but still people don't believe Him. We have record in the Bible of all the great things that Jesus did and said, but He gives us a choice. Do you believe Him? I hope for your sake you do!

....

Jesus said unto her, I am the Resurrection, and the Life: he that believeth in Me, though he were dead, yet shall he live: And whosoever liveth and believeth in Me shall never die. Believest thou this? She saith unto Him, Yea, Lord: I believe that Thou art the Christ, the Son of God, which should come into the world. And when she had so said, she went her way, and called Mary her sister secretly, saying, the Master is come, and calleth for thee. As soon as she heard that, she arose quickly, and came unto Him. John, Chapter 11, verses 25-29.

This passage reminds me of asking kids to come do something and you hear, "In a minute," "During the commercial," or "When I get around to it." Actually, I have been guilty of saying the exact same things myself. As Christians, do we jump up and respond when we feel Jesus is calling us to do something or do we tell Him, "When I get around to it"?

....

There they made Him a supper; and Martha served: but Lazarus was one of them that sat at the table with Him. Then took Mary a pound of ointment of spikenard, very costly, and anointed the feet of Jesus, and wiped His feet with her hair: and the house was filled with the odour of the ointment. Then saith one of His disciples, Judas Iscariot, Simon's son, which should betray Him. Why was not this ointment sold for three hundred pence, and given to the poor? This he said, not that he cared for the poor: but because he was a thief, and had the bag, and bare what was put therein. Then said Jesus, Let her alone: against the day of My burying hath she kept this. For the poor always ye have with you; but Me ye have not always. John, Chapter 12, verses 2-8.

Judas chastises Mary for doing something good when he really had ulterior motives. He really wanted the money for himself. How many times do we have ulterior motives but sound very self-righteous to others?

I know eating was one of the subtle ways that I let Satan sneak into my life. You wouldn't think Satan could have a stronghold on a person with something as seemingly insignificant as eating. Generally, we think about major things like drinking, taking drugs, infidelity, stealing, etc., not eating. Things that seem minor are easier for us "Self-righteous Christians" to let into our lives without noticing how it works a wedge in our relationship with God.

God showed me how important food and my compulsive eating had become when I yelled at my daughter when she was little. She had brought some of her neighborhood friends over and had given them each one of the green Pippin Apples that I had stored in our refrigerator. I yelled at her, telling her that she shouldn't have given the apples to them because there wouldn't be enough for the family. Actually, I wasn't really worried about the family. Those apples were my favorite and I had bought them for me!

I was being a terrible example of my faith! My ulterior motives interfered when I should have been complimenting my daughter for sharing with others. Instead, I was hoarding the apples for myself! It seems silly to have let something as insignificant as apples sneak in between my relationship with my daughter and my faith, but I'm ashamed to say that I did.

....

> *On the next day much people that were come to the feast, when they heard that Jesus was coming to Jerusalem, Took branches of palm trees, and went forth to meet Him, and cried, Hosanna: Blessed is the King of Israel that cometh in the Name of the Lord. And Jesus, when He had found a young ass, sat thereon; as it is written, Fear not, daughter of Zion: behold, thy King cometh, sitting on an ass's colt. These things understood not His disciples at the first: but when Jesus was glorified, then remembered they that these things were written of Him, and that they had done these things unto Him. John, Chapter 12, verses 12-16.*

This reminds me of a really good instructor who tells you beforehand what you're going to learn. That way you can identify the important information when you see it. The really good instructor gives you a variety of examples to prove a point. That's what I see happening in the Bible.

The Old Testament tells us we are looking for the Savior and what He will do and say, along with what things will happen to Him when He comes. The New Testament not only tells about Jesus fulfilling these things that had been predicted, but tells of all the miracles that He did, as proof to those who are doubtful. These things are verified through different people who described what Jesus said and how He saved us from our sins through His death and Resurrection. If a person has any doubts, reading the Bible would help them see how Jesus' life is no coincidence.

This is one of the many passages from the Old Testament that foretell of Jesus:

Rejoice greatly, O daughter of Zion; shout, O daughter of Jerusalem: behold, thy King cometh unto thee: He is just, and having Salvation: lowly, and riding upon an ass, and upon a colt the foal of an ass. Zechariah, Chapter 9, verse 9.

Here is one of the related New Testament passages that show how Jesus had fulfilled the ancient prophesy:

And when they drew nigh unto Jerusalem, and were come to Bethphage, unto the mount of Olives, then sent Jesus two disciples, Saying unto them, Go into the village over against you and straightway ye shall find an ass tied, and a colt with her: loose them, and bring them unto Me. And if any man say aught unto you, ye shall say, The Lord hath need of them; and straightway he will send them. And this was done, that it might be fulfilled which was spoken by the prophet, saying, Tell ye the daughter of Zion, Behold; thy King cometh sitting upon an ass, and a colt the foal of an ass. Matthew, Chapter 21, verses 1-5.

....

And Jesus answered them, saying, The hour is come, that the Son of Man should be glorified. Verily, verily, I say unto you, Except a corn of wheat fall into the ground and die, it abideth alone: but if it die, it bringeth forth much fruit. He that loveth his life shall lose it; and he that hateth his life in this world shall keep it unto life eternal. If any man serve Me, let him follow Me; and where I am, there shall also My servant be: if any man serve Me, him will My Father honour. Now is My soul troubled; and what shall I say? Father, save Me from this hour: but for this cause came I unto this hour. Father, glorify Thy Name. Then came there a Voice from heaven, saying, I have both glorified It, and will glorify It again. The people therefore, that stood by, and heard It said that It thundered: others said, An angel spake to Him. Jesus answered and said, This Voice came not because of Me, but for your sakes. John, Chapter 12, verses 23-30.

I love the way Jesus made the comparison between His life and a kernel of wheat that dies, but through its death brings forth much fruit. Jesus was willing to give up His life for us so that we could be forgiven from our sins. Yet, we are often skeptical which seems awfully ungrateful after all Jesus has done for us. Jesus goes on to say that those who are willing to give their lives for Him will have eternal life. Are we willing to give our worldly lives over to God and become examples of how Jesus works in us? That's what it takes!

Here is a related passage:

*He that findeth his life shall lose it: and he that loseth his life for My sake shall find it. Matthew, Chapter 10, verse 39.

....

Jesus saith unto him, I am the Way, the Truth, and the Life: no man cometh unto the Father, but by Me. If ye had known Me, ye should have known My Father also: and from henceforth ye know Him, and have seen Him. John, Chapter 14, verses 6-7.

Knowing how patient, understanding and forgiving Jesus is gives me a clear picture of God the Father who is exactly the same. Fortunately for me, since I need lots of patience and forgiveness. I tend to keep making the same mistakes over and over again by getting caught up in feeling self-righteous about things, judging other people and letting food or possessions become too important in my life (just to mention a few of my many shortcomings.)

....

Verily, verily, I say unto you. He that believeth on Me, the works that I do shall he do also; and greater works than these shall he do; because I go unto My Father. And whatsoever ye shall ask in My Name, that will I do, that the Father may be glorified in the Son. If ye shall ask any thing in My Name, I will do it. If ye love Me, Keep My Commandments. And I will pray the Father, and He shall give you another Comforter, that He may abide with you for ever. John, Chapter 14, verses 12-16.

When my son was born, he had to be rushed to a large hospital hours away from us for a life-threatening surgery. It can be pretty lonely when the nurses bring out the babies for their mothers to hold and your arms are empty. Fortunately, the Comforter (Holy Spirit) had given me what I call the Peace Which Passes All Understanding. It's a calm feeling when I would normally be really upset or extremely concerned. Instead, I felt at peace knowing that God was taking excellent care of things so that I shouldn't worry…and He did!

Here is a related passage:

Be careful for nothing; but in every thing by prayer and supplication with thanksgiving let your requests be made known unto God. And the Peace of God, Which Passeth All Understanding, shall keep your hearts and minds through Christ Jesus. Philippians, Chapter 4, verses 6-7.

....

He that hath My Commandments, and keepeth them, he it is that loveth Me: and he that loveth Me shall be loved of My Father, and I will love him, and will manifest Myself to him. John, Chapter 14, verse 21.

I have often been more of a "Do as I Say, Not as I Do Christian." It's sure a lot easier to tell others how they should live their lives according to what God tells us in the Bible, than to actually live as the example He wants.

Here is a related passage:

He that receiveth you receiveth Me, and he that receiveth Me receiveth Him that sent Me. Matthew, Chapter 10, verse 40.

....

I am the true vine, and My Father is the husbandman. Every branch in Me that beareth not fruit He taketh away: and every branch that beareth fruit, He purgeth it that it may bring forth more fruit. John, Chapter 15, verses 1-2.

I love the comparison Jesus makes in this chapter with a grapevine and His followers (Christians.) Just like the farmer in the grape vineyard who cuts down unproductive branches, God weeds out so-called Christians who aren't productive, as well. Christians who produce fruit will be trained in the ways to become better examples of how God works in their lives. I need to be a better example, because I sure wouldn't want to get pruned!

....

Abide in Me, and I in you. As the branch cannot bear fruit of itself, except it abide in the vine; no more can ye, except ye abide in Me. John, Chapter 15, verse 4.

In this comparison, Christians are the branches and Jesus is the vine. If a heavy wind had broken a branch off, that branch could not continue to produce grapes year after year on its own. People who stray away from Jesus lose their focus as Christians if they don't have an ongoing relationship with Him. The branch needs a vine with a strong root system to get nourishment up through it; into the branches and into the grapes. Christians rely heavily on the nourishment that Jesus gives them through His Word (the Bible) to help us grow as His examples for others. In this same way we rely on Jesus, who relies on us to be productive by sharing our faith with others.

....

If ye abide in Me, and My Words abide in You, ye shall ask what ye will, and it shall be done unto you. Herein is My Father glorified, that ye bear much fruit: so shall ye be My disciples. As the Father hath loved Me, so have I loved you: continue ye in My love. If ye keep My Commandments, ye shall abide in My love; even as I have kept My Father's Commandments, and abide in His love. These things have I spoken unto you, that My joy might remain in you, and that your joy might be full. This is My Commandment, That ye love one another, as I have loved you. Greater love hath no man than this that a Man lay down His life for His friends. Ye are My friends, if ye do whatsoever I command you. Henceforth I call you no servants: for the servant knoweth not what his Lord doeth: but I have called you friends; for all things that I have heard of My Father I have made known unto you. John, Chapter 15, verses 7-15.

I don't want to take this lightly, being an "Only for the Moment Christian," then falling back into my old sinful ways again. Jesus gave His life for me and for you. He deserves a little more recognition than an occasional mention on special religious holidays or when we feel the need to go to church for family traditions. He sacrificed so much for us which should warrant us trying to make a committed effort to be the Christian that Jesus would want us to be.

....

A woman when she is in travail hath sorrow, because her hour is come: but as soon as she is delivered of the child, she remembereth no more the anguish, for joy that a man is born into the world. John, Chapter 16, verse, 21.

My mother told me something like this when I was expecting my daughter. I was somewhat apprehensive since this was my first child. Ever since then, I share this with other expectant mothers who tend to be overwhelmed by all the delivery-room horror stories that their supposed friends and co-workers share with them.

I have never figured out why women do this to each other. You would think that if they had been scared by the delivery stories that other people had told them, they wouldn't want to do this to their friends. I have continued to see women do this over the years and in different parts of the country. It's almost like some female bonding ritual, where mothers get to see if the expectant mother is worthy of her newborn child by living through all the delivery-room horror stories shared with them.

My mother told me that God made childbirth very special. Although there is some pain involved, it's only for a little while and your focus is on having your new child born healthy. The pain tends to pale in comparison to the anticipation of having a happy, healthy child.

She reminded me of scars I had as a youngster. I can remember that the original cut hurt, but I can't actually feel the pain associated with those scars anymore. She told me that God made childbirth pain in much the same way since people wouldn't continue to have children if they held onto the pain.

My mother said the pain experienced disappears from your focus once you have your new child in your arms. Now, I think this is a much nicer thing to share with expectant mothers than the other delivery-room stories that I mentioned, and it's nice there is Scripture to back it up.

....

And in that day ye shall ask Me nothing. Verily, verily, I say unto you. Whatsoever ye shall ask the Father in My Name, He will give it you. John, Chapter 16, verse 23.

There have been times in my life when I have had situations larger than my plate could handle. Fortunately, God answered my prayer by providing friends and family who would support me in ways that defy explanation. I am truly blessed!

....

Behold, the hour cometh, yea, is now come, that ye shall be scattered, every man to his own, and shall leave Me alone; and yet I am not alone, because the Father is with Me. These things I have spoken unto you, that in Me ye might have peace. In the world ye shall have tribulation: but be of good cheer; I have overcome the world. John, Chapter 16, verses 32-33.

Jesus knows of the terrible travesty of justice that is about to befall Him, and yet He takes the time to reassure His disciples (and us.) This passage gives me so much hope, even when worldly things seem to get me down. Jesus has conquered the world, so it can't ever get the best of me as long as I continue to focus on Him.

....

Neither pray I for these alone, but for them also which shall believe on Me through their Word; That they all may be one; as Thou, Father, art in Me, and I in Thee that they also may be one in Us: that the world may believe that Thou has sent Me, And the glory which Thou gavest Me I have given them; that they may be one, even as We are One. John, Chapter 17, verses 20-22.

I have been trying to go back through my feeble brain to remember what this reminds me of. Well, I have finally figured it out. There is a portion of my daily prayer which is, "Dear God, please dwell with us and in us now and always, and please have us dwell with You and in You now and always." That's what it reminds me of!

The significance of this prayer is that our relationship with God is of no importance if it's only one-sided. We can ask God to dwell with us and in us, but if we choose not to act on that we are lost. If we dwell with Him and in Him, as well, we are united and open to the opportunity of growing in Christ.

....

When they therefore were come together, they asked of Him, saying, Lord, wilt Thou at this time restore again the kingdom to Israel? And He said unto them, It is not for you to know the times or the seasons which the Father hath put in His own power. Acts, Chapter 1, verses 6-7.

Although this isn't really what this passage is about, it reminds me of when one of my grandsons was younger and we would ask him if he wanted to spend the day with us. He wanted to know what we were going to do before he would commit to coming with us.

I don't think it's positive for us to foster the attitude that if we do something exciting enough, then he will grace us with his presence. Out of stubbornness, I didn't tell him what we were doing before he made his decision. If he decided to go with us, he could do all the interesting things that we were going to do. If not, that was okay too, because he has the ability to make his own choices.

Well, I think that God works in much the same way. God doesn't give us the dates of the major events of the world. Or else we might reply, "Well, if I know what's in it for me first, God, and I think it's to my advantage, then I will consider being Your follower." God wants us to be His followers out of blind faith and love.

....

> *But ye shall receive power, after that the Holy Ghost is come upon you: and ye shall be witnesses unto Me both in Jerusalem, and in all Judea, and in Samaria, and unto the uttermost part of the earth. And when He had spoken these things, while they beheld, He was taken up, and a cloud received Him out of their sight. And while they looked stedfastly toward heaven as He went up, behold, two men stood by them in white apparel; Which also said, Ye men of Galilee, why stand ye gazing up into heaven? This same Jesus, which is taken up from you into heaven, shall so come in like manner as ye have seen Him go into heaven. Acts, Chapter 1, verses 8-11.*

The last thing Jesus said to His disciples as He ascends into heaven is extremely significant. Jesus tells them to let others know what He had done to provide Salvation for everyone, not just for a specific country, nationality or race but it is to be shared, *"unto the uttermost part of the earth."*

....

> *And when the day of Pentecost was fully come, they were all with one accord in one place. And suddenly there came a sound from heaven as of a rushing mighty wind, and it filled all the house where they were sitting. And there appeared unto them cloven tongues like as of fire, and it sat upon each of them. And they were all filled with the Holy Ghost, and began to speak with other tongues, as the Spirit gave them utterance. And there were dwelling at Jerusalem Jews, devout men, out of every nation under heaven. Now when this was noised abroad, the multitude came together, and were confounded, because that every man heard them speak in his own language. And they were all amazed and marvelled, saying one to another, Behold, are not all these which speak Galileans? And how hear we every man in our own tongue, wherein we were born? Acts, Chapter 2, verses 1-8.*

The gift of the Holy Spirit makes a Grand entrance! God didn't want this to go unnoticed or He would have just given this gift subtly to the disciples. He wanted people to know that this is a gift from God so He had witnesses to this special occasion!

It tells about how the Holy Spirit came down and gave the disciples and other followers the ability to talk to different nationalities and cultures of people in their native tongue. Otherwise the disciples and followers of God would not be able to minister to anyone other than those who could understand the disciple's language.

Whether people still talk in tongues or whether it was just during the time of the disciples isn't exactly clear to me, at this point. I just know that the disciples and followers did then in order to be able to preach to everyone. God didn't want anyone excluded from the opportunity to hear His Word.

There is a lot of controversy about talking in tongues, but I don't have to get involved in disputes on that topic. It doesn't say in the Bible that a requirement for Salvation is to believe in Jesus and to talk in tongues. It just says that we are supposed to believe in Jesus as our Savior and to try to lead our lives as an example for Him. So, I don't have to know all the answers in order to have Salvation. If God wants me to know this, He'll show me what He wants me to know, when He wants me to know it. You can read more about this in 1 Corinthians, Chapter 12, Chapter 13 and Chapter 14 to make up your own mind on this matter which is definitely preferable to someone else telling you what to believe. God does have suggestions for these gifts so that they don't alienate visitors.

Here are some related passages:

**If therefore the whole church be come together into one place, and all speak with tongues, and there come in those that are unlearned, or unbelievers, will they not say that ye are mad? 1 Corinthians, Chapter 14, verse 23.*

*If any man speak in an unknown tongue, let it be by two, or at the most by three, and that by course; and let one interpret. But if there be no interpreter, let him keep silence in the church; and let him speak to himself, and to God. 1 Corinthians, Chapter 14, verses 27-28.

....

Therefore let all the house of Israel know assuredly, that God hath made that same Jesus, whom ye have crucified, both Lord and Christ. Now when they heard this, they were pricked in their heart, and said unto Peter and to the rest of

> the apostles, Men and brethren, what shall we do? Then Peter said unto them, Repent, and be baptized every one of you in the Name of Jesus Christ for the remission of sins, and ye shall receive the gift of the Holy Ghost. For the promise is unto you, and to your children, and to all that are afar off, even as many as the Lord our God shall call. And with many other Words did he testify and exhort, saying, Save yourselves from this untoward generation. Then they that gladly received his Word were baptized: and the same day there were added unto them about three thousand souls. And they continued stedfastly in the apostles' doctrine and fellowship, and in breaking of bread, and in prayers. And fear came upon every soul: and many wonders and signs were done by the apostles. Acts, Chapter 2, verses 36-43.

Jesus didn't want the apostles or us to sit back on our laurels after He ascended into heaven. He wants us to take an active stand in sharing so that others have Salvation through Jesus, as well. I'm ashamed to say that I tend to work on this when the situation feels safe and comfortable.

This isn't the Army where the drill sergeant comes up to the new recruits in line saying, "Johnson, Scott and Harris, you have just volunteered for K.P. Duty." God gives us a choice. After Jesus gave His Life for me, I want to be a much better example than I have been in the past.

....

> And all that believed were together, and had all things common; And sold their possessions and goods, and parted them to all men, as every man had need. And they, continuing daily with one accord in the temple, and breaking bread from house to house, did eat their meat with gladness and singleness of heart. Praising God, and having favour with all the people. And the Lord added to the church daily such as should be saved. Acts, Chapter 2, verses 44-47.

It's difficult for me to imagine such total dedication to sharing the Word of God. That would mean selling my house and giving the money to someone else. That would mean not having a TV, VCR, furniture, bank account, etc. Every aspect of my life would be focused on delivering the message of Salvation to others. It makes me realize what a worldly life I still am leading even though I go through the motions of being a follower of Christ.

When it's difficult to give up worldly <u>possess</u>ions, it seems like they <u>possess</u> your soul! Definitely something I need to work on, especially since I'm thinking about getting a new computer while I'm editing this rather than focusing on the message that this has for me. Boy, do I ever need to get my priorities straight!

Here are some related passages:

*And the multitude of them that believed were of one heart and of one soul: neither said any of them that aught of the things which he possessed was his own; but they had all things common. And with great power gave the apostles witness of the Resurrection of the Lord Jesus: and great grace was upon them all. Neither was there any among them that lacked: for as many as were possessors of lands or houses sold them and brought the prices of the things that were sold, And laid them down at the apostles' feet: and distribution was made unto every man according as he had need. And Joses, who by the apostles was surnamed Barnabas, (which is, being interpreted, The son of consolation,) a Levite, and of the country of Cyprus, Having land, sold it, and brought the money, and laid it at the apostles' feet. Acts, Chapter 4, verses 32-37.

*Then Peter said, Lord, we have left all, and followed Thee. And He said unto them, Verily I say unto you, There is no man that hath left house, or parents, or brethren, or wife, or children, for the kingdom of God's sake, Who shall not receive manifold more in this present time, and in the world to come life everlasting. Luke, Chapter 18, verses 28-30.

*And as ye go, preach, saying, The kingdom of heaven is at hand. Heal the sick, cleanse the lepers, raise the dead, cast out devils: freely ye have received, freely give. Provide neither gold, nor silver, nor brass in your purses, Nor scrip for your journey, neither two coats, neither shoes, nor yet staves: for the workman is worthy of his meat. Matthew, Chapter 10, verses 7-10.

....

And he [lame man] gave heed unto them, expecting to receive something of them. Then Peter said, Silver and gold have I none; but such as I have give I thee: In the Name of Jesus Christ of Nazareth rise up and walk. And he took him by the right hand, and lifted him up: and immediately his feet and ankle bones received strength. And he leaping up stood, and walked, and entered with them into the temple, walking, and leaping, and praising God. And all the people saw him walking and praising God: And they knew that it was he which sat for alms at the Beautiful gate of the temple: and they were filled with wonder and amazement at that which had happened unto him. And as the lame man which was healed held Peter and John, all the people ran together unto them in the porch that is called Solomon's, greatly wondering. And when Peter saw it, he answered unto the people, Ye men of Israel, why marvel ye at this? or why look ye so earnestly on us, as though by our own power or holiness we had made this man to walk? The God of Abraham, and of Isaac, and of Jacob, the God of our fathers, hath gloried His Son Jesus; whom ye delivered up, and denied Him in the presence of Pilate, when he was determined to let Him go. But ye denied the Holy One and the Just, and desired a murderer to be granted unto you, and killed the Prince of Life, whom God hath raised from the dead; whereof we are witnesses. And His Name through faith in His Name hath made this man strong, whom ye see and know: yea, the faith which is by him hath given him this perfect soundness in the presence of you all. Acts, Chapter 3, verses 5-16.

    In healing the lame man, Peter didn't take credit for the miracle but made sure that the people focused on this miracle coming from faith in Jesus, not through Peter's efforts. When I watch religious shows on TV, I'm appalled at the way some of them focus more on the religious leaders who get paid, than they do on Jesus Christ. Peter didn't say "I" healed the lame man through Jesus. "I" am able to do this miracle through Jesus' power. "I" need you to send me money so that "I" can continue these miracles. Peter gave the total credit to Jesus, no "I's" or "Me's".

    Sometimes, I get concerned about those who profess to be the messengers of God, but publicly draw attention to themselves. If Jesus and His apostles didn't draw attention to themselves for the miracles they did and didn't ask people for money, do you think Jesus would approve of those on TV who do? It's just something that seems noteworthy as you watch different religious shows that do this. You need to be able to discern the Will of God. Trust your instincts. He will guide you through these.

    Here are some related passages:

Be it known unto you all, and to all the people of Israel, that by the Name of Jesus Christ of Nazareth, whom ye crucified. Whom God raised from the dead, even by Him doth this man stand here before you whole. This is the stone which was set at nought of you builders, which is become the head of the corner. Neither is there Salvation in any other: for there is none other Name under heaven given among men, whereby we must be saved. Now when they saw the boldness of Peter and John and perceived that they were unlearned and ignorant men, they marvelled; and they took knowledge of them, that they had been with Jesus. And beholding the man which was healed standing with them, they could say nothing against it. Acts, Chapter 4, verses 10-14.

Even as I please all men in all things, not seeking mine own profit, but the profit of many, that they may be saved. 1 Corinthians, Chapter 10, verse 33.

....

But a certain man named Ananias, with Sapphira his wife, sold a possession, And kept back part of the price, his wife also being privy to it, and brought a certain part, and laid it at the apostles' feet. But Peter said, Ananias, why hath Satan filled thine heart to lie to the Holy Ghost, and to keep back part of the price of the land? Whiles it remained, was it not thine own? And after it was sold, was it not in thine own power? Why hast thou conceived this thing in thine heart? thou hast not lied unto men, but unto God. And Ananias hearing these words fell down, and gave up the ghost: and great fear came on all them that heard these things. And the young men arose, wound him up, and carried him out, and buried him. And it was about the space of three hours after, when his wife, not knowing what was done, came in. And Peter answered unto her, Tell me whether ye sold the land for so much? And she said, Yea for so much. Then Peter said unto her, How is it that ye have agreed together to tempt the Spirit of the Lord? Behold, the feet of them which have buried thy husband are at the door, and shall carry thee out. Then fell she down straightway at his feet, and yielded up the ghost: and the young men came in, and found her dead, and carrying her forth, buried her by her husband. And great fear came upon all the church, and upon as many as heard these things. Acts, Chapter 5, verses 1-11.

I'm very fortunate God that has this story of Ananias and his wife pop in my mind from time to time, especially at times when I'm trying to find an angle to beat the system. An example would be my planning to have my college daughter come and eat at the breakfast buffet in my hotel when I come to her town to visit. Since I've realized how I was calculating this in my heart, I now go to someone at the hotel and offer to pay for my daughter to join us for breakfast. It's not that anyone minded or would have missed the food. What matters is that I contrived this plan in order to save a few bucks on my daughter's breakfast and God knows what's in my heart. He knows when I'm making up lame excuses for why I'm not going to church on a particular occasion or why the sales person deserved my less than patient response to the store's policy, etc.

It would be nice if God didn't need to remind me so often. That's not the case. Satan works in very subtle ways and finds ways to sneak into our lives through our planning and scheming and our making excuses for our choices. I'm so thankful that God takes the time to remind me. I don't ever want to let these subtle things work into my life and slowly lead me astray. I need to maintain a focus on God and the reminders He puts in my mind (some people call it a conscience), which help to refocus me.

. . . .

There came also a multitude out of the cities round about unto Jerusalem, bringing sick folks, and them which were vexed with unclean spirits: and they were healed every one. Then the high priest rose up, and all they that were with him, (which is the sect of the Sadducees,) and were filled with indignation, And laid their hands on the apostles, and put them in the common prison. But the angel of the Lord by night opened the prison doors, and brought them forth, and said, Go, stand and speak in the temple to the people all the Words of this life. And when they heard that, they entered into the temple early in the morning and taught. But the high priest came, and they that were with him, and called the council together, and all the senate of the children of Israel, and sent to the prison to have them brought. But when the officers came, and found them not in the prison, they returned, and told. Saying, The prison truly found we shut with all safety, and the keepers standing without before the doors: but when we had opened, we found no man within. Acts, Chapter 5, verses 16-23.

Telling others about Jesus' death and Resurrection was important enough that God had an angel unlock the jail cell doors these two different times. If He went to all that trouble, don't you think He wants me to be more open about sharing my faith with others? That's one of my bigger shortcomings!

This is a related passage:

>*Now about that time Herod the king stretched forth his hands to vex certain of the church. And he killed James the brother of John with the sword. And because he saw it pleased the Jews, he proceeded further to take Peter also. (Then were the days of unleavened bread.) And when he had apprehended him, he put him in prison, and delivered him to four quaternions of soldiers to keep him; intending after Easter to bring him forth to the people. Peter therefore was kept in prison: but prayer was made without ceasing of the church unto God for him. And when Herod would have brought him forth, the same night Peter was sleeping between two soldiers, bound with two chains: and the keepers before the door kept the prison. And, behold, the angel of the Lord came upon him, and a light shined in the prison: and he smote Peter on the side, and raised him up, saying, Arise up quickly. And his chains fell off from his hands. And the angel said unto him, Gird thyself, and bind on thy sandals, And so he did. And he saith unto him, Cast thy garment about thee, and follow me. And he went out, and followed him; and wist not that it was true which was done by the angel; but thought he saw a vision. When they were past the first and the second ward, they came unto the iron gate that leadeth unto the city; which opened to them of his own accord: and they went out, and passed on through one street; and forthwith the angel departed from him. And when Peter was come to himself, he said, Now I know of a surety, that the Lord hath sent His angel, and hath delivered me out of the hand of Herod, and from all the expectation of the people of the Jews. And when he had considered the thing, he came to the house of Mary the mother of John, whose surname was Mark; where many were gathered together praying. And as Peter knocked at the door of the gate, a damsel came to hearken, named Rhoda. And when she knew Peter's voice, she opened not the gate for gladness, but ran in, and told how Peter stood before the gate. And they said unto her, Thou art mad. But she constantly affirmed that it was even so. Then said they, It is*

his angel. But Peter continued knocking: and when they had opened the door, and saw him, they were astonished. But he, beckoning unto them with the hand to hold their peace, declared unto them how the Lord had brought him out of the prison. And he said, Go show these things unto James, and to the brethren. And he departed, and went into another place. Now as soon as it was day, there was no small stir among the soldiers, what was become of Peter. And when Herod had sought for him, and found him not, he examined the keepers, and commanded that they should be put to death. And he went down from Judaea to Caesarea, and there abode. Acts, Chapter 12, verses 1-19.

....

And to him they agreed: and when they had called the apostles, and beaten them, they commanded that they should not speak in the Name of Jesus, and let them go. And they departed from the presence of the council, rejoicing that they were counted worthy to suffer shame for His Name. And daily in the temple, and in every house, they ceased not to teach and preach Jesus Christ. Acts, Chapter 5, verses 40-42.

My son was committed to raising money for "Jerry's Kids." I tried to encourage my children to be sensitive to the needs of the less fortunate. This fourth grade student went from house to house all weekend long collecting money. Undaunted by those who were unable or unwilling to contribute, his determination led him to collect a record amount for this worthy cause. Earlier, I had suggested that he had done enough and should think of quitting but he wouldn't give up until he felt he had done his very best for this cause. I need to be as dedicated to my beliefs, regardless of what others think.

....

When they heard these things, they were cut to the heart, and they gnashed on him [Stephen] with their teeth. But he, being full of the Holy Ghost, looked up stedfastly into heaven, and saw the glory of God, and Jesus standing on the right hand of God, And said, Behold, I see the heavens opened, and the Son of Man standing on the right hand of God. Then they cried out with a loud voice, and stopped their ears, and ran upon him with one accord, And cast him out of the city, and stoned him: and the witnesses laid down their clothes at a young man's feet, whose name was Saul. And they stoned Stephen, calling upon God, and saying, Lord Jesus, receive my spirit. And he kneeled down and cried with a loud voice, Lord, lay not this sin to their charge. And when he had said this, he fell asleep. Acts, Chapter 7, verses 54-60.

I was impressed with how forgiving Stephen is. They have bitten him and are in the process of stoning him to death, yet he asks God to forgive them. I have a difficult time forgiving people who have hurt my feelings ten years ago. Boy, do I ever have a lot of room for growth!

....

And there was great joy in that city. But there was a certain man, called Simon, which beforetime in the same city used sorcery, and bewitched the people of Samaria, giving out that himself was some great one: To whom they all gave heed, from the least to the greatest, saying, This man is the great power of god. And to him they had regard, because that of long time he had bewitched them with sorceries. But when they believed Philip preaching the things concerning the kingdom of God, and the Name of Jesus Christ, they were baptized, both men and women. Then Simon himself believed also: and when he was baptized, he continued with Philip, and wondered, beholding the miracles and signs which were done. Now when the apostles which were at Jerusalem heard that Samaria had received the Word of God, they sent unto them Peter and John: Who, when they were come down, prayed for them, that they might receive the Holy Ghost: (For as yet He was fallen upon none of them: only they were baptized in the Name of the Lord Jesus.) Then laid they their hands on them, and they received the Holy Ghost. And when Simon saw that through laying on of the apostles' hands the Holy Ghost was given, he offered them money, Saying, Give me also this power, that on whosoever I lay hands, he may receive the Holy Ghost. But Peter said unto him, Thy money perish with thee, because thou hast thought that the gift of God may be purchased with money. Thou hast neither part nor lot in this matter: for thy heart is not right in the sight of God. Repent therefore of this thy wickedness, and pray God, if perhaps the thought of thine heart may be forgiven thee. Acts, Chapter 8, verses 8-22.

Some of the things that amaze me in this passage are related to Simon who could use sorcery to get a whole city to be in awe of him and the things he did. If it was possible then, it makes me wonder if people in power, certain celebrities, religious leaders, etc. do the same thing now. Are we captivated by particular people who defy all our ethical reasoning?

I'm not sure on this one, but it makes me wonder about people in the media or some religions that get rich from people sending in their life savings to them. Just something to think about.

Additionally, when Simon saw the power given through the Holy Spirit when they were laying on hands, he wanted it too. Rather than become committed to his belief in Jesus, doing it the hard way through changing his life, Simon picked the easy way out and thought he could have his cake and eat it too! He thought he could live his worldly life and buy the gift of the Holy Ghost. Well, Peter saw right through that plan!

The sad part of all of this is that I somewhat identified with Simon. Sometimes I'm looking for the easy way out to accomplish God's Will with the least amount of risk on my part. I need to be more open to being the person that God wants me to be.

....

And he [Peter] became very hungry, and would have eaten: but while they made ready, he fell into a trance, And saw heaven opened, and a certain vessel descending unto him, as it had been a great sheet knit at the four corners, and let down to the earth: Wherein were all manner of four footed beasts of the earth, and wild beasts, and creeping things, and fowls of the air, And there came a Voice to him, Rise, Peter; kill, and eat. But Peter said, Not so, Lord; for I have never eaten any thing that is common or unclean. And the Voice spake unto him again the second time, What God hath cleansed, that call not thou common. This was done thrice: and the vessel was received up again into heaven. Now while Peter doubted in himself what this vision which he had seen should mean, behold the men which were sent from Cornelius had made inquiry for Simon's house, and stood before the gate. And called and asked whether Simon, which was surnamed Peter, were lodged there. Acts, Chapter 10, verses 10-18.

When I first read this, I thought it was speaking solely about people formerly not being allowed to eat pork and other foods which had been forbidden in past Bible teachings. This passage has far-reaching ramifications. Later on in the same chapter it further clarifies this passage.

And he [Peter] said unto them, Ye know how that it is an unlawful thing for a man that is a Jew to keep company, or come unto one of another nation; but God hath shown me that I should not call any man common or unclean. Acts, Chapter 10, verses 28.

It goes on to say: Send therefore to Joppa, and call hither Simon, whose surname is Peter; he is lodged in the house of one Simon a tanner by the sea side: who, when he cometh, shall speak unto thee. Immediately therefore I sent to thee; and thou hast well done that thou art come. Now therefore are we all here present before God, to hear all things that are commanded thee of God. Then Peter opened his mouth, and said, Of a truth I perceive that God is no respecter of persons: But in every nation he that feareth Him, and worketh righteousness, is accepted with Him. The Word which God sent unto the children of Israel, preaching peace by Jesus Christ: (He is Lord of all). Acts Chapter 10, verses 32-36.

Furthermore it says: And He commanded us to preach unto the people, and to testify that it is He which was ordained of God to be the Judge of the quick and dead. To Him give all the prophets witness, that through His Name whosoever believeth in Him shall receive remission of sins. Acts Chapter 10, verses 42-43.

Parts of the passage that I'm quoting are changing the way that Christians think about the social system. In the past, certain nationalities or cultures were not to associate with others. God shares His will with Peter through a dream, using food as a comparison. Previously, certain foods had been considered unclean and not to be eaten just like there had been certain cultures of people who were not to associate with each other. Through this dream, God says that all the foods are acceptable to Him in the same way that ALL people are His. God doesn't want His disciples just to preach to particular types of people or cultures. Everyone needs to hear the Word of God.

It shows that God didn't feel any one nationality, culture or race was better than another. He wants everyone to have Salvation, not just certain people. I think if this was important to God then, people should live their lives accordingly.

It's sad to see and hear some supposed Christians talk negatively about people of different ethnic backgrounds. I don't think we are being the best example of how God works in our lives when we are putting down different cultures. I don't believe God wants us to think we are better than others whether it's because they have a different ethnic background, different financial status, believe differently, etc. I think He wants us to be compassionate and supportive of everyone, being an example of how He works in our lives.

Here are some related passages:

What then? Are we better than they? No, in no wise: for we have before proved both Jews and Gentiles, that they are all under sin; As it is written, There is none righteous, no, not one: There is none that understandeth, there is none that seeketh after God. Romans, Chapter 3, verses 9-10.

For ye are all the children of God by faith in Christ Jesus. For as many of you as have been baptized into Christ have put on Christ. There is neither Jew nor Greek, there is neither bond nor free, there is neither male nor female: for ye are all one in Christ Jesus. And if ye be Christ's, then are ye Abraham's seed, and heirs according to the promise. Galatians, Chapter 3, verses 26-29.

And Jesus came and spake unto them, saying, All power is given unto Me in heaven and in earth. Go ye therefore, and teach all nations, baptizing them in the Name of the Father, and of the Son, and of the Holy Ghost: Teaching them to observe all things whatsoever I have commanded you: and, lo, I am with you always, even unto the end of the world. Amen. Matthew, Chapter 28, verses 18-20.

....

Then departed Barnabas to Tarsus, for to seek Saul: And when he had found him, he brought him unto Antioch. And it came to pass, that a whole year they assembled themselves with the church, and taught much people. And the disciples were called Christians first in Antioch. Acts, Chapter 11, verses 25-26.

I just thought this passage was interesting because it tells about the origin of the term "Christians".

....

And Herod was highly displeased with them of Tyre and Sidon: but they came with one accord to him, and having made Blastus the king's chamberlain their friend, desired peace, because their country was nourished by the king's country. And upon a set day Herod, arrayed in royal apparel, sat upon his throne, and made an oration unto them. And the people gave a shout, saying, It is the voice of a god, and not of a man. And immediately the angel of the Lord smote him, because he gave not God the glory: and he was eaten of worms, and gave up the ghost. But the Word of God grew and multiplied. Acts, Chapter 12, verses 20-24.

This makes me think of times when God gives me a clever idea. People will sometimes compliment me on them and ask how I came up with the idea. I've found that it's much better for me to say, "God just had the idea pop into my head," rather than to take the undeserved credit for it. This passage reinforces that we are supposed to make sure we always give God the glory instead of using it as an opportunity to add a few more feathers to our cap.

••

But Elymas the sorcerer (for so is his name by interpretation) withstood them, seeking to turn away the deputy from the faith. Then Saul, (who also is called Paul,) filled with the Holy Ghost, set his eyes on him, And said, O full of all subtlety and all mischief, thou child of the devil, thou enemy of all Righteousness, wilt thou not cease to pervert the right ways of the Lord? Acts, Chapter 13, verses 8-10.

If God had this person in the Bible who used sorcery called a "child of the devil," do you think He would approve of the fascination with the children's book series that has sorcery as a primary focus? This series has become so popular that both adults and children are reading them, promoting them to others. It makes me sad Satan uses children's books as a subtle way to lead people astray.

••

Then Paul and Barnabas waxed bold, and said, It was necessary that the Word of God should first have been spoken to you: but seeing ye put it from you, and judge yourselves unworthy of everlasting life, lo, we turn to the Gentiles. For so hath the Lord commanded us, saying, I have set thee to be a light of the Gentiles, that thou shouldest be for Salvation unto the ends of the earth. And when the Gentiles heard this, they were glad, and glorified the Word of the Lord: and as many as were ordained to eternal life believed. Acts, Chapter 13, verse 46-48.

There was a time when I was confused because the Bible would talk about the Jews being the promised people. I wondered how I was going to get to heaven since I'm not Jewish. But this says Salvation is for all people to the ends of the world, which includes me. A person just has to believe Jesus Christ is Lord and Savior of all in order to go to heaven. I'm so thankful! What a simple request. I don't have to be born to royalty. I don't have to be rich or on the society page. I don't have to look or dress a certain way. I just have to believe in Jesus. How much simpler could it get?

Dorothy Scott

If God conveyed this to Peter, do you think He wants us treating different races in an undignified manner? I don't think it makes Him happy to know how we have race and social class divisions. We can personally make a change in how we interact with others and serve as role models at the same time.

....

And there they preached the Gospel. And there sat a certain man at Lystra, impotent in his feet, being a cripple from his mother's womb, who never had walked: The same heard Paul speak: who steadfastly beholding him, and perceiving that he had faith to be healed. Said with a loud voice, Stand upright on thy feet. And he leaped and walked. And when the people saw what Paul had done, they lifted up their voices, saying in the speech of Lycaonia, The gods are come down to us in the likeness of men. And they called Barnabas, Jupiter; and Paul, Mercurius, because he was the chief speaker. Then the priest of Jupiter, which was before their city, brought oxen and garlands unto the gates, and would have done, sacrifice with the people. Which when the apostles, Barnabas and Paul, heard of, they rent their clothes, and ran in among the people, crying out, And saying, Sirs, why do ye these things? We also are men of like passions with you, and preach unto you that ye should turn from these vanities unto the living God, which made heaven, and earth, and the sea, and all things that are therein: Who in times past suffered all nations to walk in their own ways. Nevertheless He left not Himself without witness, in that He did good, and gave us rain from heaven, and fruitful seasons, filling our hearts with food and gladness. And with these sayings scarce restrained they the people, that they had not done sacrifice unto them. And there came thither certain Jews from Antioch and Iconium, who persuaded the people, and having stoned Paul, drew him out of the city, supposing he had been dead. Howbeit, as the disciples stood round about him, he rose up, and came into the city: and the next day he departed with Barnabas to Derbe. Acts, Chapter 14, verses 7-20.

In some bizarre way, I think I now understand why the Ancient Greeks and Romans believed in the mythical gods for so long. They must have seen the disciples doing miracles and thought they were gods. They got so caught up in these mythological gods that they never paid attention to what the disciples were telling them about Jesus and Salvation.

It's funny how over time man has created elaborate explanations for the things that God has done rather than acknowledge God. There is a religious group that professes to be Christian but can't acknowledge God. They have to have some logical explanation for miracles and other things rather than just believing in Him. Some groups feel that utilizing the "god power within them," brings about the desired things in their life. Others use the "power of positive thinking" and some "visualize" themselves getting the job they desire. They don't truly realize that they aren't giving God the credit when they think that they got the job through the "god power within them."

When I go for a job interview, I ask God to take care of the things I say and whether I get the job or not, whichever way is His will. I feel positive that God knows what is best for me and my family, so I am happy whether I get the job or not. That doesn't mean I might not be somewhat disappointed if I didn't get the job, but I only want the job that God thinks is best for my particular situation.

Although God says in the Bible that He dwells within each of us; I don't think it's this same "god power" that I hear this group speaking of. Everything I have read in the Bible, and I have read it from cover to cover 16 plus times so far, tells us that God wants us to turn to Him in everything, not to the "god power that lies within us" or "to visualize things the way we want them to be."

I really have a personal concern, because I worry that some well-meaning people may be led astray. They may believe what seems convenient or more understandable to them rather than believe in God like the people in this passage who couldn't believe that the disciples were doing these miracles on God's behalf. That defied all logical explanation so they chose to believe that the disciples were gods instead.

Here is a related passage:

*And a certain Jew named Apollos, born at Alexandria, an eloquent man, and mighty in the Scriptures, came to Ephesus. This man was instructed in the way of the Lord; and being fervent in the Spirit, he spake and taught diligently the things of the Lord, knowing only the baptism of John. And he began to speak boldly in the synagogue: whom when Aquila and Priscilla had heard, they took him unto them, and expounded unto him the way of God more perfectly. And when he was disposed to pass into Achaia, the brethren wrote, exhorting the disciples to receive *him: who, when he was come, helped them much which had believed through grace: For he mightily convinced the Jews, and that publicly, showing by the Scriptures that Jesus was Christ. Acts, Chapter 18, verses 24-28.*

....

And it came to pass, as we went to prayer, a certain damsel possessed with a spirit of divination met us, which brought her masters much gain by soothsaying: The same followed Paul and us, and cried, saying, These men are the servants of the Most High God, which show unto us the way of Salvation. And this did she many days. But Paul, being grieved, turned and said to the spirit, I command thee in the Name of Jesus Christ to come out of her. And he came out the same hour. And when her masters saw that the hope of their gains was gone, they caught Paul and Silas, and drew them into the marketplace unto the rulers. Acts, Chapter 16, verses 16-19.

I'm going to skip some verses to get to the part where Paul is imprisoned.

And when they had laid many stripes upon them, they cast them into prison, charging the jailer to keep them safely: Who, having received such a charge, thrust them into the inner prison, and made their feet fast in the stocks. And at midnight Paul and Silas prayed, and sang praises unto God: and the prisoners heard them. And suddenly there was a great earthquake, so that the foundations of the prison were shaken: and immediately all the doors were opened, and everyone's bands were loosed. And the keeper of the prison awaking out of his sleep, and seeing the prison doors open, he drew out his sword, and would have killed himself, supposing that the prisoners had been fled. But Paul cried with a loud voice, saying, Do thyself no harm: for we are all here. Then he called for a light, and sprang in, and came trembling, and fell down before Paul and Silas, And brought them out, and said, Sirs, what must I do to be saved? And they said, Believe on the Lord Jesus Christ, and thou shalt be saved, and thy house. And they spake unto him the Word of the Lord, and to all that were in his house. And he took them the same hour of the night, and washed their stripes; and was baptized, he and all his, straightway. And when he had brought them into his house, he set meat before them, and rejoiced, believing in God with all his house. And when it was

day, the magistrates sent the sergeants, saying, Let those men
go. And the keeper of the prison told this saying to Paul, The
magistrates have sent to let you go: now therefore depart, and go
in peace. Acts, Chapter 16, verses 23-36.*

There's more to the story. Paul wouldn't leave the prison because they had been publicly chastised and the magistrates were trying to secretly let them out. Paul wanted to be publicly cleared of all the charges, which eventually happened.

This passage makes me think of how perfectly God looks after the people that spread His Word. I was thinking of Daniel in the lion's den and how he wasn't harmed. It brings to mind lots of others, as well. Noah and his family were saved from the flood by God letting him know he was to build an ark. Shadrach, Meshach and Abednego, were not burned in the fiery furnace. Peter was let out of jail by the angel. The list of miracles, where God distinctly protects those that are doing His will, goes on and on. It's hard for me to imagine that anyone wouldn't want God in their corner. I sure do!

Here is a related passage:

*Take heed therefore unto yourselves, and to all the flock, over the which the Holy Ghost hath made you overseers, to feed the church of God, which He hath purchased with His Own Blood. For I know this, that after my departing shall grievous wolves enter in among you, not sparing the flock. Also of your own selves shall men arise, speaking perverse things, to draw away disciples after them. Acts, Chapter 20, verses 28-30.

....

Then Paul stood in the midst of Mars' hill, and said, Ye men of Athens, I perceive that in all things ye are too superstitious. For as I passed by, and beheld your devotions, I found an altar with this inscription, TO THE UNKNOWN GOD. Whom therefore ye ignorantly worship, him declare I unto you. God that made the world and all things therein, seeing that He is Lord of heaven and earth, dwelleth not in temples made with hands; Neither is worshipped with men's hands, as though He needed any thing, seeing He giveth to all life, and breath, and all things; And hath made of one blood all nations of men for to dwell on the face of the earth, and hath determined the times before appointed, and bounds of their habitation; That they should seek the Lord, if haply they might feel after Him, and find Him, though He be not far from every one of us: For in Him we live, and move, and have our being; as certain also of your own poets have said, For we are also His offspring. Forasmuch then as we are the offspring of God, we ought not to think that the Godhead is like unto gold, or silver, or stone, graven by art and man's device. Acts, Chapter 17, verses 22-29.

This reminds me of when my mother told me about intercourse and how babies are conceived when I was really young. I have to admit it's a pretty strange connection to make with this passage.

I was very young when my mother explained about babies being conceived. In fact, I don't really remember her telling me. The thing is, she did tell me the truth and not some story, just like Paul told them the truth about God and not some story.

Forgetting all the accurate information my mother had told me because it didn't seem to make any sense at the time, left me open to this very interesting explanation when I was a little older.

A girl in my class told me that girls got pregnant by boys touching them with their finger. I got so disturbed with this notion that I was afraid to walk through the halls at school. I thought a boy could touch you with his finger while passing in the hallway and you might not ever know who the father of your baby was.

Fortunately, I went home and asked my mother how you know who the father of your baby is? This really confused her because she had already told me the truth and I had chosen to believe a far-fetched story instead. Well, it seems very similar here. Paul told them the truth about God, but they chose to believe some far-fetched story and worship idols made by man's hands instead. How sad!

Here are some related passages:

*Lest ye corrupt yourselves, and make you a graven image, the similitude of any figure, the likeness of male or female, The likeness of any beast that is on the earth, the likeness of any winged fowl that flieth in the air, The likeness of any thing that creepeth on the ground, the likeness of any fish that is in the waters beneath the earth: And lest thou lift up thine eyes unto heaven, and when thou seest the sun, and the moon, and the stars, even all the host of heaven, shouldest be driven to worship them, and serve them, which the LORD thy God hath divided unto all nation under the whole heaven. Deuteronomy, Chapter 4, verses 16-19.

*Take heed unto yourselves, lest ye forget the covenant of the LORD your God, which He made with you, and make you a graven image, or the likeness of any thing which the LORD thy God hath forbidden thee. Deuteronomy, Chapter 4, verse 23.

*Thou shalt have none other gods before Me. Thou shalt not make thee any graven image, or any likeness of any thing that is in heaven above, or that is in the earth beneath, or that is in the waters beneath the earth: Thou shalt not bow down thyself unto them, nor serve them: for I the LORD thy God am a jealous God, visiting the iniquity of the fathers upon the children unto the third and fourth generation of them that hate Me. And showing mercy unto thousands of them that love Me and keep My Commandments. Deuteronomy, Chapter 5, verses 7-10.

*Take heed to yourselves, that your heart be not deceived, and ye turn aside, and serve gods, and worship them; And then the LORD'S wrath be kindled against you, and He shut up the heaven, that there be no rain, and that the land yield not her fruit; and lest ye perish quickly from off the good land which the LORD giveth you. Deuteronomy, Chapter 11, verses 16-17.

*Sing unto the LORD, all the earth: show forth from day to day His Salvation. Declare His glory among the heathen, His marvellous works among all nations. For great is the LORD, and greatly to be praised: He also is to be feared above all gods. For all the gods of the people are idols: but the LORD made the heavens. Glory and honor are in His presence: strength and gladness are in His place. 1 Chronicles, Chapter 16, verses 23-27.

....

Then spake the Lord to Paul in the night by a vision, Be not afraid, but speak, and hold not thy peace: For I am with thee, and no man shall set on thee to hurt thee: for I have much people in this city. Acts, Chapter 18, verses 9-10.

I don't know the exact title, but this must be where they got the idea for the song that includes: *Be not afraid, for I am with thee always...* This song is very comforting to my daughter who remembers this when she is feeling stressed.

....

For therein is the righteousness of God revealed from faith to faith: as it is written, The just shall live by faith. For the wrath of God is revealed from heaven against all ungodliness and unrighteousness of men, who hold the Truth in unrighteousness; Because that which may be known of God is manifest in them; for God hath shown it unto them. For the invisible things of Him from the creation of the world are clearly seen, being understood by the things that are made, even His eternal power and Godhead; so that they are without excuse: Because that, when they knew God, they glorified Him not as God, neither were thankful; but became vain in their imaginations, and their foolish heart was darkened. Professing themselves to be wise, they became fools, And changed the glory of the uncorruptible God into an image made like to corruptible man, and to birds, and fourfooted beasts, and creeping things. Wherefore God also gave them up to uncleanness through the lusts of their own hearts, to dishonour their own bodies between themselves: Who changed the Truth of God into a lie, and worshipped and served the creature more than the Creator, Who is blessed for ever. Amen. For this cause God gave them up unto vile affections: for even their women did change the natural use into that which is against nature: And likewise also the men, leaving the natural use of the woman, burned in their lust one toward another; men with men working that which is unseemly, and receiving in themselves that recompence of their error which was meet. And even as they did not like to retain God in their knowledge, God gave them over to a reprobate mind, to do those things which are not convenient; Being filled with all unrighteousness, fornication, wickedness, covetousness, maliciousness; full of envy, murder, debate, deceit, malignity whisperers, Backbiters, haters of God, despiteful, proud, boasters, inventors of evil things, disobedient to parents, Without understanding, covenantbreakers, without natural affection, implacable, unmerciful: Who knowing the judgment of God, that they which commit such things are worthy of death, not only do the same, but have pleasure in them that do them. Romans, Chapter 1, verses 17-32.

Throughout the Bible, God gives us direction for our lives. He lets us know through the passages which things will lead us in the direction that He wants and which things have the potential to lead us down the wrong paths. This passage is noteworthy because it mentions a variety of lifestyle and behavior choices that displease God. Although we are to pay attention to these to make our choices accordingly, God doesn't give us the right to judge others.

Who are we to cast the first stone? I think it's important to remember: *Matthew, Chapter 7, verses 1-2, Judge not, that ye be not judged. For with what judgment ye judge, ye shall be judged: and with what measure ye mete, it shall be measured to you again.*

So, although God gives us guidance, we are not to be rude or hateful to others, regardless of whether their lifestyle, sexual preferences or religious beliefs are different than ours.

....

For when the Gentiles, which have not the Law, do by nature the things contained in the Law, these, having not the Law, are a Law unto themselves: Which show the work of the Law written in their hearts, their conscience also bearing witness, and their thoughts the mean while accusing or else excusing one another. In the day when God shall judge the secrets of men by Jesus Christ according to My Gospel. Romans, Chapter 2, verses 14-16.

Our family had a policy that if our children told the truth, there would be a lighter consequence to try to reinforce their being honest. I remember hearing my pre-school aged son at the other end of the house saying, "Truth, Mommy. Truth," when he had done something that he knew he wasn't supposed to do.

I'm proud to say that my children have grown to trust the instincts that God gives them through their conscience, much more than I ever did.

Here is a related passage:

*Pray for us: for we trust we have a good conscience, in all things willing to live honestly. Hebrews, Chapter 13, verse 18.

....

Thou therefore which teachest another, teachest thou not thyself? thou that preachest a man should not steal, dost thou steal? Romans, Chapter 2, verse 21.

Actually, there is more that goes with this passage. I just took out the part that relates to me. When I was in high school, I was visiting a church one time with my mother. The sermon was especially interesting. It talked about a parent who was called to the Police Station because their child had gotten arrested for stealing some pens from a local store. The thing the parent said to the child was, "Why would you steal pens when I can get all the pens you want from my work?"

We, as Christians, may have double standards just like this parent did. Sometimes we are examples of negative things without really realizing what we're doing. When we are being examples of how God works in our lives, we need to make sure all our actions and words glorify Him. We have to realize that we are giving others a message whether it's taking things from work or laughing at jokes that put down people who are different than we are.

....

> *For circumcision verily profiteth, if thou keep the Law: but if thou be a breaker of the Law, thy circumcision is made uncircumcision. Therefore if the uncircumcision keep the righteousness of the Law, shall not his uncircumcision be counted for circumcision? Romans, Chapter 2, verses 25-26.*
>
> *But he is a Jew, which is one inwardly; and circumcision is that of the heart, in the Spirit, and not in the letter; whose praise is not of men, but of God. Romans, Chapter 2, verse 29.*

There was a time when people thought that if they were Jewish and followed some basic laws like circumcision, they could do whatever they wanted and were saved because Jews were the chosen people. This passage clarifies that just being Jewish or following rules like circumcision won't get us Salvation.

I guess what this all boils down to is, God knows what is in our hearts and whether we live as examples of how Jesus works in our lives or not. This is going to be more of a determiner of our Salvation than any outward signs like being circumcised or being of a particular ethnic or cultural group.

Here are some related passages:

> **Where is boasting then? It is excluded. By what Law? Of works? Nay: but by the Law of faith. Therefore we conclude that a man is justified by faith without the deeds of the Law. Is He the God of the Jews only? Is He not also of the Gentiles? Yes, of the Gentiles also: Seeing it is One God which shall justify the circumcision by faith, and uncircumcision through faith. Do we then make void the Law through faith? God forbid: yea, we establish the Law. Romans, Chapter 3, verses 27-31.*

*For in Jesus Christ neither circumcision availeth any thing, nor uncircumcision; but faith which worketh by love. Galatians, Chapter 5, verse 6.

*For in Christ Jesus neither circumcision availeth anything, nor uncircumcision, but a new creature. And as many as walk according to this rule, peace be on them, and mercy, and upon the Israel of God. Galatians, Chapter 6, verses 15-16.

....

And not only so, but we glory in tribulations also: knowing that tribulation worketh patience; And patience experience, and experience hope: And hope maketh not ashamed; because the love of God is shed abroad in our hearts by the Holy Ghost which is given unto us; For when we were yet without strength, in due time Christ died for the ungodly. Romans, Chapter 5, verses 3-6.

Don't you just admire people who can thank God in the midst of all types of disaster and tribulation? I remember when I would get frustrated when things didn't turn out the way I wanted. My father would tell me that those experiences gave me character. I think God is telling us the same thing in this passage that my father used to tell me. If I'm cursing God when things go wrong, am I being a good example of how Jesus works in my life?

The best example I have ever seen of people glorifying God in the midst of extreme tribulation, next to Job, goes to my aunt and her family who experienced an unusually tragic loss of loved ones. Some would have been bitter and hateful, but they were examples of their faith to all those who were touched by this loss. I'm not sure I would have fared as well, but God in His infinite mercy will bless them with The Peace Which Passes All Understanding to survive the pain of their loss.

....

Wherefore, as by one man sin entered into the world, and death by sin; and so death passed upon all men, for that all have sinned. Romans, Chapter 5, verse 12.

Nope, none of us is better or more apt to be saved than another. We are all sinners. Adam was the first man that sinned and we have continued to perpetuate that plight. Fortunately for us, Jesus has made the ultimate sacrifice so we all have the same opportunity for Salvation through our faith in Him.

Here are some related passages:

> *Therefore as by the offence of one judgment came upon all men to condemnation: even so by the righteousness of One the free Gift came upon all men unto justification of life. Romans, Chapter 5, verse 18.
>
> *For the wages of sin is death; but the Gift of God is eternal life through Jesus Christ our Lord. Romans, Chapter 6, verse 23.
>
> *For as in Adam all die, even so in Christ shall all be made alive. 1 Corinthians, Chapter 15, verse 22.

....

> For if ye live after the flesh, ye shall die: but if ye through the Spirit do mortify the deeds of the body, ye shall live. For as many as are led by the Spirit of God, they are the sons of God. For ye have not received the spirit of bondage again to fear; but ye have received the Spirit of adoption, whereby we cry, Abba, Father. The Spirit itself beareth witness with our spirit, that we are the children of God. Romans, Chapter 8, verses 13-16.

Choose Your Own Adventure books were pretty popular at one time. You would be reading an adventure story and then were given choices. If you turned to one set of pages listed, the story would end one way and if you turned to some of the other pages listed, it would end totally different ways.

We can live worldly lives of the flesh and have a less than pleasant ending or we can realize where we have gone off-track and turn our lives around to focus on God and what He wants for us. When we choose to live through the Spirit, we will have eternal life with Jesus in heaven. Which ending do you choose????

....

> For He saith to Moses, I will have mercy on whom I will have mercy, and I will have compassion on whom I will have compassion. So then it is not of him that willeth, nor of him that runneth, but of God that showeth mercy. Romans, Chapter 9, verses 15-16.

There are religious groups that believe that if they "will" things to happen, "visualize things," "use the god power within them" or use the "power of positive thinking," everything will turn out the way they want.

Things might turn out the way they want because Satan uses things like this to work a subtle wedge in their relationship with God. It's similar to what happens when people read horoscopes where they start out reading it for fun, but after awhile they become more and more dependant on it. If things turn out well after a person "wills it," or uses "the god power within them" or "visualizes" things the way they want, they are much more apt to do this again the next time rather than turn to God, asking Him to provide for their every need. They don't even realize they are drifting further and further from what God wants, as evidenced through this Bible verse.

....

That if thou shalt confess with thy mouth the Lord Jesus, and shalt believe in thine heart that God hath raised Him from the dead, thou shalt be saved. For with the heart man believeth unto righteousness; and with the mouth confession is made unto Salvation. For the Scripture saith, Whosoever believeth on Him shall not be ashamed. For there is no difference between the Jew and the Greek: for the same Lord over all is rich unto all that call upon Him. For whosoever shall call upon the Name of the Lord shall be saved. Romans, Chapter 10, verses 9-13.

The Bible doesn't say, "People who do nice things for others," are saved. It doesn't say, "People of only a particular ethnic background," are saved. It doesn't say, "Whoever uses the god-power within them is saved." It doesn't say, "People who believe in God as they understand Him," are saved. It doesn't say, "Whoever thinks positively" or "wills things" is saved.

It does say in verse nine: *"That if thou shalt confess with thy mouth the Lord Jesus, and shalt believe in thine heart that God hath raised Him from the dead, thou shalt be saved."*

Pure and simple, that's what you have to do to be saved!

....

Owe no man any thing, but to love one another: for he that loveth another hath fulfilled the Law. For this, Thou shalt not commit adultery, Thou shalt not kill, Thou shalt not steal, thou shalt not bear false witness, Thou shalt not covet; and if there be any other Commandment, it is briefly comprehended in this saying namely, Thou shalt love thy neighbour as thyself. Love worketh no ill to his neighbour: therefore love is the fulfilling of the Law. Romans, Chapter 13, verses 8-10.

I think God had this passage written for people like me who get caught up in trying to remember too many things and end up forgetting most of it. This way I don't have to remember all types of different rules about being a Christian. In order to lead my life as an example of how God works through me, I just have to remember one rule: *Love thy neighbor as thyself.* This covers everything else.

When I contemplate talking rudely to a sales person who has been less than courteous to me, all I have to do is think, "Is this how God would want me to treat someone else?" I wish I could say I always remember that before I give a sarcastic reply, but it often pops in my mind and I'm less apt to respond hatefully. I definitely am not perfect but want to work toward being a better example of how God works in my life.

....

Him that is weak in the faith receive ye, but not to doubtful disputations. For one believeth that he may eat all things: another, who is weak eateth herbs. Let not him that eateth despise him that eateth not; and let not him which eateth not judge him that eateth: for God hath received him. Who art thou that judgest another man's servant? To his own Master he standeth or falleth. Yea, he shall be holden up: for God is able to make him stand. One man esteemeth one day above another: another esteemeth every day alike. Let every man be fully persuaded in his own mind. He that regardeth the day, regardeth it unto the Lord; and he that regardeth not the day, to the Lord he doth not regard it. He that eateth, eateth to the Lord, for he giveth God thanks; and he that eateth not, to the Lord he eateth not, and giveth God thanks. Romans, Chapter 14, verses 1-6.

Let us not therefore judge one another any more: but judge this rather, that no man put a stumbling block or an occasion to fall in his brother's way. I know, and am persuaded by the Lord Jesus, that there is nothing unclean of itself: but to him that esteemeth any thing to be unclean, to him it is unclean. But if thy brother be grieved with thy meat, now walkest thou not charitably. Destroy not him with thy meat, for whom Christ died. Let not then your good be evil spoken of: For the kingdom of God is not meat and drink; but righteousness, and peace, and joy in the Holy Ghost. For he that in these things serveth Christ is acceptable to God, and approved of men. Let us therefore follow after the things which make for peace, and things wherewith one may edify another. For meat destroy not the work of God. All things indeed are pure; but it is evil for that man who eateth with offence. It is good neither to eat flesh, nor to drink wine, nor any thing whereby thy brother stumbleth, or is offended, or is made weak. Hast thou faith? have it to thyself before God. Happy is he that condemneth not himself in that thing which he alloweth. And he that doubteth is damned if he eat, because he eateth not of faith; for whatsoever is not of faith is sin. Romans, Chapter 14, verses 13-23.

These passages have influenced my life in a number of ways. I had been struggling for years about whether we should be going to church on Saturday or on Sunday, or whether it was okay to eat meat or not. I admire my aunt and uncle who are very devout Christians who go to church on a different day and eat somewhat differently than I do.

God says that whether we eat meat or not, or go to church on Saturday or Sunday doesn't determine our Salvation. Our Salvation is because of our faith in Jesus and living as an example of how He works in our lives. What matters is that we follow our beliefs.

He also tells us that we aren't supposed to taunt others because their beliefs are different than ours by putting a stumbling block before them. An example would be, having friends over for dinner who don't eat meat for religious reasons and only having meat courses, putting them in an awkward position.

We need to support others and not be judgmental. I need to keep focusing on God to lead me in the direction that He wants instead of worrying about what everyone else is doing or not doing. It sounds like these details don't matter to Him as long as they are done to glorify God.

Here are some related passages:

*But meat commendeth us not to God: for neither, if we eat, are we the better; neither if we eat not, are we the worse. But take heed lest by any means this liberty of yours become a stumbling block to them that are weak. 1 Corinthians, Chapter 8, verses 8-9.

*Notwithstanding thou mayest kill and eat flesh in all thy gates, whatsoever thy soul lustest after, according to the blessing of the LORD thy God which He hath given thee: the unclean and the clean may eat thereof, as of the roebuck, and as of the hart. Only ye shall not eat the blood; ye shall pour it upon the earth as water. Deuteronomy, Chapter 12, verses 15-16.

> *For whatsoever things were written aforetime were written for our learning, that we through patience and comfort of the Scriptures might have hope. Now the God of patience and consolation grant you to be likeminded one toward another according to Christ Jesus: That ye may with one mind and one mouth glorify God, even the Father of our Lord Jesus Christ. Romans, Chapter 15, verses 4-6.*

When I get upset about things or worried about family situations, I will often pick up the Bible. I don't usually open it to the spot where I left off the last time. I pick up the Bible with both hands and open it and read whatever is on those pages. I always say a little prayer first for God to take care of my understanding, comprehension and retention. Although it doesn't happen every time, it's amazing how many times I open the Bible to pages that specifically relate to my particular situation. I feel God guides me to the particular pages He wants me to read which calm me down and comfort me, just like this passage says.

....

> *Know ye not that ye are the temple of God, and that the Spirit of God dwelleth in you? If any man defile the temple of God, him shall God destroy; for the temple of God is holy, which temple ye are. 1 Corinthians, Chapter 3, verses 16-17.*

I have heard that some religions have interpreted this passage to say that Christians shouldn't get their ears pierced or get tattoos but that isn't what this passage means to me. This passage is telling me that I'm a Christian 24/7 (24 hours a day/7 days a week) and God dwells in me all the time.

My actions, thoughts, words and deeds make me a walking billboard for God. A billboard works as an advertisement to draw people toward a particular business. If the sign were sloppy, had misspellings or poor grammar, the billboard would reflect poorly on the owner of the business.

Now, if I go out and get drunk, take drugs, am rude to others or use God's Name in vain, it's like I've used bad grammar on my billboard which would reflect poorly on God who dwells in me. I need to make sure that I'm attempting to live in a manner that makes me a good example of how God works in my life.

Here is a related passage:

> **I am crucified with Christ: nevertheless I live; yet not I, but Christ liveth in me: and the life which I now live in the flesh I live by the faith of the Son of God, who loved me, and gave Himself for me. Galatians, Chapter 2, verse 20.*

> *I wrote to you in an epistle not to company with fornicators: Yet not altogether with the fornicators of this world, or with the covetous, or extortioners, or with idolaters; for then must ye needs go out of the world. But now I have written unto you not to keep company, if any man that is called a brother be a fornicator, or covetous, or an idolater, or a railer, or a drunkard, or an extortioner; with such an one no not to eat. For what have I to do to judge them also that are without? Do not ye judge them that are within? But them that are without God judgeth. Therefore put away from among yourselves that wicked person.*
> *1 Corinthians, Chapter 5, verses 9-13.*

I think God talks to us through Paul like a parent talks to their teenager about people who might be poor influences on them. A parent might say something like, "I think it's very important for you to be cautious about what type of people you hang around with at school. Now, I want you to be polite to everyone, because we aren't to be judgmental of others, but we are supposed to be aware of the lifestyle choices others make.

"Although you may have the best of intentions, sometimes other people's bad habits rub off on us even without our being aware of it. So, it's important that you don't hang with kids that you think do drugs, drink, and party or are rude and crude. I know it's hard because some of the kids who make poor choices are the ones who seem the most popular. I hope you know that I'm only telling you this because I love you. I just don't want to see you get involved with the wrong type of people." Well, I think God often guides us like a loving parent, as well.

Here is a related passage:

> **Be ye not unequally yoked together with unbelievers: for what fellowship hath righteousness with unrighteousness? and what communion hath Light with darkness? And what concord hath Christ with Belial? or what part hath he that believeth with an infidel? 2 Corinthians, Chapter 6, verses 14-15.*

> *And the woman which hath an husband that believeth not, and if he be pleased to dwell with her, let her not leave him. For the unbelieving husband is sanctified by the wife, and the unbelieving wife is sanctified by the husband: else were your children unclean; but now are they holy. But if the unbelieving depart, let him depart. A brother or a sister is not under*

bondage in such cases: but God hath called us to peace. For what knowest thou, O wife, whether thou shalt save thy husband? or how knowest thou, O man whether thou shalt save thy wife? 1 Corinthians, Chapter 7, verses 13-16.

God gives His approval for staying in a good marriage with a non-Christian spouse, because you might be able to lead your spouse to Christianity through your relationship with God. On the other hand, I think it says that if you're in an unhealthy relationship, whether the person does or doesn't profess to be a Christian, God absolves us from our marital commitment.

Now, some may think this passage doesn't apply to them because God only absolves them if their partner is a non-Christian. Do you really think a person is a Christian just because they say they are? Don't you think they are supposed to be a "Put Their Money Where Their Mouth Is Christian," by really living a life that reflects their belief in Jesus?

So, if a spouse drinks up all the money in the house and there's no money to pay for food or clothes for the children, do you really think God considers this person a Christian? If a spouse is so involved in drugs or other vices and causes constant turmoil in the family, do you really think God considers this person a Christian? If a spouse has a hard day at work and hits the kids or you, do you really think God considers this person a Christian just because they profess to be one?

I think that God is saying the "till death do you part" portion of your marriage vow doesn't apply because God said, *"A brother or a sister is not under bondage in such cases."* Sure, God would like all marriages to work out and doesn't want people to leave just because they feel they may have missed out on all the fun that they think their single friends are having. That isn't what this is discussing.

God loves the non-Christian, the alcoholic, the drug addict and the abusive person, all of which can turn their lives around and become Christian. This would have to be more than just saying they are a Christian. They would have to really live their lives as a Christian.

Sometimes we just aren't the ones who can bring these people to God. Male or female, we have to be able to assess whether we are in a healthy environment for ourselves and our children. If we aren't, we are absolved from the "till death do you part" commitment, because being in an unhealthy or life-threatening environment isn't what God would want for any of us.

....

Now all these things happened unto them for examples: and they are written for our admonition, upon whom the ends of the world are come. Wherefore let him that thinketh he standeth take heed lest he fall. There hath no temptation taken you but such as is common to man: but God is faithful, who will not suffer you to be tempted above that ye are able; but will with the temptation also make a way to escape, that ye may be able to bear it. 1 Corinthians, Chapter 10, verses 11-13.

As Christians, we will have our share of temptations. Do you really think Satan just sits back and says, "Oh, they're Christians. I'll leave them alone. Well, God's got one up on me." That isn't my impression of Satan. I feel he tries to lead Christians astray in a wide variety of ways. Sometimes they are really obvious ways like: money, drinking, drugs, gambling, infidelity, etc.

Sometimes, Satan works in very subtle ways like: eating, control issues, gossiping, etc. God is telling us that although He knows we are going to be tempted, we will never be tempted beyond our capabilities as long as we focus on Him. He will never leave us, but we are in control of the choices we make. I pray that I always choose God rather than the temptations that Satan dangles in front of me.

....

All things are lawful for me, but all things are not expedient: all things are lawful for me, but all things edify not. Let no man seek his own, but every man another's wealth. 1 Corinthians, Chapter 10, verses 23-24.

I think God says that "Balance in All Things" is good. Having money, a house and a car are alright to own, but too much focus on any of these can lead us astray.

In addition to that, focusing on worldly goods makes us poor examples of how God works in our lives. We are supposed to focus on helping others rather than "Getting Ahead in the World."

....

For as often as ye eat this Bread, and drink this Cup, ye do show the Lord's death till He comes. Wherefore whosoever shall eat this Bread, and drink this Cup of the Lord, unworthily, shall be guilty of the Body and Blood of the Lord. But let a man examine himself, and so let him eat of that Bread, and drink of that Cup. For he that eateth and drinketh unworthily, eateth and drinketh damnation to himself, not discerning the Lord's Body. For this cause many are weak and sickly among you, and many sleep. For if we would judge ourselves, we should not be judged. But when we are judged, we are chastened of the Lord, that we should not be condemned with the world. 1 Corinthians, Chapter 11, verses 26-32.

God wants me to do some self-reflection before I have communion. It's important, especially for "Self-righteous Christians" like me, to have some humbling time to think about all my shortcomings. It doesn't only mean the major vices. Some of us get big heads because we don't think we have those obvious vices that others might have. We often need to be taken down a notch because we are just as sinful.

We aren't to think our sins aren't as great as someone else's and feel that we are more worthy than they are. We are just as sinful by the subtle things we allow to creep into our lives. These keep us from being the Christian that God wants us to be. Times when we were less than patient and loving with our families, the times we yelled at someone on the freeway, the times we were gossiping with others, etc.

God is saying it is better for us to have periodic reflective time now, judging ourselves rather than continuing to live our sinful, self-righteous lives. That is preferable to finding out later from God on the Last Day that we didn't make the "final cut." That's one eye opener I don't want, so I need to start by making changes in my life today!

....

There are diversities of gifts, but the same Spirit. There are differences of administrations, but the same Lord. And there are diversities of operations, but it is the same God which worketh all in all. But the manifestation of the Spirit is given to every man to profit withal: For to one is given by the Spirit the Word of wisdom; to another Word of knowledge by the same Spirit. To another faith by the same Spirit; to another the gifts of healing by the same Spirit; To another the working of miracles; to another prophecy; to another discerning of spirits; to another divers kinds of tongues; to another the interpretation of tongues: But all these worketh that one and the selfsame Spirit, dividing to every man severally as He will. For as the body is one, and hath many members, and all the members of that one body, being many, are one body: so also is Christ. For by One Spirit are we all baptized into One Body, whether we be Jews or Gentiles, whether we be bond or free; and have been all made to drink into One Spirit. For the Body is not one member, but many. 1 Corinthians, Chapter 12, verses 4-14.

God wants us to know that He gives everyone particular talents in which to glorify Him. He doesn't want us to become big headed thinking we are better than someone who doesn't have our particular talent. God tells us that we are all working together as one unit on His behalf. Similarly, there are many different body parts that work together for the good of the whole, just as each member of the body has a different function. No particular body member is greater than another.

This particular passage talks about speaking in tongues as being one of the gifts. I don't really know enough about this to really address it. What I do know is this passage tells me that although God may have given me particular talents to glorify Him, I should not be judging people who have talents that I don't understand. Just because their talents are different, doesn't make them wrong. Christians should be supportive of one another, regardless.

....

Though I speak with the tongues of men and of angels, and have not charity, I am become as sounding brass, or a tinkling cymbal. And though I have the gift of prophecy, and understand all mysteries, and all knowledge; and though I have all faith, so that I could remove mountains, and have not charity, I am nothing. And though I bestow all my goods to feed the poor and though I give my body to be burned, and have not charity, it profiteth me nothing. Charity suffereth long, and is kind; charity envieth not; charity vaunteth not itself; is not puffed up, Doth not behave itself unseemly, seeketh not her own, is not easily provoked, thinketh no evil; Rejoiceth not in iniquity, but rejoiceth in the Truth; Beareth all things, believeth all things, hopeth all things, endureth all things. Charity never faileth: but whether there be prophecies, they shall fail; whether there be tongues, they shall cease; whether there be knowledge, it shall vanish away. For we know in part, and we prophesy in part. 1 Corinthians, Chapter 13, verses 1-9.

And now abideth faith, hope, charity, these three; but the greatest of these is charity. 1 Corinthians, Chapter 13, verse 13.

I love this passage. It tells me that I can profess to be a good Christian and do all kinds of things that look generous to others. Unless I live the life of a Christian by being genuinely charitable in my actions, loving my neighbors, my enemies or those that believe differently than I do, then I'm all talk.

There was a song we learned in Vacation Bible School years ago called *If You're a Christian and You Know It*. Well, it says that if you were a Christian then your face would really show it, clap your hands. I think it should say instead that if you were a Christian, then your life will really show it. That's the true indicator of being a Christian, not what we look like on the outside to others.

....

O death, where is thy sting? O grave, where is thy victory? The sting of death is sin; and the strength of sin is the law. But thanks be to God, which giveth us the victory through our Lord Jesus Christ. Therefore, my beloved brethren be ye steadfast, unmovable, always abounding in the work of the Lord, forasmuch as ye know that your labour is not in vain in the Lord. 1 Corinthians, Chapter 15, verse 55-58.

I remember my father and I being in the hospital with each of us -holding one of my grandmother's hands as she passed away. She didn't fight it and she seemed to be at peace with the idea of joining God in heaven.

Here is a related passage:

*Come unto Me, all ye that labour and are heavy laden, and I will give you rest. Take My yoke upon you and learn of Me; for I am meek and lowly in heart: and ye shall find rest unto your souls. For My yoke is easy, and My burden is light. Matthew, Chapter 11, verses 28-30.

....

Grace be to you and peace from God our Father, and from the Lord Jesus Christ. Blessed be God, even the Father of our Lord Jesus Christ, the Father of mercies, and the God of all comfort; who comforteth us in all our tribulation, that we may be able to comfort them which are in any trouble, by the comfort wherewith we ourselves are comforted of God. 2 Corinthians, Chapter 1, verses 2-4.

There were times in my life when things were not as smooth as they are now. I was fortunate that I had family members and friends to comfort me and to remind me that God would get me through them...and He did!

....

For God, who commanded the Light to shine out of darkness, hath shined in our hearts, to give the Light of the knowledge of the glory of God in the face of Jesus Christ. But we have this Treasure in earthen vessels, that the excellency of the power may be of God, and not of us. 2 Corinthians, Chapter 4, verses 6-7.

This is another one of the Bible passages that confirms my focus on God rather than us: "willing" things, using the "power of positive thinking", "using the god power within me" or "visualizing" things the way you want them to be. It's not just someone's opinion or someone's philosophy. God tells us in this passage and throughout the Bible that He wants us to focus on Him.

I think it's important for you to know that I'm not just giving my opinion, because there is a religious basis for my belief related to passages in the Bible. It's very important as a Christian, to check things out. A lot of different religious beliefs sound really good or plausible. Some have isolated passages from the Bible to support them. That's using the Bible out of context. I doubt if all who do this mean to be deceitful, but concepts and beliefs out of alignment with the Bible may possibly be leading people astray, no matter how plausible the belief sounds. Remember to check these things out for yourself. It's YOUR Salvation that's in question!

....

We are troubled on every side, yet not distressed; we are perplexed, but not in despair; Persecuted, but not forsaken; cast down, but not destroyed. 2 Corinthians, Chapter 4, verses 8-9.

Part of this passage is in a song my church sings. I like the message that Christians don't let things get the best of us, because we know God is there on our side.

....

For our light affliction, which is but for a moment, worketh for us a far more exceeding and eternal weight of glory; While we look not at the things which are seen, but at the things which are not seen: for the things which are seen are temporal; but the things which are not seen are eternal. 2 Corinthians, Chapter 4, verses 17-18.

Sometimes I get caught up in feeling sorry for myself. When I think of this, my troubles are very insignificant compared to the suffering Jesus went through to save us from our sins. After I think of all He went through on my behalf, I feel guilty for the petty things I worry about.

Here is a related passage:

*For I the Lord thy God will hold thy right hand, saying unto thee, Fear not; I will help thee. Isaiah, Chapter 41, verse 13.

....

Therefore if any man be in Christ, he is a new creature: old things are passed away: behold, all things are become new. 2 Corinthians, Chapter 5, verse 17.

I know my comparison can't come anywhere close to the impact this passage has on our lives as Christians. In my second grade class I have a Good Choices Chart. Those who are making good choices have their clothes pins in a particular area of the chart. There is another area of the chart where students move their clothes pin if they make poor choices as a reminder for them to refocus. I like to empower students so that they feel capable of turning things around. I let them do things to help around the class to earn it off. Afterwards, they can put their clothespin back in the good choices section. Students start all over with their clothespins in the Good Choices section each and every day.

Well, Salvation is kind of like this chart. When we are behaving in sinful ways and are caught up in a self-focused lifestyle, our clothespins would be in the poor choices section. Sometimes God will have things happen in our lives, drawing our attention to our need to refocus. Once we ask God for forgiveness and try to turn our lives around, we don't have to do something tangible to earn off the clothespin. Jesus did that for us through His death and Resurrection! We just need to do our best to continue to live as examples of how God works in our lives. When we slip, just like the chart, everyday we have a fresh start. God never gives up on us.

....

But what I do, that I will do, that I may cut off occasion from them which desire occasion; that wherein they glory, they may be found even as we. For such are false apostles, deceitful workers, transforming themselves into the apostles of Christ. And no marvel; for Satan himself is transformed into an angel of light. Therefore it is no great thing if his ministers also be transformed as the ministers of righteousness; whose end shall be according to their works. 2 Corinthians, Chapter 11, verses 12-15.

This passage reminds us to be careful to not be deceived. There will be people who say they are Christians, proposing beliefs that sound good but will lead many astray. It goes on to say that Satan transforms himself into a minister of righteousness to mislead people.

I always remember Jim Jones who was a minister years ago. He took a group of "believers" to Jonestown, Guyana. These people must have been very devoted to their "beliefs." I'm not sure that if push came to shove that I would leave my home and family to go to another country just because someone told me this is what God wanted me to do. Anyway, they must have been very dedicated to leave everything and everyone behind.

Jim Jones either convinced or tricked these "believers" into committing suicide when the authorities got too involved. Well, although these were very committed "believers" who gave up all for their faith in God, it was for nothing. They gave up all their things, friends, family and lives for a very disturbed minister who led these people to believe he was doing the will of God. (If you want more details; look up the Jonestown Massacre in Guyana during 1978.) Did these people find Salvation? I can't speak to that, but it's highly questionable.

We don't want to find ourselves misled by others who profess to be followers of God. I think it's very important for all Christians to check things out in the Bible. Don't take things for granted just because someone else says them, whether it's a minister, a devoted Christian, me, someone on a Christian Channel or Radio Station. It's very easy to take a verse or two out of the Bible and make it support just about anything. That's considered using the Bible passages out of context.

Reading a chapter before the passage and after the passage is beneficial. Each chapter is about a page or two. This gives you a better idea of what the quoted Bible verses really mean. That's why I always tell you where I get the Bible passages. I want you to be able to look them up and verify them. It's a very important thing to do.

You need to look at the people who have an influence on your religious life. What type of lifestyle do they lead? Are they running in the fast lane? Are they preaching something that has become very popular or a fad type of belief? Are they taking too much credit for things rather than keeping the focus on God? Are they putting an undue emphasis on giving money? Be cautious about who you give ultimate control of your religious life. Check things out. Passages like this one remind me that very dedicated believers can still be misled by others as in the Jonestown Massacre. It pays to check things out. It may have a direct impact on your Salvation.

Here are some related passages:

But though we, or an angel from heaven, preach any other gospel unto you than that which we have preached unto you, let him be accursed. As we said before, so say I now again, If any man preach any other gospel unto you than that ye have received, let him be accursed. Galatians, Chapter 1, verses 8-9.

Whoso causeth the righteous to go astray in an evil way, he shall fall himself into his own pit: but the upright shall have good things in possession. Proverbs, Chapter 28, verse 10.

Then the Lord said unto me, The prophets prophesy lies in My Name: I sent them not, neither have I commanded them, neither spake unto them: they prophesy unto you a false vision and divination, and a thing of nought, and the deceit of their heart. Therefore thus saith the Lord concerning the prophets that prophesy in My Name, and I sent them not, yet they say, Sword and famine shall not be in this land; By sword and famine shall those prophets be consumed. And the people to whom they prophesy shall be cast out in the streets of Jerusalem because of the famine and the sword; and they shall have none to bury them, them, their wives, nor their sons, nor their daughters: for I will pour their wickedness upon them. Jeremiah, Chapter 14, verses 14-16.

For many shall come in My Name, saying I am Christ; and shall deceive many. Matthew, Chapter 24, verse 5.

. . . .

For this thing I besought the Lord thrice, that it might depart from me. And He said unto me, My grace is sufficient for thee: for My strength is made perfect in weakness. Most gladly therefore will I rather glory in my infirmities, that the power of Christ may rest upon me. 2 Corinthians, Chapter 12, verses 8-10.

This is really from Paul speaking about a vision he had from God. Even though he asked Jesus to take away his burden, His reply was, "*My grace is sufficient for thee: for My strength is made perfect in weakness.*"

It reminds me of when God asked Moses to talk to the Pharaoh to let God's people go and for Moses to lead these people to the Promised Land. Moses told God that he wouldn't make a very good leader because he wasn't a good speaker. God told him not to worry about it because he was the person that God wanted to lead His people. (Paraphrased)

I'm ashamed to say that there have been times when God has led me to be a witness to someone else and I told God through my actions, "That's not my thing, God. I'm not the type who is good at confronting people and telling them about you. Why don't you save it for someone else from those other religions that don't mind being embarrassed by going door to door and confronting people? Now, if you need someone to do a low-risk thing like saying a prayer for someone or giving a little money to the needy, then I'm your person."

I need to remember that God will take care of my weaknesses if I let Him, and will provide the strength necessary to do whatever He wants, just like He did for Moses.

....

> *Knowing that a man is not justified by the works of the Law, but by the faith of Jesus Christ, even we have believed in Jesus Christ, that we might be justified by the faith of Christ, and not by the works of the Law: for by the works of the Law shall no flesh be justified. Galatians Chapter 2, verse 16.*

There are people who think that if they are good people they will have Salvation, but they don't actively believe in Jesus Christ. This doesn't necessarily mean they have to attend church regularly. There are some people who attend church regularly that may or may not receive Salvation because of their lifestyle choices. Attending church isn't a sole indicator of a person's belief in Christ. That is a personal matter between God and them. Isn't it neat that God makes all of these decisions on an individual basis?

Anyway, the requirement for Salvation is to believe that Jesus Christ is Savior of all. Now, this isn't an isolated thing. That belief needs to be an active part of our life. It's not just something we should think about every six years when a relative dies and you think about them going to heaven to be with God. It's supposed to be a daily part of our lives. That's what I mean. This passage is saying that we don't get Salvation by just following the Law; it's our faith in Jesus Christ that saves us, but we are still supposed to be examples of how Jesus works in our lives.

Here are some related passages:

> **Neither yield ye your members as instruments of unrighteousness unto sin: but yield yourselves unto God, as those that are alive from the dead, and your members as instruments of righteousness unto God. For sin shall not have dominion over you: for ye are not under the Law, but under grace. What then? Shall we sin, because we are not under the Law, but under grace? God forbid. Romans 6, verses 13-15.*

Therefore by the deeds of the Law there shall no flesh be justified in His sight: for by the Law is the knowledge of sin. But now the righteousness of God without the Law is manifested, being witnessed by the Law and the prophets; Even the righteousness of God which is by faith of Jesus Christ unto all and upon all them that believe: for there is no difference: For all have sinned, and come short of the glory of God; Being justified freely by His grace through the redemption that is in Christ Jesus. Romans, Chapter 3, verses 20-24.

Now, it was not written for his sake alone, that it was imputed to him; But for us also, to whom it shall be imputed, if we believe on Him that raised up Jesus our Lord from the dead: Who was delivered for our offences, and was raised again for our justification. Romans, Chapter 4, verses 23-25.

Therefore being justified by faith, we have peace with God through our Lord Jesus Christ. By whom also we have access by faith into this grace wherein we stand, and rejoice in hope of the glory of God. Romans, Chapter 5, verses 1-2.

But that no man is justified by the Law in the sight of God, it is evident; for, The just shall live by faith. Galatians, Chapter 3, verse 11.

That in the ages to come He might show the exceeding riches of His grace in His kindness toward us through Christ Jesus. For by grace are ye saved through faith; and that not of yourselves: it is the gift of God. Not of works, lest any man should boast. For we are His workmanship, created in Christ Jesus unto good works, which God hath before ordained that we should walk in them. Ephesians, Chapter 2, verses 7-10.

....

For, brethren, ye have been called unto liberty; only use not liberty for an occasion to the flesh, but by love serve one another. Galatians, Chapter 5, verse 13.

Our faith in God gives us a lot of freedom. I know I don't have to worry about my kids starving because I know that God will provide food for my family since He says so in the Bible. Realizing things like this has freed up my life so much that it's difficult to explain.

Recognizing this, we have some choices. We could say, "Well, I know that God won't let us starve, so I could take the money I used to set aside from the budget for food and go out drinking with my friends who have been asking me for some time. In the past, I had told them no because I couldn't afford it. Now, I can go out and party with them because God will make sure the kids don't go hungry." I'm not sure that God would be pleased with this decision.

It's a choice that God gives us. Instead, I could say, "Since I don't have to spend so much time worrying about my family having enough to eat the way I used to, I can spend my extra time helping the elderly neighbor across the street by cleaning her house or watering her plants."

....

> *Now the works of the flesh are manifest, which are these; Adultery, fornication, uncleanness, lasciviousness, Idolatry, witchcraft, hatred, variance, emulations, wrath, strife, seditions, heresies, Envyings, murders, drunkenness, revellings, and such like: of the which I tell you before, as I have also told you in time past, that they which do such things shall not inherit the kingdom of God. But the fruit of the Spirit is love, joy, peace, longsuffering, gentleness, goodness, faith, Meekness, temperance: against such there is no Law. Galatians, Chapter 5, verses 19-23.*

When others react to my not wanting to watch shows with witchcraft, demonic or satanic themes, I feel vindicated when I read this passage. When it says people who demonstrate those negative choices won't inherit the kingdom of God, it doesn't sound like God is just mildly annoyed if people do the things listed in this passage. My desire is to stay committed to what I know God wants rather than to buckle under when I know they disapprove.

....

> *If we live in the Spirit, let us also walk in the Spirit. Let us not be desirous of vain glory, provoking one another, envying one another. Galatians, Chapter 5, verses 25-26.*

In high school, I remember running for Sophomore Secretary. (I always remember how to spell secretary, because I spelled it incorrectly on every banner I displayed throughout the school.) My opponent was also a member of the Drill Team. I had tried out for the Drill Team but wasn't selected.

My envy of my opponent led me to tell others that she really didn't deserve the Sophomore Secretary position that I coveted. I told them that her other obligations were too time consuming for her to do a good job for the Sophomore Class.

It was a very humbling experience for me when she won the election for Sophomore Secretary. I hate to think of how spiteful I had been, because I let that position become too important in my life. I definitely wasn't being a very good example to others.

....

Be not deceived; God is not mocked: for whatsoever a man soweth, that shall he also reap. For he that soweth to his flesh shall of the flesh reap corruption; but he that soweth to the Spirit shall of the Spirit reap life everlasting. And let us not be weary in well doing: for in due season we shall reap, if we faint not. As we have therefore opportunity, let us do good unto all men, especially unto them who are of the household of faith. Galatians, Chapter 6, verses 7-10.

This reminds me of the rock stars who have gotten caught up in all the fame and money and end up has-beens because of drug, alcohol and counterproductive choices they make in their lives.

Then I think of Mother Teresa and all the wonderful, selfless things she did for others during her life. Although, I wouldn't be the envy of all my neighbors, I would rather work toward having similar attributes as Mother Teresa, with my focus on God's Will for me rather than living and dying in the fast lane.

....

In whom we have redemption through His Blood, the forgiveness of sins, according to the riches of His grace. Ephesians, Chapter 1, verse 7.

Sometimes I get a little arrogant and self-righteous and think about the good things that I think I'm doing for others. Passages like this are very humbling. They remind me of how Jesus gave His life for us. That's why I have my Salvation, not from any things I do to earn it. The things that we do for others need to be for God, out of love. They shouldn't be to draw attention to ourselves or for us to become smug, thinking we are good Christians because we do these things.

....

That Christ may dwell in your hearts by faith; that ye, being rooted and grounded in love. Ephesians, Chapter 3, verse 17.

I like the mental picture that I get when I think of Christ dwelling in my heart. I break His heart when I focus on making worldly choices. I get caught up in looking at all the angles to save a dime, not necessarily because I need to. It's more of an intellectual challenge to find my very best deal and it's exhilarating to find a bargain!

When I go to purchase things, I often look at all the prices that are stamped on the items. Sometimes they mislabel them, pricing an item considerably lower than all the rest. I know it must be some type of error but I've taken it to the cash register, exhilarated because I have found this great deal.

I try to rationalize it in my mind, saying that it's the store's fault for mislabeling things and they have to live up to their error or it is false advertising. Then I usually get a strong, intense feeling that I'm doing something against my religious principals. I know that I'm not being a good example of how God works in my life and I generally tell the cashier about the price difference.

I say generally, because writing this has made me aware that I just did this recently and I didn't draw it to the cashier's attention. We were driving through Kansas on the way to see my grandkiddos for Christmas. I have a very good friend whose daughter collects Wizard of Oz memorabilia. I saw this figurine I wanted to get for her daughter and I found one that was marked $3.00 less than all the others on the shelf. I rationalized this by telling myself that it's from an older shipment that was marked the lower price, thinking the newer ones were marked the higher price. This time, I never told the cashier.

I feel terrible about this, because I feel like I am being a hypocrite as I write this to you. It just so happened that I still had the receipt. I just went to see if it had an address on it, but it didn't. Of course, that would have been the chicken way out! It would have been pretty easy to send this person $3.00 in the mail. It did have the phone number on the receipt, so I called.

I apologized and wanted her address to send her the money. (They don't have mail service for the turnpike businesses.) When she told me that wasn't necessary, I explained that I consider myself a Christian and needed to live by my Christian ethics and I hadn't. I knew there had been a $3.00 difference in the price of the figurines and hadn't brought it to her attention.

She told me not to worry about it, but I do—not because of the $3.00. It bothers me that I could find it so easy to backslide into old worldly ways when I think I'm making great strides at being the person that God wants me to be.

This has been a very humbling experience for me. Satan can sneak into our lives through very subtle things and I let him do it without even batting an eye! Fortunately, Jesus dwells in my heart and lets me know when I'm not living the life that He wants.

....

And to know the love of Christ, which passeth knowledge, that ye might be filled with all the fullness of God. Ephesians, Chapter 3, verse 19.

It truly is difficult to comprehend how God works in our lives. I remember growing up thinking that God was this distant, glorious being who was there to take care of us when we had important issues. Now, I have found that if I pray to Him with little things like the key not turning over in the ignition or ask Him to find something I'm looking for, He is there taking care of even the smallest of my worries.

....

And to know the love of Christ; which passeth knowledge, that ye might be filled with all the fullness of God. Now unto Him that is able to do exceeding abundantly above all that we ask or think, according to the power that worketh in us. Unto Him be glory in the church by Christ Jesus throughout all ages, world without end. Amen. Ephesians, Chapter 3, verses 19-21.

I was concerned that this passage might be one that people who focus on using "the god power within them" might use to support their belief in this erroneous concept. This passage has listed Colossians, Chapter 1, verse 29 as a cross-reference. It is really helpful to read this for clarification of what the passage in Ephesians really means.

Whereunto I also labour, striving according to His working, which worketh in me mightily. Colossians, Chapter 1, verse 29.

These two passages aren't talking about using "the god power within me" to acquire the things you wish to attain or to accomplish. What this is talking about, from what I understand, is that God works through us for His glory when we are the examples He wants us to be. An illustration might be that we are there to support a friend or a co-worker who is at a major turning point in their life. God was there working through us by our example. He was there through our support, our comforting words and our telling them of how our faith in God gets us through the tough times. He works through us in our explanation of the positive impact that God has had on our lives.

Being an instrument that God can use to touch the lives of others is a wonderful experience! God works through different people in different ways, just like the passage I wrote about earlier that says God gives us each different types of gifts to glorify Him. (Paraphrased)

....

> *But unto every one of us is given grace according to the measure of the gift of Christ. Wherefore He saith, When He ascended up on high, He led captivity captive, and gave gifts unto men. (Now that He ascended, what is it but that He also descended first into the lower parts of the earth? He that descended is the same also that ascended up far above all heavens, that He might fill all things.) And He gave some, apostles; and some, prophets; and some, evangelists; and some pastors and teachers; For the perfecting of the saints, for the work of the ministry, for the edifying of the Body of Christ: Till we all come in the unity of the faith, and of the knowledge of the Son of God, unto a perfect Man, unto the measure of the stature of the fullness of Christ. Ephesians, Chapter 4, verses 7-13.*

This makes me think about a watch with its back taken off. There are all kinds of mechanisms and gears in a watch. Each gear and mechanism looks a little different from each other and does something a little different, but all the gears and mechanisms of the watch work together with one ultimate goal.

I think Christians are like the gears and mechanisms of the watch. We all have different gifts and abilities, but should all have the one unifying and ultimate goal of being the examples God wants us to be. We might all do this in different ways. Some might go door to door sharing their love for Jesus, while someone else does this by asking a friend to go to church with them. Some accomplish this by giving their money, their time or their talents to do God's work. Still others do God's work through being a good example of how Christ works in their life.

Hopefully all, regardless of their gifts, take the time to pray for those who don't know Christ in their lives, since they all have the same ultimate and unifying goal.

Here is a related passage:

> **As every man hath received the gift, even so minister the same one to another, as good stewards of the manifold grace of God. If any man speak, let him speak as the oracles of God, if*

any man minister, let him do it as of the ability which God giveth: that God in all things may be glorified through Jesus Christ, to whom be praise and dominion for ever and ever. Amen. 1 Peter, Chapter 4, verses 10-11.

....

That we henceforth be no more children, tossed to and fro, and carried about with every wind of doctrine, by the sleight of men, and cunning craftiness, whereby they lie in wait to deceive; but speaking the Truth in love, may grow up into Him in all things, which is the head, even Christ. Ephesians, Chapter 4, verses 14-15.

Some people appear to act as if they are marionettes like Pinocchio and others act like real people. The ones who act like marionettes, similar to Pinocchio, seem to blame everyone else and circumstances for all the things that happen in their lives. They act as if they are powerless puppets and others are pulling all their marionette strings, controlling their lives.

The ones who seem to be real people realize that they make choices in their lives that impact the things that happen to them. If things don't turn out the way they want, they look at the choices they are making and make changes that ultimately turn their lives around.

I think that God wants us, as Christians, to be real people. Ones who can change our choices if we find our lives aren't going in the direction that would glorify God. He doesn't want us to be marionettes like Pinocchio, being led astray by those who promise the fun and excitement of the worldly life. He doesn't want us to feel like we have no control over our choices and are powerless to change our lives.

If you have spent your life feeling powerless like Pinocchio, God is here to cut the strings that bind you and lead you astray. He can make you the real Christian you want to be. You can turn to Him to help you make the necessary changes…no strings attached! (I couldn't resist adding that!)

....

That ye put off concerning the former conversation the old man, which is corrupt according to the deceitful lusts; And be renewed in the Spirit of your mind; And that ye put on the new man, which after God is created in righteousness and true holiness. Wherefore putting away lying, speak every man Truth with his neighbour for we are members one of another. Ephesians, Chapter 4, verses 22-25.

This passage is basically saying that once you become a Christian, you should start living the life of a Christian, putting away your old sinful behaviors. It makes me think of a time when I went to the grocery store with coupons in hand; ready to cut my expenses big time! I remember having a coupon for ten cents off of a particular brand of raisins. I didn't want that brand of raisins, though. It probably was considerably more expensive even with the ten cent off coupon. I ended up getting the cheaper box of raisins, knowing it wasn't the right brand for the coupon.

I rationalized my actions, thinking it was only a dime. I gave the cashier the ten cent off coupon deliberately mixed in between all my other coupons, hoping she didn't realize that I had substituted the cheaper brand for the more expensive one.

She told me the total for my groceries and I started writing my check and had to stop. This situation impacted my life! The cashier didn't realize I was lying and was stealing by substituting the cheaper brand of raisins for the coupon I used. I knew and what was worse, God knew! Was my loss of integrity worth the ten cents I was saving? (It's funny how Satan can sneak up on some of us "Self-righteous Christians," in very subtle ways.)

I immediately gave her ten cents for the raisins, telling her that I was sorry I had gotten a more expensive brand than the coupon stated. She told me not to worry about it, it was just a dime. I told her that I wanted her to take the dime anyway, saying I knew I had taken the wrong raisins and I wouldn't feel right unless she took the money. Actually, I thought she would be horrified that I would do such a thing. I was prepared to be totally embarrassed by the cashier's reaction because I really deserved it, but it didn't happen that way.

I didn't have an obvious consequence for my actions. It was more the realization that I was lying to God and myself. I was jeopardizing my Salvation over money. I'm fortunate that God has this situation pop back in my mind as a reminder from time to time. It's especially helpful when I'm a "Looking at the Angles Christian," figuring out some kind of angle to beat the system or I'm wording things very carefully so that I'm not telling the whole truth in situations, but not exactly telling a lie, either.

I'm very thankful that God gives me a conscience to remind me when I start slipping into old human ways again.

....

Be ye angry, and sin not: let not the sun go down upon your wrath. Ephesians, Chapter 4, verse 26.

Dorothy Scott

I have always heard this Bible verse used in relation to marriage. I really believe whole-heartedly that this is good advice for both adults and children. There have been nights when I have gone to bed frustrated with a family member and then this verse pops into my head. (I'm so glad God looks after me that way!) I get back up and work things out with whichever family member I need to. I get a good night's sleep, feeling the situation has been peacefully resolved, which sets a good example for the rest of the family. When we hold onto grudges and anger, it eats away at us and doesn't make us very good examples of how God works in our lives.

Here is a related passage:

Be not hasty in thy spirit to be angry: for anger resteth in the bosom of fools. Ecclesiastes, Chapter 7, verse 9.

....

Let him that stole steal no more: but rather let him labour, working with his hands the thing which is good, that he may have to give to him that needeth. Ephesians, Chapter 4, verse 28.

When I was about ten years old, I talked a neighbor into going to the local "Candy Store." I talked him into stealing some candy, graham crackers and gum ball rings with me. I even talked him into going back to do the same thing a second time.

I stopped doing that. No, I never got caught and no one ever told on me. I just didn't feel right inside. I knew I had stolen and so did God. No matter what I did, I couldn't rationalize things. God knew it and I knew it. It was as simple as that! All I could think to do at the time was to stop stealing and to become a better example of how God works in my life. (I guess I should have gone to make amends to the store owner, but that didn't cross my mind until about 20 years later.)

Now, as a school teacher, I remember this situation when I find one of my students stealing something. (It's kind of funny, every year I have a student who takes a big handful of the play money that I use for math. When I talk to them, they always try to tell me that a relative gave it to them.) Then, I tell them about when I was about their age and stole too. I talk about how I didn't like how I felt inside because I knew I stole, so I stopped stealing. I ask them if I'm a bad person now. (They always tell me no.) Then, I ask them if stealing was a poor choice? I tell them they are right. Stealing is a poor choice, but we don't have to continue to steal. I tell them that I have confidence that they can turn things around just like I did.

Sometimes I get concerned when youngsters do something wrong and label themselves as "bad people". I think they sometimes start behaving like they think "bad people" behave. It's so important for kids to realize that they aren't "bad people," but have just made poor choices and are able to turn it around and to make better choices. This is important to remember the next time a child does something that upsets you. We want them to realize how to make better choices in the future, rather than staying focused on all the poor choices that they have made in their lives. I'm so glad that God has been much more forgiving of me than I have been of others.

....

And be not drunk with wine, wherein is excess; but be filled with the Spirit. Ephesians, Chapter 5, verse 18.

I know a lot of churches are against drinking. I'm not especially fond of it myself and I'm very concerned for those who have family members who drink to excess. I do toast the bride and groom at weddings, but I really just don't like the taste of alcohol. Based on this passage and several others in the Bible, I don't think that having a drink every now and then is against God's principles. I think it's that some people don't just have one drink every now and then…or their every now and then becomes an all too regular pattern. I think God doesn't want anyone to drink to excess or, for that matter, to do anything to excess.

I'm not including this verse to support "those who drink a little too regularly". That's not what this is about. I feel that it's my privilege in writing this book to be able to convey things to the best of my ability that have influenced my life. Knowing God gave me permission to have an occasional drink but not to do it to excess, has helped be a guide for my life. I don't think I have hardly ever had a second drink or a third. I just don't see any point in trying to find out just how many drinks it takes to lead to drinking in excess. Getting caught up in repetitive social drinking would not make me a very good example of how God works in my life.

....

Speaking to yourselves in psalms and hymns and Spiritual songs, singing and making melody in your heart to the Lord. Giving thanks always for all things unto God and the Father in the Name of our Lord Jesus Christ. Ephesians, Chapter 5, verses 19-20.

I know that over the years I have heard people comment on music, thinking a wide variety of things. Some of these comments were less than supportive of music. While this passage isn't speaking to all types of music for pleasure, it does sound like God likes us to be singing hymns and songs that focus on Him and our love for Him.

I love to sing old familiar hymns from time to time or make up songs which are prayers in my mind when I'm driving somewhere. There are some songs that are supposed to be religious songs but come from a wide variety of religious beliefs, some of which aren't compatible with my belief in God. So, I try to be careful, checking out the music I listen to, especially through the media. I wouldn't want to find myself singing along with some song on the radio only to find out the person who wrote that song believes in Buddha. That would mean I'm unknowingly singing along with a song about Buddha instead of God. It pays to check things out.

One of the things to remember is that when we sing to God, it's one more form of praying. It's another one of the many ways that we can glorify God and thank Him for all He's done.

Here are some related passages:

Then sang Moses and the children of Israel this song unto the LORD, and spake, saying, I will sing unto the LORD, for He hath triumphed gloriously: the horse and his rider hath He thrown into the sea. The Lord is my strength and song, and He is become my Salvation: He is my God and I will prepare Him an habitation; my father's God, and I will exalt Him. Exodus, Chapter 15, verses 1-2.

All the earth shall worship Thee, and shall sing unto Thee; they shall sing to Thy Name. Psalm, Chapter 66, verse 4.

O let the nations be glad and sing for joy: for Thou shalt judge the people righteously, and govern the nations upon the earth. Selah. Psalm, Chapter 67, verse 4.

Sing unto God, sing praises to His Name: extol Him that rideth upon the heavens by His Name JAH, and rejoice before Him. Psalm, Chapter 68, verse 4.

Sing unto God, ye kingdoms of the earth; O sing praises unto the Lord. Selah: Psalm, Chapter 68, verse 32.

I will sing of the mercies of the LORD forever: with my mouth will I make known Thy faithfulness to all generations. Psalm, Chapter 89, verse 1.

*Come, let us sing unto the LORD: let us make a joyful noise to the Rock of our Salvation. Let us come before His presence with thanksgiving and make a joyful noise unto Him with psalms. For the LORD is a great God, and a great King above all gods. Psalm, Chapter 95, verses 1-3.

*O sing unto the LORD a new song: sing unto the LORD, all the earth. Sing unto the LORD, bless His Name; show forth His Salvation from day to day. Declare His glory among the heathen, His wonders among all people. For the LORD is great, and greatly to be praised: He is to be feared above all gods. Psalm, Chapter 96, verses 1-4.

*O sing unto the LORD a new song; for He hath done marvellous things: His right Hand, and His holy Arm, hath gotten Him the victory. Psalm, Chapter 98, verse 1.

*Make a joyful noise unto the LORD, all the earth: make a loud noise, and rejoice, and sing praise. Sing unto the LORD with the harp; and the voice of a psalm. With trumpets and sound of cornet make a joyful noise before the LORD, the King. Psalm, Chapter 98, verses 4-6.

*O give thanks unto the LORD, call upon His Name: make known His deeds among the people. Sing unto Him, sing psalms unto Him; talk ye of all His wondrous works. Glory ye in His holy Name: let the heart of them rejoice that seek the LORD. Psalm, Chapter 105, verses 1-3.

*Then was our mouth filled with laughter, and our tongue with singing: then said they among the heathen, The LORD hath done great things for them. The LORD hath done great things for us; whereof we are glad. Psalm, Chapter 126, verses 2-3.

*Praise the LORD, for the LORD is good: sing praises unto His Name; for it is pleasant. Psalm, Chapter 125, verse 3.

*All the kings of the earth shall praise Thee, O LORD, when they hear the Words of Thy mouth. Yea, they shall sing in the ways of the LORD; for great is the glory of the LORD. Psalm, Chapter 138, verses 4-5.

*Praise Ye the LORD. Praise the LORD, O my soul. While I live will I praise the LORD: I will sing praises unto my God while I have any being. Psalm, Chapter 146, verses 1-2.

*Sing unto the LORD with thanksgiving; sing praise upon the harp unto our God. Psalm, Chapter 147, verse 7.

*In the transgression of an evil man there is a snare: but the righteous doth sing and rejoice. Proverbs, Chapter 29, verse 6.

*Praise ye the LORD. Sing unto the LORD a new song, and His praise in the congregation of saints. Let Israel rejoice in Him that made him: let the children of Zion be joyful in their King. Let them praise His Name in the dance: let them sing in the dance: let them sing praises unto Him with the timbrel and harp. For the LORD taketh pleasure in His people: He will beautify the meek with Salvation. Let the saints be joyful in glory: let them sing aloud upon their beds. Psalm, Chapter 149, verses 1-5.

*In that day shall this song be sung in the land of Judah; We have a strong city; Salvation will God appoint for walls and bulwarks. Isaiah, Chapter 26, verse 1.

*The Lord was ready to save me: therefore we will sing my songs to the stringed instruments all the days of our life in the house of the Lord. Isaiah, Chapter 38, verse 20.

*Sing unto the LORD a new song, and His praise from the end of the earth, ye that go down to the sea, and all that is therein; the isles, and the inhabitants thereof. Let the wilderness and the cities thereof lift up their voice, the villages that Kedar doth inhabit: let the inhabitants of the rock sing, let them shout from the top of the mountains. Let them give glory unto the LORD, and declare His praise in the islands. Isaiah, Chapter 42, verses 10-12.

*Sing, O ye heavens; for the LORD hath done it: shout, ye lower parts of the earth: break forth into singing, ye mountains, O forest, and every tree therein: for the LORD hath redeemed Jacob, and glorified Himself in Israel. Isaiah, Chapter 44, verse 23.

*Go ye forth of Babylon, flee ye from the Chaldeans, with a voice of singing declare ye, tell this, utter it even to the end of the earth; say ye, The LORD hath redeemed His servant Jacob. Isaiah, Chapter 48, verse 20.

*Sing, O heavens; and be joyful, O earth; and break forth into singing, O mountains: for the LORD hath comforted His people, and will have mercy upon His afflicted. Isaiah, Chapter 49, verse 13.

*Thy watchmen shall lift up the voice; with the voice together shall they sing: for they shall see eye to eye, when the LORD shall bring again Zion. Break forth into joy, sing together, ye waste places of Jerusalem: for the LORD hath comforted His people, He hath redeemed Jerusalem. The LORD hath made bare His Holy Arm in the eyes of all the nations; and all the ends of the earth shall see the Salvation of our God. Isaiah, Chapter 52, verses 8-10.

*For as the rain cometh down, and the snow from heaven, and returneth not thither, but watereth the earth, and maketh it bring forth and bud, that it may give seed to the sower, and bread to the eater: So shall My Word be that goeth forth out of My Mouth: it shall not return unto Me void, but it shall prosper in the thing whereto I sent it. For ye shall go out with joy, and be led forth with peace: the mountains and the hills shall break forth before you into singing, and all the trees of the field shall clap their hands. Instead of the thorn shall come up the fir tree, and instead of the brier shall come up the myrtle tree: and it shall be to the LORD for a Name, for an everlasting sign that shall not be cut off. Isaiah, Chapter 55, verses 10-13.

Behold My servants shall sing for joy of heart, but ye shall cry for sorrow of heart, and shall howl for vexation of spirit. Isaiah, Chapter 65, verse 14.

*Sing unto the LORD, praise ye the LORD: for He hath delivered the soul of the poor from the hand of evildoers. Jeremiah, Chapter 20, verse 13.

*For thus saith the LORD; Sing with gladness for Jacob, and shout among the chief of the nations: publish ye, praise ye, and say, O LORD, save Thy people, the remnant of Israel. Jeremiah, Chapter 31, verse 7.

*The LORD thy God in the midst of thee is mighty; He will save, He will rest in His love, He will joy over thee with singing. Zephaniah, Chapter 3, verse 17.

*And when they had sung an hymn, they went out into the mount of Olives. Matthew, Chapter 26, verse 30.

....

Giving thanks always for all things unto God and the Father in the Name of our Lord Jesus Christ: Submitting yourselves one to another in the fear of God: Wives, submit yourselves unto your own husbands, as unto the Lord. For the husband is the head of the wife, even as Christ is the head of the church: and He is the Saviour of the Body. Therefore as the church is subject unto Christ, so let the wives be to their own husbands in everything. Husbands, love your wives, even as Christ also loved the church, and gave Himself for it: That He might sanctify and cleanse it with the washing of water by the Word. That He might present it to Himself a glorious church, not having spot, or wrinkle, or any such thing; but that it should be Holy and without blemish. So ought men to love their wives as their own bodies. He that loveth his wife loveth himself. For no man ever yet hated his own flesh; but nourisheth and cherisheth it, even as the Lord the church: For we are members of His Body, of His Flesh, and of His Bones. For this cause shall a man leave his father and mother, and shall be joined unto his wife, and they two shall be one flesh. This is a great mystery: but I speak concerning Christ and the church. Nevertheless let every one of you in particular so love his wife even as himself; and the wife see that she reverence her husband. Ephesians, Chapter 5, verses 20-33.

Ease up, now! I realize that this appears to be a passage that sets the Women's Movement back 100 years, but it's not! This passage isn't about women having the right to vote. It's not about women having equal pay for equal jobs. This passage is about a husband and wife being respectful of each other's needs and treating each other with the same courtesy and respect that they want. God put man and woman together to support each other as a UNIT. The marriage wasn't meant for two totally separate entities to be fighting to maintain their ability to be in control of the other.

When God says that the man is the head of the household doesn't mean that the man is supposed to arbitrarily make all the decisions regardless of his wife's opinions, or vice versa. If the husband and the wife are to be a UNIT, it should involve discussions on decisions, being respectful of each person's opinion.

If the man is to treat the woman as he would treat his own body and the woman is to do the same, then that means they should be respectful of each other in all matters. A husband or a wife wouldn't beat up their own body, so they should not beat up their spouse. A husband or a wife wouldn't be calling themselves names or saying put-downs about themselves, so they shouldn't do it to their spouse-even if it's funny. It undermines the marriage.

A husband or a wife wouldn't be yelling at themselves, so they shouldn't do it to their spouse. A husband or a wife wouldn't deprive themselves of their basic needs, so they shouldn't do it to their spouse. A husband or a wife wouldn't want their spouse to be unfaithful to them, so they shouldn't do it to their spouse. A husband or a wife wouldn't be hateful and unforgiving to themselves and their own faults, so they shouldn't do it to their spouse. This passage has nothing to do with the Women's Movement. It has only to do with the husband and the wife treating each other with the same respect and support that they would want to get within the marriage.

Here is a related passage:

And He answered and said unto them, Have ye not read, that He which made them at the beginning made them male and female, And said, For this cause shall a man leave father and mother, and shall cleave to his wife: and they twain shall be one flesh? Wherefore they are no more twain, but one flesh. What therefore God hath joined together, let not man put asunder. Matthew, Chapter 19, verses 4-6.

....

Children, obey your parents in the Lord: for this is right. Honour thy father and mother; which is the first Commandment with promise; That it may be well with thee, and thou mayest live long on the earth. And ye fathers, provoke not your children to wrath: but bring them up in the nurture and admonition of the Lord. Ephesians, Chapter 6, verses 1-4.

This passage also goes both ways. Children are to be respectful of their parents and to obey their rules. I think all too many parents only focus on this part of the passage. They forget that they aren't supposed to provoke their children to wrath; instead they are to nurture them. This DOES mean that parents are to be supportive of their children, which does NOT mean that they are to raise their children by telling them how stupid they are and how they can't do anything right.

This DOES mean that parents are to appropriately discipline their children, which does NOT mean that they are to take all their frustrations out on their children, yelling at them, hitting them or sexually abusing them. This DOES mean that parents are to provide for their children's physical and emotional needs and well-being, which does NOT mean that they are supposed to ignore their child's basic needs. This DOES mean that parents are to nurture their children, which does NOT mean overindulging them with their every wish. This DOES mean that parents are to set clear and appropriate rules, which does NOT mean being harshly strict with them or being too lenient either. This DOES mean that it's reasonable for parents to expect children to do chores as a member of the household, but it does NOT mean that they are to expect their children to do all the household chores, or that the parents do everything for the child so the child never develops a sense of responsibility.

The child, under the appropriate conditions set forth in the Bible, is supposed to obey their parents, but the parent isn't to provoke them to anger and is to nurture them. In other words, the parents and the children are to work together in mutual respect of one another and of God.

....

As ye have therefore received Christ Jesus the Lord, so walk ye in Him: Rooted and built up in Him, and stablished in the faith, as ye have been taught, abounding therein with thanksgiving. Beware lest any man spoil you through philosophy and vain deceit, after the tradition of men, after the rudiments of the world, and not after Christ. Colossians, Chapter 2, verses 6-8.

I'm not to get caught up in counterproductive philosophical discussions with other people regarding my faith. There have been times when I have done this and I began to doubt my own faith or became uncertain about particular issues.

I have found that when I read the Bible, so many things are clarified for me in a way that no person was able to do. I know these answers come from God and are not some person or group's philosophical interpretation of the Bible. My faith becomes vulnerable when I let other people tell me what I should and shouldn't believe and how I should do it.

It's kind of like a painting. You spend hours creating a painting and it's just right for you. You show it to some friends and they tell you that you should change the painting in a particular way. You show the painting to an artist and he tells you that you should really change these other aspects of the painting. Lastly, you show the painting to an art teacher.

He tells you that the painting really should be altered in some totally new way. By the time you ask all of these different people's advice, you can't remember why you painted the painting in that particular fashion and what your original goals for the painting were. Your mind is so muddled by all these interpretations of the right way to paint that the painting doesn't seem like the same painting you felt excited about in the beginning.

As an artist, I have found it's much better when I don't ask for other people's opinions and I paint for my own pleasure. As a Christian, I have found I can't get involved in other people's philosophical discussions of how they think religion is supposed to be. There are millions of different people with millions of different interpretations. If I get caught up in listening to other people's opinions, I can get confused and possibly lose my focus on God. I find it much better to bow out of philosophical discussions and read the Bible on my own and to trust the instincts that God gives me.

....

If ye then be risen with Christ, seek those things which are above, where Christ sitteth on the right hand of God. Set your affection on things above, not on things on the earth. Colossians, Chapter 3, verses 1-2.

I don't know how you do it, but you should see me clean the house. I start with one aspect of house cleaning. I get off on a tangent when I see something that needs to be put away in another room. When I'm in that room, I am reminded of something else that I forgot to do. After I do that thing, I try to remember what I had originally started to do, because by that time I've lost my focus. Sometimes I remember and sometimes I don't! This passage reminds me that I am to continue to focus on God and His will for me instead of going off on tangents and getting caught up in worldly issues which can pull my focus away from Him.

....

But now ye also put off all these; anger, wrath, malice, blasphemy, filthy communication out of your mouth. Lie not one to another, seeing that ye have put off the old man with his deeds; And have put on the new man, which is renewed in knowledge after the image of Him that created Him. Colossians, Chapter 3, verses 8-10.

They say you can't tell a book by its cover, but this passage is kind of the reverse of that. It tells me that people look at Christians to see if they really behave the way they think Christians should. God reminds me now that I'm a Christian; I'm to behave as a Christian. I'm not to be hateful, gossip, use vulgar speech or use God's Name in vain (even though it has become so commonplace that people don't realize that they're even doing it.) When people see me, my cover needs to reflect the way God has changed my life.

Here is a related passage:

> *Little children, let no man deceive you: he that doeth righteousness is righteous, even as He is righteous. He that committeth sin is of the devil: for the devil sinneth from the beginning. For this purpose the Son of God was manifested, that He might destroy the works of the devil. Whosoever is born of God doth not commit sin; for His seed remaineth in Him: and He cannot sin, because He is born of God. In this the children of God are manifest, and the children of the devil: whosoever doeth not righteousness is not of God, neither he that loveth not his brother. 1 John, Chapter 3, verses 7-10.

....

> Put on therefore, as the elect of God, holy and beloved, bowels of mercies, kindness, humbleness of mind, meekness, longsuffering; Forbearing one another and forgiving one another, if any man have a quarrel against any: even as Christ forgave you, so also do ye. And above all these things put on charity, which is the bond of perfectness. And let the peace of God rule in your hearts, to the which also ye are called in one body; and be ye thankful. Let the Word of Christ dwell in you richly in all wisdom; teaching and admonishing one another in psalms and hymns and Spiritual songs, singing with grace in your hearts to the Lord. And whatsoever ye do in word or deed, do all in the Name of the Lord Jesus, giving thanks to God and the Father by Him. Colossians, Chapter 3, verses 12-17.

Actually, Christians are really fortunate, these days. You don't commonly hear of them throwing Christians to the lions anymore. I think it's more about us being willing to live as God wants us to by being examples of how He works in our lives, regardless of what other people think or say.

Are we resentful when we are presented with an opportunity to make a donation to a worthy cause or are we giving to others and thankful for what we have? Do we get caught up in reading the latest fad or do we find time to grow in our faith as we read the Bible and learn more about God? Do we get caught up in listening to music with a worldly theme or do we sing Spiritual songs and hymns? Do we respond hatefully to cashiers who seem less than sensitive to our concerns or do we remember all our actions and words reflect our faith in God? Are we resentful that we don't have the newest and the best of worldly items like others or are we thankful for all God provides for us? Food for thought!

....

And whatsoever ye do, do it heartily, as to the Lord, and not unto men; Knowing that of the Lord ye shall receive the reward of the inheritance: for ye serve the Lord Christ. Colossians, Chapter 3, verses 23-24.

This makes me think about Random Acts of Simple Kindness and Love. This is when people secretly do nice things for others (this could be for people you know or complete strangers.) These anonymous acts aren't done for any reward or praise, but are just for the pleasure it brings to do nice things for others.

I think God is saying that because we love Him, we are to have that same attitude in all we do. We should take pleasure in doing nice things for others, not for any reward or praise, but because we enjoy doing nice things for God. Actually, it's exhilarating when you do nice things for others without letting anyone know you did them! It's really very special to know that you have been allowed to be an instrument for God by being involved in one of His little miracles for someone else. If you have never done things like this before, you should try it! There is nothing quite like the pure joy of doing something nice for another person without getting caught up in bragging to others about what you did. You do it just because it's something God would like you to do. Try it!

....

But of the times and the seasons, brethren, ye have no need that I write unto you. For yourselves know perfectly that the day of the Lord so cometh as a thief in the night. 1 Thessalonians, Chapter 5, verses 1-2.

We are told over and over again in the Bible that no one knows when the end of the world will be. It will sneak up on us just like a thief is able to sneak around in the night without anyone knowing. We need to be examples of how God works in our lives, not just in ten or twenty years from now, when we have finished sowing our wild oats, but always. God is forgiving but we should not push Him too far, either. We can't go around manipulating God and our faith by saying that I'm sinful and God will forgive me anyway, so I will just go ahead and do this sinful thing and ask for forgiveness later.

Well, God knows what is in our hearts. He knows when we are trying to manipulate Him and when we are genuinely trying to be Christians. Although none of us is perfect, we need to attempt to be the best examples we can of how God works in our lives.

....

Now we exhort you, brethren, warn them that are unruly, comfort the feebleminded, support the weak, be patient toward all men. See that none render evil for evil unto any man; but ever follow that which is good, both among yourselves, and to all men. Rejoice evermore. Pray without ceasing. In every thing give thanks: for this is the Will of God in Christ Jesus concerning you. 1 Thessalonians, Chapter 5, verses 14-18.

There are times in our lives when we can share our genuine concern for those who are making self-destructive choices. You never know if the things you say may be at a time that will help refocus that person. (I always like to ask God to provide the words when I'm in a situation like this. He always provides the right things for me to say.)

We are to be patient, tolerant and supportive of those who are mentally disabled, as well as those with any other disability. We are to be patient with everyone because we are supposed to be examples of how God works in our lives.

Have you ever overheard someone saying, "Yeah, they profess to be a Christian. You should have seen him out drinking the night away in the local bars. Some Christian, huh?" Or, "You should have seen the way she was yelling at her kids and she says she's a Christian. If that's what Christians do, I want no part of it."

Did you realize that our example could either lead people to God or push them away from having a relationship with Him? Well, it can! Sometimes our example is as close as anyone gets to knowing Jesus and the impact that He leaves on our lives.

....

Prove all things; hold fast that which is good. Abstain from all appearance of evil. And the very God of peace sanctify you wholly, and I pray God your whole Spirit and soul and body be preserved blameless unto the coming of our Lord Jesus Christ. 1 Thessalonians, Chapter 5, verses 21-23.

I think the "Prove all things" is good sound advice. We aren't to believe everything someone says is in the Bible just because someone who sounds knowledgeable says it's in there. It means we are to check it out first.

This passage also says that we should make sure we are in situations that are good for us and to stay away from anything that is evil or could lead us astray. Sometimes when I'm angry with someone, I ask God to take care of it, but in reality I still really want to be angry a little longer. When I ask God to take care of my willingness to let Him take my anger away, then I'm surrendering my need to stay angry.

....

> *Now we command you, brethren, in the Name of our Lord Jesus Christ, that ye withdraw yourselves from every brother that walketh disorderly, and not after the tradition which he received of us. For yourselves know how ye ought to follow us; for we behaved not ourselves disorderly among you; Neither did we eat any man's bread for nought; but wrought with labour and travail night and day, that we might not be chargeable to any of you: Not because we have not power, but to make ourselves an ensample unto you to follow us. For even when we were with you, this we commanded you, that if any would not work, neither should he eat. For we hear that there are some which walk among you disorderly, working not at all, but are busybodies. Now them that are such we command and exhort by our Lord Jesus Christ, that with quietness they work, and eat their own bread. But ye, brethren, be not weary in well doing. And if any man obey not our Word by this Epistle, note that man, and have no company with him, that he may be ashamed. Yet count him not as an enemy, but admonish him as a brother. Now the Lord of Peace Himself give you peace always by all means. The Lord be with you all. 2 Thessalonians, Chapter 3, verses 6-16.*

Apostle Paul was talking about how the followers of Jesus didn't want to be beholding to anyone or to be perceived as taking advantage of others. When they stayed with people as they went around spreading the Word of God, they worked for their food. Paul was saying that this is the way it should be and those who didn't work shouldn't eat.

He was into "Reality Therapy". Those Christians who didn't work and let others do all the work while they found time to be busybodies and visit, shouldn't be given food. He thought this would motivate them to talk less and to work more, that is…if they planned on eating.

He said that Christians shouldn't hang around people who were not obeying the Word of God. Maybe this shame might motivate others to change their behavior, but goes on to say that they shouldn't treat that person like their enemy either. They are doing these things to help motivate the person to make changes in their behavior choices, in the same way you might treat a brother who was going astray.

....

But if any provide not for his own, and specially for those of his own house, he hath denied the faith, and is worse than an infidel. 1 Timothy, Chapter 5, verse 8.

I remember hearing this over the years, "They take care of their own." Well, God is telling us this is exactly what we are supposed to do. There is a big difference between empowering and enabling, though. So, our help should be supportive in a way that maintains the person's self-respect, encouraging them always to make positive choices in their lives.

....

Perverse disputings of men of corrupt minds, and destitute of the Truth, supposing that gain is godliness: from such withdraw thyself. But godliness with contentment is great gain. For we brought nothing into this world, and it is certain we can carry nothing out. And having food and raiment let us be therewith content. But they that will be rich fall into temptation and a snare, and into many foolish and hurtful lusts, which drown men in destruction and perdition. For the love of money is the root of all evil: which while some coveted after, they have erred from the faith, and pierced themselves through with many sorrows. But thou, O man of God, flee these things; and follow after righteousness, Godliness, faith, love, patience, meekness. Fight the good fight of faith, lay hold on eternal life, whereunto thou art also called, and hast professed a good profession before many witnesses. 1 Timothy, Chapter 6, verses 5-12.

God is reminding us to stay away from people who have corrupt minds or those who distort the Word of God. There are some who feel the proof of being a good Christian would be having all the worldly possessions they want. Actually, there are people who believe that way today. They feel God would want them to have all types of nice things (possessions) and they actively pray for them. I know someone who looks at a picture of her dream car each day and then visualizes God giving it to her. I know God said that He would take care of our every need, but I don't think that means we are going to eat steak and prime rib every night because we are Christians, and we aren't guaranteed we'll drive fancy cars.

In fact, a big portion of this passage talks about how a lot of Christians get caught up in trying to attain money, status and worldly possessions which corrupt them. He says we are to be content with the food and the clothes we have, not visualizing ourselves being given fancy cars, high level jobs and lots of money. The desire for these things could very well lead us astray.

....

Therefore I endure all things for the elect's sakes, that they may also obtain the Salvation which is in Christ Jesus with eternal glory. It is a faithful saying: For if we be dead with Him, we shall also live with Him: If we suffer, we shall also reign with Him: if we deny Him, He also will deny us. 2 Timothy, Chapter 2, verses 10-12.

Boy, this passage always makes me sit up and take notice. It makes me think of all those times when I have the opportunity to say something to someone else about how God works in my life and I don't. I'm afraid of what they might think of me, but I'm really denying God. I would sure hate for Him to deny me in much the same way.

This is something I have to continue to work on. Yeah, I'm typing this book right now about how God works in my life, but I'm not taking any big time risk. For me, risking is when I need to share my faith personally with someone else, taking the chance that they may reject me for standing up for my beliefs.

Actually, whenever I have taken that risk, I haven't had people reject me. Most everyone I've talked to has been very respectful of my beliefs. Most of them have even shared situations from their lives that have ended up strengthening my faith. I think the point is that we need to be willing to stand up for God if the situation arises, instead of leaving it to someone else.

Here are some related passages:

*But whosoever therefore shall confess Me before men, him will I confess also before My Father which is in heaven. But whosoever shall deny Me before men, him will I also deny before My Father which is in heaven. Matthew, Chapter 10, verses 32-33.

*And blessed is he, whosoever shall not be offended in Me. Matthew, Chapter 11, verse 6.

....

> *Who concerning the Truth have erred, saying that the resurrection is past already; and overthrow the faith of some. Nevertheless the foundation of God standeth sure, having this seal, The Lord knoweth them that are His. And, Let every one that nameth the Name of Christ depart from iniquity. 2 Timothy, Chapter 2, verses 18-19.*

I think this passage speaks to people who try to confuse us by saying things like, "Heaven is here on earth, right now," or "You can make your life a heaven or a hell by the choices you make." Your choices do bring about logical consequences. If you make poor lifestyle choices, you usually have a life that reflects those choices. If you make lifestyle choices that reflect your faith in God, you won't have steak on the table every night, but God will take care of you.

My concern is that people can get confused by others and lose their focus on God when they engage in philosophical religious debates with them. Even though some profess to be devout Christians, reading the Bible is one of the best ways to find out God's Will for us.

God wants us to leave behind our sinful ways and to live a life that reflects how He has influenced us. We don't have to get public notoriety as a Christian in order to have Salvation. God knows who the Christians are and who just says they are.

....

> *For the time will come when they will not endure sound doctrine; but after their own lusts shall they heap to themselves teachers, having itching ears; And they shall turn away their ears from the Truth, and shall be turned unto fables. 2 Timothy, Chapter 4, verses 3-4.*

This passage has special significance because I first got interested in the Bible due to the erroneous quote from the Bible that really was from an Aesop's Fable (god helps him who helps himself.) I did not capitalize the "g" on god because the god they are talking about is a Mythological god, not the One True God. I try to always capitalize the "g" on God out of respect for our Heavenly Father.

....

> *But speak thou the things which become sound doctrine: That the aged men be sober, grave, temperate, sound in faith, in charity, in patience. The aged women likewise, that they be in behaviour as becometh holiness, not false accusers, not given to much wine, teachers of good things; That they may teach the young women to be sober, to love their husbands, to love their*

children, To be discreet, chaste, keepers at home, good, obedient to their own husbands, that the Word of God be not blasphemed. Young men likewise exhort to be sober minded. In all things shewing thyself a pattern of good works: in doctrine shewing uncorruptness, gravity, sincerity. Titus, Chapter 2, verses 1-7.

Have you ever been in a situation where someone is griping about their husband or wife? After a few minutes it seems that the rest of the people in the group start pointing out the flaws of their spouse, as well. On the ride home, these petty little flaws seem to be magnified because they have been publicly brought to your attention. God tells us in this passage that we are to be good examples to younger generations and should not get caught up in such discussions.

The younger generation learns by example and so did we. If their parents, grandparents or elders have a drink every time there is some type of problem, it sets a bad example. I'm not saying that an occasional drink is wrong, but it can become a crutch for all of the little problems that arise in life. It sends a real negative message when our children, grandchildren and friends see us turn to the bottle every time we have a problem or we have a disagreement with our spouse. They think that is the way things are supposed to be handled.

If they see us always complaining about our spouse, they are more apt to do the same with their spouse. I don't know about you, but I really don't want my children arguing with their spouses or turning to the bottle or recreational drugs to help them escape the problems that arise. I would much rather be a positive example of how God works in my daily life and in my marriage.

．．

That being justified by His grace, we should be made heirs according to the hope of eternal life. This is a faithful saying, and these things I will that thou affirm constantly, that they which have believed in God might be careful to maintain good works. These things are good and profitable unto men. But avoid foolish questions, and genealogies, and contentions, and strivings about the Law; for they are unprofitable and vain. Titus, Chapter 3, verses 7-9.

I remember hearing that some people seem to feel that they deserve a certain amount of prestige because they have followed their family roots all the way back to those who landed on Plymouth Rock. I know following your family tree can be interesting, but I think God is saying that even if we checked our genealogy and found we were related to the Apostle Paul himself, we would be wasting our time. It's not who you know that gets you into heaven, it's our love for Jesus and trying to lead the life He wants for us. That's what makes the difference!

....

> *God Who hath at sundry times and in divers manners spake in time past unto the fathers by the prophets. Hath in these last days spoken unto us by His Son, whom He hath appointed Heir of all things, by Whom also He made the worlds; Who being the brightness of His glory, and the express image of His person, and upholding all things by the Word of His power, when He had by Himself purged our sins, sat down at the right hand of the Majesty on High; Being made so much better than the angels, as He hath by inheritance obtained a more excellent Name than they. For unto which of the angels said He at any time, thou art My son, this day have I begotten thee? And again, I will be to him a Father, and he shall be to Me a son? And again, when He bringeth in the First Begotten into the world, He saith, And let all the angels of God worship Him. And of the angels He saith, Who maketh His angels spirits, and His ministers a flame of fire. But unto the Son He saith, Thy throne, O God, is for ever and ever: a sceptre of righteousness is the sceptre of Thy kingdom. Hebrews, Chapter 1, verses 1-8.*

This passage reinforces my concern that people might get led astray by focusing on angels rather than focusing on God. Angels have become popular in the last few years. There are some shows focused on angels and some catalogs and stores filled primarily with angels. The thing is, God doesn't want us worshipping angels or giving them undue attention. I think some people get confused and think they are really focusing on God when they pay so much attention to angels. Some people even pray to their guardian angel rather than praying to God, thinking it's one and the same thing, but it isn't.

If the angel in Revelation forbade John to bow down to him (last asterisk), then I would think we should pay attention to this. We are to focus on God and not the angels even though they are God's ministering spirits. Our focus is to always be on God the Father, Son and Holy Spirit; none other.

Here are some related passages:

*But to which of the angels said He at any time, Sit on My right hand, until I make thine enemies thy footstool: Are they not all ministering spirits, sent forth to minister for them who shall be heirs of Salvation? Hebrews, Chapter 1, verses 13-14.

*And Manoah said unto the angel of the LORD, I pray thee, let us detain thee, until we shall have made ready a kid for thee. And the angel of the LORD said unto Manoah. Though thou detain me, I will not eat of thy bread: and if thou wilt offer a burnt offering, thou must offer it unto the LORD. For Manoah knew not that he was an angel of the LORD. Judges, Chapter 13, verse 15-16.

*And I John saw these things, and heard them, And when I had heard and seen, I fell down to worship before the feet of the angel which showed me these things. Then saith he unto me, See thou do it not: for I am thy fellowservant, and of thy brethren the prophets, and of them which keep the sayings of this book: worship God. Revelation, Chapter 22, verses 8-9.

....

For He spake in a certain place of the seventh day on this wise, and God did rest the seventh day from all His works. Hebrews, Chapter 4, verse 4.

I like the way that God looks out for my family in spite of our weaknesses. He knows that I work intensely all week and I spend all weekend either caught up in doing the things I took home from work or I get involved in other projects. If I spend all my spare time focused on work and projects, then I'm not spending my time focused on God and my family.

I have an aunt and an uncle who don't work on the day that they go to church. I always thought it was admirable, but I would come up with twenty billion reasons why I needed to do these projects instead. When I read the Bible, I realized that God says over and over again (mostly in the Old Testament) that we aren't supposed to work on the Sabbath and are to have a day of rest, focusing on God and our family.

I got to thinking about this. If He went out of His way to make sure that this was in the Bible so many times, there must be a good reason for it. The more I thought about it, I realized that if we are doing things from work or other projects all week, we will rarely find quality time for God and our family. God wants us to have priorities in our lives. After

God who is our first priority, our families should come next and then our work. Think of how many children rarely get to spend time with their parents because they are too busy working late or they are involved in work related projects at home.

God also gives us added benefits for not working on the Sabbath. Taking this day to focus on God and our families allows us to be refreshed for the new week. When we stay busy all weekend after a hectic week, we are more apt to become impatient with our family members over the little things that arise. Additionally, when we get caught up in our work and projects, we are more apt to find excuses for not going to church with our family.

The worst part is that we are poor examples to our children. If we stay busy working all the time, they won't grow up learning how to pace themselves either. Everyone needs to maintain a healthy balance in their lives. If work becomes the sole focus, then our families are bound to lose out-not to mention us.

Someday our kids will be grown and out of the house. Will they come and visit us regularly when we are older? Did we model the importance of family time while they were growing up? Will they be too busy doing their own projects and work that they have no time for us? What's worse is the possibility that they will have no time for their own families. Are we perpetuating a cycle of super busy people who have little time to interact with others? Something to think about.

As I said, God has this stated and restated throughout the Bible. I'm going to list some of the Bible passages that support this so you can see the lengths that God went to in order to remind us to have a day of rest to focus on Him and our families.

Here are some related passages:

*Six days thou shalt do thy work, and on the seventh day thou shalt rest: that thine ox and thine ass may rest, and the son of thy handmaid, and the stranger, may be refreshed. Exodus, Chapter 23, verse 12.

*Speak thou also unto the children of Israel, saying, Verily My Sabbaths ye shall keep: for it is a sign between Me and you throughout your generations; that ye may know that I am the Lord that doth sanctify you. Ye shall keep the Sabbath therefore; for it is holy unto you: every one that defileth it shall surely be put to death: for whosoever doeth any work therein, that soul shall be cut off from among his people. Six days may work be done; but in the seventh is the Sabbath of rest, holy to

Bible Passages That Can Influence Your Life

the LORD: whosoever doeth any work in the Sabbath day, he shall surely be put to death. Wherefore the children of Israel shall keep the Sabbath, to observe the Sabbath throughout their generations, for a perpetual covenant. It is a sign between Me and the children of Israel for ever: for in six days the LORD made heaven and earth, and on the seventh day He rested, and was refreshed. Exodus, Chapter 31, verses 13-17.

*And Moses gathered all the congregation of the children of Israel together, and said unto them, These are the Words which the Lord hath commanded, that ye should do them. Six days shall work be done, but on the seventh day there shall be to you an holy day, a Sabbath of rest to the LORD, whosoever doeth work therein shall be put to death. Ye shall kindle no fire throughout your habitations upon the Sabbath day. Exodus, Chapter 35, verses 1-3.

*Ye shall keep My Sabbaths, and reverence My sanctuary: I am the LORD. Leviticus, Chapter 19, verse 30.

*Speak unto the children of Israel, and say unto them, Concerning the feasts of the LORD, which ye shall proclaim to be holy convocations, even these are My feasts. Six days shall work be done: but the seventh day is the Sabbath of rest, an holy convocation; ye shall do no work therein: it is the Sabbath of the LORD in all your dwellings. Leviticus, Chapter 23, verses 2-3.

*Ye shall keep My Sabbaths, and reverence My sanctuary. I am the LORD. Leviticus, Chapter 26, verse 2.

*There dwelt men of Tyre also therein, which brought fish, and all manner of ware, and sold on the Sabbath unto the children of Judah, and in Jerusalem. Then I contended with the nobles of Judah, and said unto them, What evil thing is this that ye do, and profane the Sabbath day? Did not your fathers thus, and did not our God bring all this evil upon us, and upon this city? yet ye bring more wrath upon Israel by profaning the Sabbath. Nehemiah, Chapter 13, verses 16-18.

*Thus saith the LORD; Take heed to yourselves, and bear no burden on the Sabbath day, nor bring it in by the gates of Jerusalem; Neither carry forth a burden out of your houses on the Sabbath day, neither do ye any work, but hallow ye the Sabbath day, as I commanded your fathers. But they obeyed not, neither inclined their ear, but made their neck stiff, that *they might not hear, nor receive instruction. And it shall come to pass, if ye diligently hearken unto Me saith the Lord, to bring in no burden through the gates of this city on the Sabbath day, but hallow the Sabbath day, to do no work therein; Then shall there enter into the gates of this city kings and princes sitting upon the throne of David, riding in chariots and on horses, they, and their princes, the men of Judah, and the inhabitants of Jerusalem: and this city shall remain for ever. And they shall come from the cities of Judah, and from the places about Jerusalem, and from the land of Benjamin, and from the plain, and from the mountains, and from the south, bringing burnt offerings, and sacrifices, and meat offerings, and incense and bringing sacrifices of praise, unto the house of the LORD. But if ye will not hearken unto Me to hallow the Sabbath day, and not to bear a burden, even entering in at the gates of Jerusalem on the Sabbath day; then will I kindle a fire in the gates thereof, and it shall devour the palaces of Jerusalem, and it shall not be quenched. Jeremiah, Chapter 17, verses 21-27.*

....

That by two immutable things, in which it was impossible for God to lie, we might have a strong consolation, who have fled for refuge to lay hold upon the hope set before us. Hebrews, Chapter 6, verse 18.

I just like this passage because it says that it's impossible for God to lie. That way I know if it says in the Bible that God will take care of me, He will!

Here are some related passages:

**Let your conversation be without covetousness; and be content with such things as ye have: for He hath said, I will never leave thee, nor forsake thee. So that we may boldly say, the Lord is my Helper, and I will not fear what man shall do unto me. Hebrews, Chapter 13, verses 5-6.*

**The Words of the LORD are pure Words: as silver tried in a furnace of earth, purified seven times. Thou shalt keep them, O LORD, Thou shalt preserve them from this generation for ever. Psalm, Chapter 12, verses 6-7.*

....

> *How much more shall the Blood of Christ, who through the eternal Spirit offered Himself without spot to God, purge your conscience from dead works to serve the living God?*
> *Hebrews, Chapter 9, verse 14.*

I remember referring to God guiding us through our conscience at an earlier point. I just wanted to include this passage because it supports what I said. Sometimes I tell people to listen to the instincts that God gives them about things, because He guides us through these.

I'm not sure if the instinct He gives us and our conscience are the exact same thing or not. What I do know is: God DOES GUIDE US if we listen to Him. Every time I listen, I have been amazed at how well things turn out. Every time I didn't listen, I always remember wishing I had. Well, this has happened enough times that I don't want to ignore God when He is guiding me anymore.

The other thing I like about this is that God takes the time for me and my problems on a personal level, when there are millions and billions of people in the world. If God gives of His time to guide me, then I <u>definitely</u> want to listen!

....

> *But without faith it is impossible to please Him: for he that cometh to God must believe that He is, and that He is a rewarder of them that diligently seek Him. By faith, Noah, being warned of God of things not seen as yet, moved with fear, prepared an ark to the saving of his house; by the which He condemned the world, and became heir of the righteousness which is by faith. By faith Abraham, when he was called to go out into a place which he should after receive for an inheritance, obeyed; and he went out, not knowing whither he went.*
> *Hebrews, Chapter 11, verses 6-8.*

You really should read all of Hebrews, Chapter 11. It tells of person after person throughout Biblical history who did the Will of God based on faith alone. It makes me think about how these accomplishments would never have happened if they hadn't listened to God because they were worried what their friends and neighbors would think of them.

It makes me wonder if I would be willing to take these same risks if God asked me. Would I have the blind faith necessary, trusting God would take care of everything? Hopefully, God would give me the willingness to respond to His requests. Where would we be right now if Noah had said to God that he wasn't quite sure whether he should build the ark because he was afraid his friends and neighbors would be talking about him and he didn't want to risk the embarrassment? Food for thought!

....

> *Let brotherly love continue. Be not forgetful to entertain strangers: for thereby some have entertained angels unawares. Hebrews, Chapter 13, verses 1-2.*

After reading forwarded emails telling how people's lives have been changed by reaching out to someone less fortunate, I am more reflective about my lack of action. When approached by the needy, I have to admit my response has not always been of Christian love to my fellow human beings. This definitely is something I need to work on, being mindful about how I would feel if people ignored and rejected me. I only hope God continues to be patient with me and brings me to the level of brotherly love that He wants us all to show to each other.

....

> *Remember them that are in bonds, as bound with them; and them which suffer adversity, as being yourselves also in the body. Hebrews, Chapter 13, verse 3.*

I need to work on being more compassionate to those who have been imprisoned. It's easy for me to sit back in my comfortable house and forget about the plight of others less fortunate. I can rationalize that they have made poor choices and have been removed from society as a consequence for these actions. In reality, I'm not sure I agree with that philosophy anymore. Sure, I think rapists, child molesters and mass murders should be kept from returning to society. Often these people get released from prison on parole after a certain amount of time and some therapy, only to rape, molest and kill again. This makes no sense when the prisons are full of other people who have done much less and may never get out. I just don't understand.

There are people who are in prison indefinitely for stealing food or cigarettes, doing stupid pranks and generally making poor choices. Are these people a threat to society? I'm sure there are some sociopaths who pose a threat, but I think there are many prisoners who would be more help to society on the outside than behind bars.

There is a Bible passage that says: *Men do not despise a thief, if he steal to satisfy his soul when he is hungry; But if he be found, he shall restore sevenfold; he shall give all the substance of his house. Proverbs, Chapter 6, verses 30-31.* God is talking about having him make restitution rather than imprisoning him.

With our country's financial situation, we can't afford to hire enough people to clean our parks and waterways, assist the aged, work with the handicapped and provide productive services for the community.

These options would allow prisoners to maintain their dignity while making restitution at the same time. It sure beats having people in a penal system where they are more apt to become corrupted by the quantity of negative influences they encounter than to be rehabilitated. Many of those imprisoned have the potential to be productive members of society with some assistance and guidance. (As I said before, I'm not including people who are rapists, molesters and killers in this category.)

It saddens me to think that there is no real equity in the penal system. There are people who were CEO's for multimillion dollar firms, who embezzled the funds of their company. Many of their co-workers have since lost their jobs, their retirements and their livelihoods because of the impact the embezzlement had on the company's finances. Often these people don't go to jail, because they have enough money to hire expensive attorneys. If they do go to jail, it's for a short amount of time in a swanky prison. They write their memoirs and make a fortune.

It's sad that the system doesn't make them make restitution to all those who lost their retirements. Don't you think it would be an excellent logical consequence if they had to take the royalties from their memoirs to pay for the retirements of those hard workers whose retirement funds had been embezzled?

Then there are minorities who are imprisoned and are doing hard time because they didn't have a ritzy lawyer defending them for things that pale in comparison. They end up spending a big portion their lives in prisons that could never compare to the swanky ones of those who embezzled millions. This just doesn't seem equitable to me.

I need to remember to keep prisoners in my prayers, but there may be other things we can do. There are organizations that we could contact that would tell us ways that we could help the families of prisoners. A monumental way we can help is by being willing to hire someone who has formerly been in prison. How are they ever going to support their family and become a productive member of society if no one hires them? We could make a difference in their lives.

....

Let no man say when he is tempted, I am tempted of God: for God cannot be tempted with evil, neither tempteth He any man: But every man is tempted, when he is drawn away of his own lust, and enticed. Then when lust hath conceived, it bringeth forth sin: and sin, when it is finished, bringeth forth death. Do not err, my beloved brethren. James, Chapter 1, verses 13-16.

It was very interesting for me to read this. Somehow, I was under the impression that God tempted us to test us, but I was wrong. It's our own sinful human nature that is tempted by things. Our choice to follow these temptations or to turn to God is what makes the difference.

....

Wherefore, my beloved brethren, let every man be swift to hear, slow to speak, slow to wrath: For the wrath of man worketh not the righteousness of God. Wherefore lay apart all filthiness and superfluity of naughtiness, and receive with meekness the engrafted Word, which is able to save your souls. But be ye doers of the Word, and not hearers only deceiving your own selves. James, Chapter 1, verses 19-22.

But whoso looketh into the perfect Law of liberty, and continueth therein, he being not a forgetful hearer, but a doer of the work, this man shall be blessed in his deed. James, Chapter 1, verse 25.

This is of special importance to me right now, because a minor matter has worked a wedge between my relationship with someone I care about. God didn't put these Words in the Bible to be something nice for us to read. He had the Bible written to provide guidelines for our lives and to remind us how things like anger, resentment and hatred can subtly interfere with our relationship with God and others. I can read this passage and just say, "Yeah, God is right. I shouldn't let wedges develop between others and me," and then do nothing further about it. Or I can be an example of how God works in my life by taking the first step, however awkward it might be to set things right. The choice is up to us.

....

If any man among you seem to be religious, and bridleth not his tongue, but deceiveth his own heart, this man's religion is vain. Pure religion and undefiled before God and the Father is this, To visit the fatherless and widows in their affliction, and to keep himself unspotted from the world. James, Chapter 1, verses 26-27.

It's easy to be a "Back-Seat Christian," becoming complacent in our relationship with God. In doing so, we are letting everyone else take care of God's work while we focus on ourselves. God says He wants us to take an active role as Christians. He wants us to visit the fatherless, those grieving and we are not to get caught up in worldly values.

With so many single parent families, visiting the fatherless could be a relatively easy thing to do. If we each took the time to touch the life of one child, we could make a major difference. Some might think that they don't have the time, but you could include neighbor kids in your game of basketball with your child. Family board games are nice to invite other kids to play. Even if you don't have children of your own, you can take a child you know with you to the library. You can invite them over to bake or BBQ. Even doing routine chores seem special when you've invited a child to help you. It gives them a sense of accomplishment and helps them feel like they are contributing. When you take your child to a scouting, church or school activity; include a child who wouldn't have been able to attend otherwise.

Going to a school once a week for 30 minutes, can positively impact the life of a child. (When I was a teacher in a low income school, I tried to get volunteers to come and read for 30 minutes a week with my students who had behavior problems. Within days, I would notice a positive change in the behavior choices that these children made. Interestingly, I wasn't having the volunteer focus on teaching the child to read or anything else academic. The vast majority of these kids are quite capable of doing academic tasks. They just have so many other things going on in their lives that it's often difficult for them to focus on academics. The time with the volunteers was really meant to be a positive time for the adult and the child to spend together. Isn't it amazing that 30 minutes of contact with a child each week could make such a difference?)

I'm not suggesting that everyone should volunteer to spend time with kids who have behavior problems, although that's not a bad idea. I'm using this as an example. If we each took the time to be with a child for 30 minutes a week, just think of the positive impact we could have on the children of our country. It has the added benefit of making us positive role models of our Christian values to our own children.

....

My brethren, have not the faith of our Lord Jesus Christ, the Lord of Glory, with respect of persons. For if there come unto your assembly a man with a gold ring, in goodly apparel, and there come in also a poor man in vile raiment; And ye have respect to him that weareth the gay clothing, and say unto him, Sit thou here in a good place; and say to the poor, Stand thou there, or sit here under my footstool; Are ye not then partial in yourselves, and are become judges of evil thoughts? Hearken, my beloved brethren, Hath not God chosen the poor of this world

> *rich in faith and heirs of the kingdom which He hath promised to them that love Him? But ye have despised the poor. Do not rich men oppress you, and draw you before the judgment seats? Do not they blaspheme that worthy Name by the which ye are called? If ye fulfil the royal Law according to the Scripture, Thou shalt love thy neighbour as thyself, ye do well. James, Chapter 2, verses 1-8.*

We have become "The Lives of the Rich and Famous Christians," catering to those with status who look and dress a particular way. I wish I could say that I didn't fall into this category, but I can't. I think our society has fallen prey to this, as well. If we were on a bus, train or subway; would we stand to give our seat to someone who looks down and out or would we stand for someone who was either rich or famous? I have a feeling I know which answer I would get if people were really being honest.

If you really think about it, our human logic is backward. Some of the people with wealth don't do as much physical labor and are not exposed to the weather conditions as much as those who are needier. Those who are less fortunate probably need our seat more than those with wealth. Well, the same goes with our kindness. The wealthy often have others who treat them courteously, but do we extend that same courtesy to the poor? I'm ashamed to say that I don't always. I wouldn't want God to treat me as indifferently as I sometimes treat those who are less fortunate. Sure, I give clothes that I no longer want to the needy, but that takes minimal effort. That is giving out of my excess and I don't think that's the same as treating others with the respect and the courtesy that they deserve.

....

> *But the tongue can no man tame; it is an unruly evil, full of deadly poison. Therewith bless we God, even the Father; and there with curse we men, which are made after the similitude of God. Out of the same mouth proceedeth blessing and cursing. My brethren, these things ought not so to be. Doth a fountain send forth at the same place sweet water and bitter? Can the fig tree, my brethren, bear olive berries? either a vine, figs? so can no fountain both yield salt water and fresh. Who is a wise man and endued with knowledge among you? let him show out of a good conversation his works with meekness of wisdom. But if ye have bitter envying and strife in your hearts, glory not, and lie not against the Truth. This wisdom descendeth not from above, but is earthly, sensual, devilish. For where envying and strife is, there is confusion and every evil work. But the wisdom that*

is from above is first pure, then peaceable, gentle, and easy to be entreated, full of mercy and good fruits, without partiality, and without hypocrisy. And the fruit of righteousness is sown in peace of them that make peace. James, Chapter 3, verses 8-18.

I think God is asking us if a Christian can truly be two-faced. You wouldn't consider someone a true friend who is nice to your face but works against you, behind your back.

I think God is telling us through this passage that we can't truly be both. Can we truly be a Christian one day a week, but participate in a worldly life with no attempt to change the rest of the week? I think God tells us that if we truly profess to be a Christian, we will be examples of our faith seven days a week instead of just one.

....

But He giveth more grace. Wherefore He saith, God resisteth the proud, but giveth grace unto the humble. Submit yourselves therefore to God. Resist the devil, and he will flee from you. Draw nigh to God, and He will draw nigh to you. Cleanse your hands, ye sinners; and purify your hearts, ye double minded. James, Chapter 4, verses 6-8.

I think that God is looking for a few good men and women just like the Marines. They don't want proud, boastful people who go around saying they are better than others. They want people who show their worth by their behavior and choices all the time.

....

But now ye rejoice in your boastings: all such rejoicing is evil. Therefore to him that knoweth to do good, and doeth it not, to him it is sin. James, Chapter 4, verses 16-17.

This passage makes me sad because I know I have been guilty of this more times than I would like to mention. I was teaching in a suburb of a larger city with more affluent families. A friend who teaches there asked me to go to the city with her to read with some "inner city" kids after school. Instead, I chose to co-sponsor the Art Club, doing projects with those more affluent. I regret being so shallow.

....

Grudge not one against another, brethren, lest ye be condemned: behold, the judge standeth before the door. James, Chapter 5, verse 9.

You know, it seems that our character flaws have been ingrained in us for so long that they would be almost impossible to change, but not so with God. I have found that since I'm focusing on God's Will for my life, the thought about God judging me like I judge others pops into my mind when I'm being critical of others, allowing me to make the changes that He wants.

....

> But above all things, my brethren, swear not, neither by heaven, neither by the earth, neither by any other oath: but let your yea be yea; and your nay, nay; lest ye fall into condemnation. James, Chapter 5, verse 12.

This passage lets me know that I can tell the truth when I'm talking to people without saying, "It's the truth, too-Swear to God," or, "It's the truth, too-I Swear it on the Bible." These extra sayings for emphasis aren't necessary and aren't what God wants.

Here is a related passage:

> *But I say unto you, Swear not at all; neither by heaven; for it is God's throne: Nor by the earth: for it is His footstool: neither by Jerusalem: for it is the city of the great King, Neither shalt thou swear by thy head, because thou canst not make one hair white or black, But let your communication be, Yea, yea; Nay, nay: for whatsoever is more than these cometh of evil. Matthew, Chapter 5, verses 34-37.

....

> Is any among you afflicted? let him pray. Is any merry? let him sing psalms. Is any sick among you? let him call for the elders of the church; and let them pray over him, anointing him with oil in the Name of the Lord: And the prayer of faith shall save the sick, and the Lord shall raise him up; and if he have committed sins, they shall be forgiven him. Confess your faults one to another, and pray one for another, that ye may be healed. The effectual fervent prayer of a righteous man availeth much. James, Chapter 5, verses 13-16.

I like the way that some of the churches I have gone to have a prayer chain. When someone brings a special need to the attention of this group, they call the next person on their list and then there are a multitude of people praying for this same cause. Having the additional prayers of the prayer chain gave me a sense of relief when I asked them to pray for my friend's husband and my uncle when they both had bypass surgery.

I have since realized that if I think the prayer chain is such a positive thing, I should try to give something back by volunteering to be a member of the prayer chain, as well.

....

Brethren, if any of you do err from the Truth, and one convert him; Let him know, that he which converteth the sinner from the error of his way shall save a soul from death, and shall hide a multitude of sins. James, Chapter 5, verses 19-20.

When I was about 11 or 12, I remember being horrified by hearing how a bunch of people saw a car drive over the levee in a nearby community. They stood by and watched the whole family drown without ever making an attempt to save them. I didn't know how those people could live with themselves. If a person had made an effort but had been unable to save them, they would have at least known they had tried.

I feel like Christians often do the same thing. We see people who are making lifestyle choices where they are apt to "drown" in their worldly ways, but we just sit back and watch without even attempting to save them. If we make an attempt, at least we will know that we tried and didn't just sit back and do nothing. Who knows, maybe we will be the person who plants the seed of change in their life.

....

But as He which hath called you is Holy, so be ye Holy in all manner of conversation; Because it is written, Be ye Holy; for I am Holy. 1 Peter, Chapter 1, verses 15-16.

It's easy to become complacent and to let a few off color words slip out every now and then. Yes, God will forgive us for these shortcomings if we ask Him, but are we being the example He wants us to be?

....

And if ye call on the Father, who without respect of persons judgeth according to every man's work, pass the time of your sojourning here in fear: Forasmuch as ye know that ye were not redeemed with corruptible things, as silver and gold, from your vain conversation received by tradition from your fathers; But with the precious Blood of Christ, as of a Lamb without blemish and without spot: Who verily was foreordained before the foundation of the world, but was manifest in these last times for you, Who by Him do believe in God, that raised Him up from the dead, and gave Him glory; that your faith and hope might be in God. 1 Peter, Chapter 1, verses 17-21.

Christians don't have a "free ride on the gravy train." God is going to judge us by our faith and our actions which should be examples of our devotion to Him. Our Salvation wasn't purchased for us by some worldly thing like money. We can't pay a fine when we are caught sinning, like a person who has been speeding pays a fine as restitution. Our Salvation is earned through Jesus' suffering, death and Resurrection on our behalf.

....

Seeing ye have purified your souls in obeying the Truth through the Spirit unto unfeigned love of the brethren, see that ye love one another with a pure heart fervently: Being born again, not of corruptible seed, but of incorruptible, by the Word of God, which liveth and abideth for ever. For all flesh is as grass, and all the glory of man as the flower of grass. The grass withereth, and the flower thereof falleth away: But the Word of the Lord endureth for ever. And this is the Word which by the Gospel is preached unto you. 1 Peter, Chapter 1, verses 22-25.

Think of a brand new computer in the box. Look inside the box and you would see machinery with potential, but of no use unless it is plugged in. Similarly, we have potential that becomes realized once we develop a relationship with Jesus.

When the computer is properly hooked up, just as a Christian who is focused on God, the machinery works at optimum capacity. Once a virus corrupts our files like worldly choices corrupt our lives, the machinery performs inconsistently, at best. Both the computer and the Christian can continue to get progressively worse. After we realize that help is needed and turn to a computer technologist to repair the hard drive, in much the same way a Christian turns to God for assistance, both can get started running "like new" again. I need to turn to God for periodic "overhauls," making sure my faith and my lifestyle choices are running smoothly and are attuned with what God wants.

....

And who is he that will harm you, if ye be followers of that which is good? But and if ye suffer for righteousness' sake, happy are ye: and be not afraid of their terror, neither be troubled: But sanctify the Lord God in your hearts: and be ready always to give an answer to every man that asketh you a reason of the hope that is in you with meekness and fear: Having a good conscience; that, whereas they speak evil of you, as of evildoers, they may be ashamed that falsely accuse your good conversation in Christ. For it is better, if the Will of God be so, that ye suffer for the well doing, than for evil doing. 1 Peter, Chapter 3, verses 13-17.

As Christians, we might get laughed at, stigmatized or even isolated from others but that's a small price to pay for our belief in God. I would much rather suffer this ridicule than to give in for momentary peace, giving up my eternal peace and Salvation. I'm a "Pick Your Battles Christian." If I look at my two options, I could live life in the fast lane now and be popular but go to hell, or I can risk some ridicule by living up to my Christian ethics and go to heaven. I plan to put my money where there is the greatest chance for reward-heaven!

....

But let none of you suffer as a murderer, or as a thief, or as an evildoer, or as a busybody in other men's matters. Yet if any man suffer as a Christian, let him not be ashamed; but let him glorify God on this behalf. 1 Peter, Chapter 4, verses 15-16.

It's easy to become self-righteous thinking, "Well, at least I haven't killed anyone or stolen anything." It's humbling to read how God feels that busybodies are just as sinful. Getting caught up in talking about others is one of the ways that Satan works a subtle wedge in the lives of Christians. It's easy to get caught up in gossip, but we need to take a stand. Sometimes just ignoring a situation is condoning that behavior. It's not always easy to let people know that you feel uncomfortable talking about others, but God will give you the words, if you let Him.

Here are some related passages:

*Let no corrupt communication proceed out of your mouth, but that which is good to the use of edifying, that it may minister grace unto the hearers. Ephesians, Chapter 4, verse 29.

*Let all bitterness, and wrath and anger, and clamour, and evil speaking, be put away from you, with all malice: and be ye kind one to another, tenderhearted, forgiving one another, even as God for Christ's sake hath forgiven you. Ephesians, Chapter 4, verses 31-32.

....

Likewise, ye younger, submit yourselves unto the elder. Yea, all of you be subject one to another, and be clothed with humility: for God resisteth the proud, and giveth grace to the humble. Humble yourselves therefore under the mighty hand of God, that He may exalt you in due time: Casting all your care upon Him; for He careth for you. 1 Peter, Chapter 5, verses 5-7.

    I remember becoming frustrated with people who were older who gave me common sense advice. I thought that they must think I'm stupid.

    Later, God showed me that I needed to listen respectfully to the advice of my elders. It didn't hurt me to listen, even though I already knew what they were telling me. It made them feel better, because they were passing on some insight that they felt would be helpful to me. I now realize that they do this out of love.

    When I'm older, I sure wouldn't want younger people treating me as if my advice didn't matter. I think this passage is important to remember. If we aren't good role models to the younger generation about being respectful to our elders, how will they know to be respectful to us when we're older?

....

We have also a more sure Word of prophecy; where unto ye do well that ye take heed, as unto a Light that shineth in a dark place, until the day dawn, and the day star arise in your hearts: Knowing this first, that no prophecy of the Scripture is of any private interpretation. For the prophecy came not in old time by the will of man: but holy men of God spake as they were moved by the Holy Ghost. 2 Peter, Chapter 1, verses 19-21.

    The ability to interpret the Bible's message doesn't belong to any one person or group, especially if they feel that they are the only ones who know what God's Will is. It's important for me to remember this because there are religious fads, cults, trends and religious leaders who may suggest beliefs that sound good but are really contrary to God's Will, as stated in the Bible. It's easier to interpret the Bible than many lead you to believe. Trust the instincts that God gives you and He will guide you as you read the Bible for yourself.

....

For if God spared not the angels that sinned, but cast them down to hell, and delivered them into chains of darkness, to be reserved unto judgment; And spared not the old world, but saved Noah the eighth person, a preacher of righteousness, bringing in the flood upon the world of the ungodly; And turning the cities of Sodom and Gomorrha into ashes condemned them

> with an overthrow, making them an example unto those that after should live ungodly; And delivered just Lot vexed with the filthy conversation of the wicked: (For that righteous man dwelling among them, in seeing and hearing, vexed his righteous soul from day to day with their unlawful deeds;) The Lord knoweth how to deliver the godly out of temptations, and to reserve the unjust unto the day of judgment to be punished. *2 Peter, Chapter 2, verses 4 -9.*

I'm reminded that God didn't spare the fallen angels (Satan and his followers). He did spare Noah and his family and the rest of the people in the world perished in the flood due to their beliefs and lifestyle choices. God saved Lot and the rest of Gomorrha perished due to their beliefs and lifestyle choices.

God is definitely <u>not</u> telling me that it's okay to be a "So-so Christian" and that I'll get to heaven anyway. I feel He's telling me that all these people perished for their wayward beliefs and choices. Only those who were dedicated to God were saved. I need to be equally dedicated to my belief in God if I want to be saved too. God knows that I won't be perfect, but He also knows what's in my heart and if I'm genuinely trying be an example of how He works in my life.

....

> For when they speak great swelling words of vanity, they allure through the lusts of the flesh, through much wantonness, those that were clean escaped from them who live in error. While they promise them liberty, they themselves are the servants of corruption: for of whom a man is overcome, of the same is he brought in bondage. *2 Peter, Chapter 2, verses 18-19.*

This passage reminds me of the story *Pinocchio*. Pinocchio was encouraged to go with the others boys to the Land of Toys where they had no responsibilities. People could do worldly things and have fun all the time. Well, Pinocchio was led astray just as some people are led astray by false prophets.

Pinocchio and the others had extreme consequences for living the worldly life. They started turning into donkeys. Well, I think people who lead the same type of worldly lives today end up not only looking like donkeys to others, but lose their chance for Salvation in the process.

Fortunately, if we turn our lives around after having lived the life of Pinocchio, God will forgive us and guide us. This isn't something to be manipulated. "Oh, I'll lead a worldly life now, while I'm younger. Then, when I'm older, I will settle down because I know God will forgive me for making these choices."

> God tells us in this passage to not be taken in like Pinocchio was. *Ye therefore, beloved, seeing ye know these things before, beware lest ye also, being led away with the error of the wicked, fall from your own stedfastness. But grow in grace, and in the knowledge of our Lord and Savior Jesus Christ. To Him be glory both now and for ever. Amen. 2 Peter, Chapter 3, verses 17-18.*

....

> *But, beloved, be not ignorant of this one thing, that one day is with the Lord as a thousand years, and a thousand years as one day. 2 Peter, Chapter 3, verse 8.*

I think this passage is important for us to remember when we read Bible passages that refer to specific amounts of time, so that we don't take the dates too literally.

This makes me think about how insignificant time can be. When I was younger, I used to spend some time in the summers with my grandmother. The weeks with her sped by so quickly that before I knew it, I was leaving to return home. She approached everything with enthusiasm, whether it was trying to figure out answers on game shows or reading.

She had a zest for everything she did and her enthusiasm was contagious. She is the person who developed my love for reading. She read thick novels and when I was about 8 years old I told her that I wished I could read big books like she did. She told me that I could and took me to the public library. She helped me pick out a humorous adult novel that would interest me. I took great pride in reading that novel, encouraged by her confidence in my abilities. I'm not sure that I would have attempted something like that, otherwise.

Well, I think the same is true for Christians. Our enthusiasm for our relationship with God can be contagious, as well. We can share this with others with confidence in their ability to be open to all God has for them. Our moral support and encouragement can make all the difference in their developing this important relationship that might not have happened otherwise.

....

> *This then is the message which we have heard of Him and declare unto you, that God is Light, and in Him is no darkness at all. If we say that we have fellowship with Him, and walk in darkness, we lie, and do not the Truth: But if we walk in the Light, as He is in the Light, we have fellowship one with another and the Blood of Jesus Christ His Son cleanseth us from all sin. If we say that we have no sin, we deceive ourselves, and the Truth is not in us. If we confess our sins, He*

is faithful and just to forgive us our sins, and to cleanse us from all unrighteousness. If we say that we have not sinned, we make Him a liar, and His Word is not in us. 1 John, Chapter 1, verses 5-10.

This reminds me of being lost in a cave with lots of different tunnels. If we know that God is the Light that we see at the end of the tunnel, we are relieved. If we move confidently toward that Light, we will be saved. The darkness is all types of worldly things like: greed, drugs, infidelity, gossip and a variety of other things that can lead us away from our focus on Jesus, who is our Light and Salvation.

Now, if we tell ourselves that the Light at the end of the tunnel is too far away and give up, we can lose our way by getting lost running down the wrong tunnels, trying to navigate the worldly temptations in darkness and lose our focus on God.

Salvation is ours if we look down the tunnel and see the path that God provides for us as He illuminates the way, if we'd only let Him.

....

He that saith, I know Him, and keepeth not His Commandments, is a liar, and the Truth is not in him. But whoso keepeth His Word in him verily is the love of God perfected: hereby know we that we are in Him. He that saith he abideth in Him ought himself also so to walk, even as He walked.
1 John, Chapter 2, verses 4-6.

I need to be a "Do as I say and as I do Christian" and be more than boastful talk. We need to be examples for others to see how God works in our lives.

Here are some related passages:

*For verily I say unto you, Till heaven and earth pass, one jot or one tittle shall in no wise pass from the Law, till all be fulfilled. Whosoever therefore shall break one of these least Commandments, and shall teach men so, he shall be called the least in the kingdom of heaven: but whosoever shall do and teach them, the same shall be called great in the kingdom of heaven. Matthew, Chapter 5, verses 18-19.

*I am the Alpha and Omega, the Beginning and the End, the First and the Last. Blessed are they that do His Commandments, that they may have right to the tree of life, and may enter in through the gates into the city. For without are dogs, and sorcerers, and whoremongers, and murderers, and idolaters, and whosoever loveth and maketh a lie. Revelation, Chapter 22, verses 13-15.

....

> *He that saith he is in the Light, and hateth his brother, is in darkness even until now. He that loveth his brother abideth in the Light, and there is none occasion of stumbling in him. But he that hateth his brother is in darkness, and walketh in darkness, and knoweth not whither he goeth, because that darkness hath blinded his eyes. 1 John, Chapter 2, verses 9-11.*

We can go through all the motions of being good Christians, but if we hate another human being, we aren't walking in the Light of God. It doesn't matter if our hate is directed to a relative or somebody with skin, beliefs or lifestyles that are different than ours.

Hate takes up too much space in our hearts and squeezes God out. In order to allow God to totally Light up our lives, we have to let go of our hatred and biases. I know that isn't always as easy as it sounds. If we turn to God with this, He will truly take care of it, if we ask Him to.

Here are some related passages:

> **Beloved, if God so loved us, we ought also to love one another. 1 John, Chapter 4, verse 11.*

> **No man hath seen God at anytime. If we love one another, God dwelleth in us, and His love is perfected in us. Hereby know we that we dwell in Him, and He in us, because He hath given us of His Spirit. And we have seen and do testify that the Father sent the Son to be the Savior of the world. Whosoever shall confess that Jesus is the Son of God, God dwelleth in him, and he in God. And we have known and believed the love that God hath to us. God is love; and he that dwelleth in love dwelleth in God, and God in him. 1 John, Chapter 4, verses 12-16.*

> **We love Him, because He first loved us. If a man say, I love God, and hateth his brother, he is a liar: for he that loveth not his brother whom he hath seen, how can he love God Whom he hath not seen? And this Commandment have we from Him, That he who loveth God love his brother also. 1 John, Chapter 4, verses 19-21.*

....

> *BEHOLD, WHAT manner of love the Father hath bestowed upon us, that we should be called the sons of God: therefore the world knoweth us not, because it knew Him not. Beloved, now are we the sons of God, and it doth not yet appear*

what we shall be: but we know that, when He shall appear, we shall be like Him: for we shall see Him as He is. And every man that hath this hope in Him purifieth himself, even as He is pure. 1 John, Chapter 3, verses 1-3.

    Christians can't expect this big pat on their back and an "Atta Boy" from society for all their dedication to their faith. The majority of society is too busy living worldly lives to focus on acknowledging people who make sacrifices because of their commitment to God. They wouldn't understand what is involved because they don't know God in their lives. Their worldly choices cloud the Light that God provides to lead them to Salvation.

....

Marvel not, my brethren, if the world hate you. We know that we have passed from death unto life, because we love the brethren. He that loveth not his brother abideth in death. Whosoever hateth his brother is a murderer: and ye know that no murderer hath eternal life abiding in him. Hereby perceive we the love of God, because He laid down His life for us: and we ought to lay down our lives for the brethren. 1 John, Chapter 3, verses 13-16.

    I have spent most of my life trying to be a good person and I got a certain amount of attention from others for the "Good Dorothy's". I hope God has helped me grow beyond needing that type of attention and approval from others.

    I still find that I'm hurt when someone doesn't really care for me, because of who I am, my beliefs or what I represent. I have to remember that not everyone in the world is going to like Christians and it's okay.

    It would be easy to respond to these people that don't care for us through retaliation or resentment, but God wants us to love everyone, not just the ones that are nice to us.

....

My little children, let us not love in word, neither in tongue; but in deed and in Truth. And hereby we know that we are of the Truth, and shall assure our hearts before Him. For if our heart condemn us, God is greater than our heart, and knoweth all things. Beloved, if our heart condemn us not, then have we confidence toward God. And whatsoever we ask, we receive of Him, because we keep His Commandments, and do those things that are pleasing in His sight. 1 John, Chapter 3, verses 18-22.

We could go around bragging about all our Christian deeds, but God knows what's in our hearts. He knows if we harbor resentments or biases toward others. He knows if we are hateful and rude to our family members and people who are different than we are.

He knows if we give to others through our actions and our finances with a willing heart. (Although I have tried to help others, I have often been guilty of being resentful for the amount of time or money I have given. Fortunately, God has taken the time to show me this. I do know that He would much rather that I do these things for Him with a willing heart.)

God can see what really is in our hearts and minds, although we can disguise it from others. We need to truly believe in God and not just in outward ways. We are to love Him with our whole heart and He will be there to answer our prayers and to take care of our every need. (Of course, getting the high-level position you want at work may not fall into the category of basic needs. God, alone, knows what is best for us.)

....

For many deceivers are entered into the world, who confess not that Jesus Christ is come in the flesh. This is a deceiver and an antichrist. 2 John, Chapter 1, verse 7.

This was an interesting passage for me because I have heard people talk over the years of the antichrist. I think their comments were always directed to the reference of the antichrist in Revelation. This passage makes me aware that the antichrist isn't just one particular person. It's anyone who deceives people and leads them astray from God.

Here are some related passages:

*For false Christs and false prophets shall rise, and shall show signs and wonders, to seduce, if it were possible, even the elect. But take ye heed: behold I have foretold you all things. Mark, Chapter 13, verses 22-23.

*Beloved, believe not every spirit, but try the spirits whether they are of God: because many false prophets are gone out into the world. Hereby know ye the Spirit of God: Every Spirit that confesseth that Jesus Christ is come in the flesh is of God: And every spirit that confesseth not that Jesus Christ is come in the flesh is not of God: and this is that spirit of antichrist, whereof ye have heard that it should come; and even now already is in the world. 1 John, Chapter 4, verses 1-3.

For there shall arise false Christs, and false prophets, and shall show great signs and wonders; insomuch that, if it were possible, they shall deceive the very elect. Behold, I have told you before. Wherefore if they shall say unto you, Behold, He is in the desert; go not forth: behold, He is in the secret chambers; believe it not. For as the lightning cometh out of the east, and shineth even unto the west; so shall also the coming of the Son of Man be. Matthew, Chapter 24, 24-27.

....

Whosoever transgresseth, and abideth not in the doctrine of Christ, hath not God. He that abideth in the doctrine of Christ, he hath both the Father and the Son. If there come any unto you, and bring not this doctrine, receive him not into your house, neither bid him God speed: For he that biddeth him God speed is a partaker of his evil deeds. 2 John, Chapter 1, verses 9-11.

There are groups that say "Your higher power as you understand him,"or, " god as you understand him." At first, I thought this was a polite way of acknowledging people's different beliefs. Then, as I read the Bible more, I realized that every time I said this, I was condoning the other people's concept of god as being God, but that wasn't right. The Bible lets me know that I'm not supposed to condone any other concept of god. There is only One True God. Facsimiles just won't work! (That doesn't mean that I'm supposed to be rude or judgmental of people who believe differently than I do.) It does mean that I shouldn't give credit to their version of god as being The One True God.

Here are some related passages:

*And in all things that I have said unto you be circumspect: and make no mention of the name of other gods, neither let it be heard out of thy mouth. Exodus, Chapter 23, verse 13.

*Before the mountains were brought forth, or ever Thou hadst formed the earth and the world, even from everlasting to everlasting, Thou art God. Psalm, Chapter 90, verse 2.

*Unto thee it was shown that thou mightest know that the LORD He is God, there is none else beside Him. Deuteronomy, Chapter 4, verse 35.

*For all the gods of the nations are idols: but the LORD made the heavens. Psalm, Chapter 96, verse 5.

*I am the LORD: that is My Name: and My glory will I not give to another, neither My praise to graven images. Isaiah, Chapter 42, verse 8.

*Thus saith the LORD the King of Israel, and his Redeemer the LORD of Hosts; I am the First, and I am the Last; and beside Me there is no God. Isaiah, Chapter 44, verse 6.

*Fear ye not, neither be afraid: have not I told thee from that time, and have declared it? ye are even My witnesses. Is there a God beside Me? yea, there is no God; I know not any. Isaiah, Chapter 44, verse 8.

*Thus saith the LORD, thy Redeemer, and He that formed thee from the womb, I am the LORD that maketh all things; that stretcheth forth the heavens alone; that spreadeth abroad the earth by Myself. Isaiah, Chapter 44, verse 24.

*I am the LORD, and there is none else, there is no God beside Me: I girded thee, though thou hast not known Me: that they may know from the rising of the sun and from the west, that there is none beside Me. I am the LORD, and there is none else. Isaiah, Chapter 45, verses 5-6.

*For thus saith the LORD that created the heavens; God Himself that formed the earth and made it; He hath established it, He created it not in vain, He formed it to be inhabited: I am the LORD; and there is none else. I have not spoken in secret, in a dark place of the earth: I said not unto the seed of Jacob, Seek ye Me in vain: I the LORD speak righteousness, I declare things that are right. Isaiah, Chapter 45, verses 18-19.

*Remember the former things of old: for I am God, and there is none else: I am God, and there is none like Me. Isaiah, Chapter 46, verse 9.

*Hearken unto Me, O Jacob and Israel, My called; I am He; I am the First, I also am the Last. Mine hand also hath laid the foundation of the earth, and My right hand hath spanned the heavens: when I call upon them, they stand up together. Isaiah, Chapter 48, verses 12-13.

*What profiteth the graven image that the maker thereof hath graven it; the molten image, and a teacher of lies, that the maker of his work trusteth therein, to make dumb idols? Woe unto him that saith to the wood, Awake; to the dumb stone, Arise, it shall teach! Behold, it is laid over with gold and silver,

and there is no breath at all in the midst of it. But the Lord is in His holy temple: let all the earth keep silence before Him. Habakkuk, Chapter 2, verses 18-20.

*There is one body, and one Spirit, even as ye are called in one hope of your calling; One Lord, one faith, one baptism, One God and Father of all, Who is above all, and through all, and in you all. Ephesians, Chapter 4, verses 4-6.

You wouldn't think God should have to repeat it over and over throughout the Bible, but people are weak. They get distracted and become vulnerable to other people and other religious groups and cultures. Since He knows we are very forgetful, He keeps reminding us that He and He alone is the only God as you can see through all of these Bible passages.

. . . .

And one of the elders answered, saying unto me, What are these which are arrayed in white robes? And whence came they? And I said unto him, Sir, thou knowest. And he said to me, These are they which came out of great tribulation, and have washed their robes, and made them white in the Blood of the Lamb. Therefore are they before the throne of God, and serve Him day and night in His temple: and He that sitteth on the throne shall dwell among them. They shall hunger no more, neither thirst any more; neither shall the sun light on them, nor any heat. For the Lamb which is in the midst of the throne shall feed them, and shall lead them unto living fountains of waters: and God shall wipe away all tears from their eyes. Revelation, Chapter 7, verses 13-17.

I'm not totally sure of the exact meaning of this passage, but I still like it because it's comforting. I feel that when we're in heaven with Jesus, we won't have any more stress and tribulation, because He will take care of our every need.

. . . .

And he exerciseth all the power of the first beast before him, and causeth the earth and them which dwell therein to worship the first beast whose deadly wound was healed. And he doeth great wonders, so that he maketh fire to come down from heaven on the earth in the sight of men, And deceiveth them that dwell on the earth by the means of those miracles which he had power to do in the sight of the beast; saying to them that dwell on the earth, that they should make an image to the beast, which had the wound by a sword and did live. And he had power to give life unto the image of the beast, that the image of the beast should both speak, and cause that as many as would not worship the image of the beast should be killed. Revelation, Chapter 13, verses 12-15.

Of course I don't truly understand all of this, but this passage makes me think of horses that lead carriages. They put blinders on the horses so that they don't get distracted and lose their focus and literally get led astray. I think, as Christians, we need to have the blinders on that only Jesus can provide for us. Then we won't be led astray by people appearing to do miraculous things, by cults and other things that could potentially lead us off course.

....

And he causeth all, both small and great, rich and poor, free and bond, to receive a mark in their right hand or in their foreheads: And that no man might buy or sell, save he that had the mark, or the name of the beast, or the number of his name. Here is wisdom. Let him that hath understanding count the number of the beast: for it is the number of a man; and his number is Six hundred threescore and six. Revelation, Chapter 13, verses 16-18.

And the smoke of their torment ascendeth up for ever and ever: and they have no rest day nor night who worship the beast and his image, and whosoever receiveth the mark of his name. Revelation, Chapter 14, verse 11.

You don't have to truly understand things to be careful. I don't truly understand why I shouldn't microwave food in plastic bowls, but credible people have said that this can be harmful, so I just don't do it!

I can't attest to understanding all of Revelation or Daniel, Chapter 10 through Chapter 12, but I do know enough to be careful when I see a warning. It talks about people losing their Salvation by getting the mark of the beast in either their right hand or their forehead. People won't able to buy or sell things unless they get this mark. Every now and then I get concerned when I hear about discussions within the government to take security precautions that might be similar to the mark of the beast.

It's very commonplace for people to use credit cards to purchase things in stores or over the Internet. The papers and magazines are riddled with columns about rampant identity theft, not to mention hackers who are

Bible Passages That Can Influence Your Life

hacking into computer systems to get vital information. I'm concerned that they will institute security measures that are similar to the mark of the beast, whether it's a number, a computer chip or something else to protect people from identity theft.

What worries me even more, is that I think people will be so excited about having this extra security that protects them, they won't even realize that they are getting the mark of the beast and are losing their Salvation in the process. We are warned to have wisdom. Be cautious about what you do and trust the instincts that God gives you. He will guide you by these.

....

Now, I will include the passages from the Old Testament that have positively influenced my Life. It's not written this way deliberately. I just started writing *Bible Passages That Can Influence Your Life* where I was reading in the Bible at the time. I had just started to read Matthew.

....

And Jacob sod pottage [made something like lentil stew]: and Esau came from the field, and he was faint: And Esau said to Jacob, Feed me, I pray thee, with that same red pottage; for I am faint: therefore was his name called Edom. And Jacob said, Sell me this day thy birthright. And Esau said, Behold, I am at the point to die: and what profit shall this birthright do me? And Jacob said, Swear to me this day; and he sware unto him: and he sold his birthright unto Jacob. Then Jacob gave Esau bread and pottage of lentils; and he did eat and drink, and rose up, and went his way: thus Esau despised his birthright. Genesis, Chapter 25, verses 29-34.

Unfortunately, I can identify with Esau. I've been a "Sell-out Christian," selling out my ethics more times than I can mention for food. Food and control are my two biggest vices. Satan loves to dangle very subtle things in front of us to pull us into his control.

It's so easy to sell out our Christian ethics without even realizing it. It might be by things like spending too much time on the computer that our family goes without our presence. The computer temporarily becomes a priority over our family. It might be by telling only partial truths. Of course, we always tell ourselves that we are doing it to protect others. Do we come up with reasons why we don't have time to pray, but spend hours in front of the TV?

There are lots of subtle ways we sell out our Christian ethics without ever noticing. Esau lived to regret selling his birthright. I don't want to live to regret selling out my Christian ethics either. I don't want God telling me on the Last Day, "Dorothy, I have other accommodations waiting for you, because you don't deserve a spot in heaven. You were too busy doing your own thing to be bothered with leading your life as an example of your love for Me."

....

And six years thou shalt sow thy land, and shalt gather in the fruits thereof: But the seventh year thou shalt let it rest and lie still; that the poor of thy people may eat: and what they leave the beasts of the field shall eat. In like manner thou shalt deal with thy vineyard, and with thy oliveyard. Exodus, Chapter 23, verses 10-11.

I know there is a lot of talk about Welfare Reform. I, too, want us empowering people instead of enabling them, destroying their work ethic. We have to be prayerful about what we choose to do with this system. This passage says that God wants us to provide for the poor. You're right; most of us don't have fields or vineyards to leave fallow the seventh year so they're available to the less fortunate. Instead, we provide for the less fortunate through our taxes, giving to related charities and making donations to causes. We also provide for the needy by giving at church and through legislation to fund these causes. We need to be careful about how we change this system. It's vital that we continue to provide adequate food and medical care for those less fortunate, especially children.

That doesn't mean giving monthly disability payments to people with learning disabilities or drug and alcohol addictions. In this case, we may be enabling people because they aren't motivated to become literate or substance free for fear of losing that income. Yes, we do need to change things so some people don't have multiple fictitious addresses to rake in the Welfare checks. The Welfare Reform needs to allow the Welfare recipient to make the necessary changes with dignity.

Although there are issues to be resolved within the Welfare System, we can't lose sight of what God has told us to do. It would be very easy to "throw the baby out with the bath water" while making the necessary changes to the Welfare System. We need to continue to provide food, medical attention and other needed services for those less fortunate, because that's what God would want us to do.

Here are some related passages:

*And when ye reap the harvest of your land, thou shalt not make clean riddance of the corners of thy field when thou reapest, neither shalt thou gather any gleaning of thy harvest: thou shalt leave them unto the poor, and to the stranger: I am the LORD your God. Leviticus, Chapter 23, verse 22.

*For the LORD your God is God of gods, and Lord of lords, a great God, a mighty, and a terrible, which regardeth not persons, nor taketh reward. He doth execute the judgment of the fatherless and widow, and loveth the stranger, in giving him food and raiment. Love ye therefore the stranger: for ye were strangers in the land of Egypt. Deuteronomy, Chapter 10, verses 17-19.

*If there be among you a poor man of one of thy brethren within any of thy gates in thy land which the LORD thy God giveth thee, thou shalt not harden thine heart, nor shut thine hand from thy poor brother: But thou shalt open thine hand wide unto him, and shalt surely lend him sufficient for his need, in that which he wanteth. Deuteronomy, Chapter 15, verses 7-8.

*When thou cuttest down thine harvest in thy field, and hast forgot a sheaf in the field, thou shalt not go again to fetch it: it shall be for the stranger, for the fatherless, and for the widow: that the LORD thy God may bless thee in all the work of thine hands. When thou beatest thine olive tree, thou shalt not go over the boughs again: it shall be for the stranger, for the fatherless, and for the widow. When thou gatherest the grapes of thy vineyard, thou shalt not glean it afterward: it shall be for the stranger, for the fatherless, and for the widow. And thou shalt remember that thou wast a bondman in the land of Egypt: therefore I command thee to do this thing. Deuteronomy, Chapter 24, verses 19-22.

*For the needy shall not always be forgotten: the expectation of the poor shall not perish for ever. Psalm, Chapter 9, verse 18.

*Blessed is he that considereth the poor: the LORD will deliver him in time of trouble. The LORD will preserve him, and keep him alive; and he shall be blessed upon the earth: and Thou wilt not deliver him unto the will of his enemies. Psalm, Chapter 41, verses 1-2.

> *The poor is hated even of his own neighbour: but the rich hath many friends. He that despiseth his neighbour sinneth: but he that hath mercy on the poor, happy is he. Proverbs, Chapter 14, verses 20-21.

> *When the poor and needy seek water, and there is none, and their tongue faileth for thirst, I the LORD will hear them, I the God of Israel will not forsake them. Isaiah, Chapter 41, verse 17.

....

> It shall be a perpetual statute for your generations throughout all your dwellings, that ye eat neither fat nor blood. Leviticus, Chapter 3, verse 17.

I just thought this was interesting. I never liked eating fat to start with, but this makes me glad that I don't eat it. I thought that the part about not eating meat with the blood in it had more to do with God protecting us from health problems that could arise from the blood. I recently heard a minister say that Christians weren't to eat meat with the blood in it, because the blood is the life of the animal and it was used in the sacrifices. There is a passage below that explains this more. I don't really know much about all of this. I just know that if God tells me not to eat fat or meat with the blood in it, then I don't want to do it. I don't have to know all the reasons why.

It's kind of like when we tell our children that they shouldn't drink and drive. We don't want them to challenge our authority and try to find out first hand about all the consequences that could possibly come from drinking and driving. It's not an issue about whether we trust that they know when to stop drinking prior to driving. It's not an issue of whether we think they are safe drivers. (That doesn't mean that we shouldn't try to explain some of these consequences to our children.) What we really want them to do is trust our judgment about this situation and just not drink and drive. Well, I think God wants us to follow certain things just because He has asked us to. I think that is a sign of our faith in Him.

Here are some related passages:

> *Moreover ye shall eat no manner of blood, whether it be of fowl or of beast, in any of your dwellings. Whatsoever soul it be that eateth any manner of blood, even that soul shall be cut off from his people. Leviticus, Chapter 7, verses 26-27.

And whatsoever man there be of the house of Israel, or of the strangers that sojourn among you, that eateth any manner of blood; I will even set My face against that soul that eateth blood, and will cut him off from among his people. For the life of the flesh is in the blood: and I have given it to you upon the altar to make an atonement for your souls: for it is the blood that maketh an atonement for the soul. Therefore I said unto the children of Israel, No soul of you shall eat blood, neither shall any stranger that sojourneth among you eat blood. And whatsoever man there be of the children of Israel, or of the strangers that sojourn among you, which hunteth and catcheth any beast or fowl that may be eaten; he shall even pour out the blood thereof, and cover it with dust. For it is the life of all flesh; the blood of it is for the life thereof: therefore I said unto the children of Israel, Ye shall eat the blood of no manner of flesh: for the life of all flesh is the blood thereof: whosoever eateth it shall be cut off. Leviticus, Chapter 17, verses 10-14.

And they smote the Philistines that day from Michmash to Aijalon: and the people were very faint. And the people flew upon the spoil, and took sheep, and oxen, and calves, and slew them on the ground: and the people did eat them with the blood. Then they told Saul, saying, Behold the people sin against the LORD, in that they eat with the blood. And he said, Ye have transgressed: roll a great stone unto me this day. 1 Samuel, Chapter 14, verses 31-33.

....

Thou shalt not hate thy brother in thine heart: thou shalt in any wise rebuke thy neighbour, and not suffer sin upon him. Thou shalt not avenge, nor bear any grudge against the children of thy people, but thou shalt love thy neighbour as thyself: I am the LORD. Leviticus, Chapter 19, verses 17-18.

This is one of many passages where God tells us that we are to love each other. He <u>doesn't</u> put a stipulation in there that says, "You are to love each other ONLY IF: they have the right skin color, they have the same sexual preference, they come from the right side-of-the tracks or they have similar beliefs and goals. We are to be Christians and love everyone!

There are people that don't believe in God. Although, I don't have to support their beliefs because there is only One God, I'm to love them, to be considerate of them and to not hold grudges against them because their beliefs are different than mine. If I'm resenting them or treat them in a less than kind manner, I'm the one who isn't being a good example of how Christ works in my life.

....

Ye shall not eat any thing with the blood: neither shall ye use enchantment, nor observe times. Leviticus, Chapter 19, verse 26.

In addition to the part about not eating things with the blood in it, God is also letting us know that He doesn't want us using enchantments (casting spells-things like witchcraft) or observing time (like horoscopes, etc.). I get concerned when I see how many weekly television series and movies are devoted to witchcraft or Satanic themes. It concerns me that this may become so commonplace that people think nothing of it-the same way that using God's Name in vain has become so common that people don't even realize they are doing it.

....

Ye shall not make any cuttings in your flesh for the dead, nor print any marks upon you: I am the LORD. Leviticus, Chapter 19, verse 28.

I'm not sure I totally understand this verse, but I thought it was noteworthy because I think it's possibly talking about tattoos and things like body piercing, although I'm not totally positive.

....

Regard not them that have familiar spirits, neither seek after wizards, to be defiled by them: I am the LORD your God. Leviticus, Chapter 19, verse 31.

This tells me that God doesn't want me watching TV shows where people are trying to get in contact with my deceased loved ones. He, also, doesn't want me reading books about wizards and sorcery even though there are many books written for children these days that are very popular with adults, as well.

Here are some related passages:

*And the soul that turneth after such as have familiar spirits, and after wizards, to go a-whoring after them, I will even set My face against that soul, and will cut him off from among his people. Sanctify yourselves therefore, and be ye holy: for I am the LORD your God. And ye shall keep My Statutes, and do them: I am the LORD which sanctify you. Leviticus, Chapter 20, verses 6-8.

A man also or woman that hath a familiar spirit, or that is a wizard, shall surely be put to death: they shall stone them with stones: their blood shall be upon them. Leviticus, Chapter 20, verse 27.

....

Therefore shall ye observe all My Statutes, and all My judgments, and do them: I am the LORD. Leviticus, Chapter 19, verse 37.

God didn't say to follow the rules that sound good to us or are convenient for us and leave the rest. We are to observe them all!

Here are some related passages:

*Know therefore that the LORD thy God, He is God, the faithful God, which keepeth covenant and mercy with them that love Him and keep His Commandments to a thousand generations. And repayeth them that hate Him to their face, to destroy them: He will not be slack to him that hateth Him, He will repay him to his face. Thou shalt therefore keep the Commandments, and the Statutes, and the judgments, which I command thee this day, to do them. Wherefore it shall come to pass, if ye hearken to these judgments, and keep, and do them, that the LORD thy God shall keep unto thee the covenant and the mercy which He sware unto thy fathers. Deuteronomy, Chapter 7, verses 9-12.

*But if ye will not obey the Voice of the LORD, but rebel against the Commandment of the LORD, then shall the hand of the LORD be against you, as it was against your fathers. 1 Samuel, Chapter 12, verse 15.

*The LORD trieth the righteous: but the wicked and him that loveth violence His soul hateth. Upon the wicked He shall rain snares, fire and brimstone, and an horrible tempest: this shall be the portion of their cup. For the righteous LORD loveth righteousness; His countenance doth behold the upright. Psalm, Chapter 11, verses 5-7.

*The FOOL hath said in his heart, There is no God. Corrupt are they, and have done abominable iniquity: there is none that doeth good. God looked down from heaven upon the children of men, to see if there were any that did understand, that did seek God. Every one of them is gone: they are altogether become filthy; there is none that doeth good, no, not one. Psalm, Chapter 53, verses 1-3.

> *Evil pursueth sinner: but to the righteous good shall be repaid. Proverbs, Chapter 13, verse 21.
>
> *A prudent man foreseeth the evil, and hideth himself; but the simple pass on, and are punished. Proverbs, Chapter 27, verse 12.

....

> If a man vow a vow unto the LORD, or swear an oath to bind his soul with a bond; he shall not break his word, he shall do according to all that proceedeth out of his mouth. Numbers, Chapter 30, verse 2.

After reading this, it became very apparent to me that God really wants us to take our vows seriously and to actually do what we say we are going to do. We aren't to say things in a stressful situation like, "God, if you just get me through this IRS audit, I promise I will give money to the poor." When the audit is over, the person is relieved and forgets all about the vow they made. We don't have to make promises to God when we pray, but if we do, we are to make sure that we take our vows seriously.

Here is a related passage:

> *When thou vowest a vow unto God, defer not to pay it; for He hath no pleasure in fools: pay that which thou hast vowed. Better is it that thou shouldest not vow, than that thou shouldest vow and not pay. Ecclesiastes, Chapter 5, verses 4-5.

....

> And the LORD shall scatter you among the nations, and ye shall be left few in number among the heathen, whither the LORD shall lead you. And there ye shall serve gods, the work of men's hands, wood and stone, which neither see, nor hear, nor eat, nor smell. But if from thence thou shalt seek the LORD thy God, thou shalt find Him. If thou seek Him with all thy heart and with all thy soul. When thou art in tribulation, and all these things are come upon thee, even in the latter days, if thou turn to the LORD thy God, and shalt be obedient unto His Voice: (For the LORD thy God is a merciful God;) He will not forsake thee, neither destroy thee, nor forget the covenant of thy fathers which He sware unto them. Deuteronomy, Chapter 4, verses 27-31.

I love reading passages like this. God tells us how angry He is when we turn away from Him, but He also loves us and is willing to forgive us if we turn back to Him. I think it's appropriate that we call Him, God the Father, because He loves us as a parent would, only in a much more pure and consistent way.

When we were kids and ran through the house, knocking over a lamp and breaking it, our parents were unhappy. We might have had a consequence for not following the rules, but our parents still loved us. That was even more evident after we came to them to apologize for breaking the rules.

God is always willing to take us back and forgive us no matter how many times we missed church, used His Name in vain or acted in unchristian ways. If we truly turn to Him, God is always there to forgive us and accept us, but we need to be committed enough to try to be examples of how He works in our lives.

Here are some related passages:

Go and proclaim these Words toward the north, and say, Return, thou backsliding Israel, saith the LORD; and I will not cause Mine anger to fall upon you: for I am merciful, saith the LORD, and I will not keep anger for ever. Only acknowledge thine iniquity, that thou hast transgressed against the LORD thy God, and hast scattered thy ways to the strangers under every green tree, and ye have not obeyed My Voice, saith the LORD. Jeremiah, Chapter 3, verses 12-13.

If so be they will hearken, and turn every man from his evil way, that I may repent Me of the evil, which I purpose to do unto them because of the evil of their doings. Jeremiah, Chapter 26, verse 3.

Wherewith shall I come before the Lord, and bow myself before the high God? shall I come before Him with burnt offerings, with calves of a year old? Will the Lord be pleased with thousands of rams, or with ten thousands of rivers of oil? shall I give my firstborn for my transgression, the first of my body for the sin of my soul? He hath shown thee, O man, what is good; and what doth the Lord require of thee, but to do justly, and to love mercy, and to walk humbly with thy God? Micah, Chapter 6, verses 6-8.

....

Hear, O Israel: The LORD our God is one LORD: And thou shalt love the LORD thy God with all thine heart, and with all thy soul, and with all thy might. And these Words, which I command thee this day, shall be in thy heart: And thou

> *shalt teach them diligently unto thy children, and shalt talk of them when thou sittest in thine house, and when thou walkest by the way, and when thou liest down, and when thou risest up. Deuteronomy, Chapter 6, verses 4-7.*

God wants us not only to love Him with all our heart, all our soul and all our might; but He wants us to raise our children with this same love of Him. I have heard all too many people say that they aren't raising their children with any religious education because they are letting their children decide for themselves when they're older.

Since I'm an educator, I'm in the position of hearing lots of conversations about what is happening to the youth of today and concerns for their well-being. If the parents don't set the foundation for their child's religious beliefs when they are young, how will the child learn to turn to God when they are faced with issues like drinking, smoking, drugs, sexual involvement, etc?

Children learn by their parent's example and those around them. If they don't see the people around them making God a priority in their lives, then the example they follow may be of peers who say that doing a little "Meth," "Ecstasy" or other drug will help them unwind and get more in touch with themselves. I've watched all too many talk shows where parents are tearfully expressing their regrets about their child who was lost to an overdose.

Maybe we are doing a huge disservice to our children by waiting until they are old enough to make their own choices about God. Maybe we need to take an active role in our children's religious education now!

Here is a related passage:

> **Therefore shall ye lay up these My Words in your heart and in your soul, and bind them for a sign upon your hand, that they may be as frontlets between your eyes. And ye shall teach them your children, speaking of them when thou sittest in thine house, and when thou walkest by the way, when thou liest down, and when thou risest up. Deuteronomy, Chapter 11, verses 18-19.*

. . . .

> *And it shall be, when the LORD thy God shall have brought thee into the land which He sware unto thy fathers, to Abraham, to Isaac, and to Jacob, to give thee great and goodly cities, which thou buildest not, And houses full of all good things, which thou filledst not, and wells digged, which thou diggedst not, vineyards and olive trees, which thou plantest not; when*

thou shalt have eaten and be full; Then beware lest thou forget the LORD which brought thee forth out of the land of Egypt, from the house of bondage. Deuteronomy, Chapter 6, verses 10-12.

We may read this Bible passage and think it really doesn't apply to us and our daily lives, but that's incorrect. How many times do we turn to God when things are going badly in our lives, our jobs or when a loved one is very ill? We ask God to take care of these desperate situations and He does so in the way that He determines is best. When things are resolved, do we spend the same amount of time focusing on God, or do we leave Him in the background until the next traumatic situation arises? Something to think about.

....

And He humbled thee, and suffered thee to hunger, and fed thee with manna, which thou knewest not, neither did thy fathers know; that He might make thee know that man doth not live by bread only, but by every Word that proceedeth out of the mouth of the LORD doth man live. Thy raiment waxed not old upon thee, neither did thy foot swell, these forty years. Deuteronomy, Chapter 8, verses 3-4.

Can you imagine how the Israelites could have walked and lived in the wilderness for forty years and their clothes and shoes never wore out? It's so awe inspiring when I think of how God took care of their every need, like manna from the sky-because they wanted bread and flocks of quail-when they wanted meat. He took care of all their basic needs, despite the fact that they turned away from Him many times in the forty years that they were in the wilderness.

God never stopped loving them, the same way that God is never going to stop loving us, even when we do some really sinful things. God knows what's in our hearts and will forgive us our sins if we have a penitent spirit and try to make the necessary changes that reflect our love of Jesus..

Here is a related passage:

*And I have led you forty years in the wilderness: your clothes aren't waxen old upon you, and thy shoe is not waxen old upon thy foot. Deuteronomy, Chapter 29, verse 5.

....

> *Then thine heart be lifted up, and thou forget the LORD thy God which brought thee forth out of the land of Egypt, from the house of bondage; Who led thee through that great terrible wilderness, wherein were fiery serpents, and scorpions, and drought, where there was no water; Who brought thee forth water out of the rock of flint; Who fed thee in the wilderness with manna, which thy fathers knew not, that He might humble thee, and that He might prove thee, to do thee good at thy latter end; And thou say in thine heart, my power and the might of mine hand hath gotten me this wealth. But thou shalt remember the LORD thy God: for it is He that giveth thee power to get wealth, that He may establish His covenant which He sware unto thy fathers, as it is this day. And it shall be, if thou do at all forget the LORD thy God, and walk after other gods, and serve them, and worship them, I testify against you this day that ye shall surely perish. Deuteronomy, Chapter 8, verses 14-19.*

It's kind of like a high school student who buys a term paper from another student rather than doing their own assignment. They are tickled when the teacher hands back their paper and they have received an A. When the teacher refers to their paper as an example of exemplary work and dedication, they puff up with pride as if they had written the term paper themselves, but they hadn't.

God knew how human we were. He knew that the Israelites would see all the miracles that He had provided for them in the wilderness and the bounty He provided in the Promised Land. God knew that they would take credit for it, as if they had accomplished these on their own. He also knew that they would forget to thank Him and they would take credit for all their good fortune, and He was right.

Do we do this in our own lives? I have, more times than I care to mention. God has gotten me through many difficult situations and when they're over, I either forget about what God had done for me, or what is even worse, I take credit for them myself.

Some people make it hard to give God the credit. People have complimented me for particular ideas or actions. I tell them that God gave me the idea or God got me through the particular situation but they argue with me, telling me, "No, god helps him who helps himself." Well, you already know how I stand on that one!

We can easily fall into the trap of not appreciating all that God has done for us. God can lead us out this trap if we let Him, just like He led the Israelites to the Promised Land.

....

> *Judges and officers shalt thou make thee in all thy gates, which the LORD thy God giveth thee, throughout thy tribes: and they shall judge the people with just judgment. Thou shalt not wrest judgment; thou shalt not respect persons, neither take a gift: for a gift doth blind the eyes of the wise, and pervert the Words of the righteous. Deuteronomy, Chapter 16, verses 18-19.*

I wish all politicians and judges adhered to rules like these; not that there aren't some who do. It would make everything much easier if nothing interfered with the political decisions that are made.

I read a book written by someone who used to work in a prison. He talked about how some of the prisoners would deliberately make friends with the guards. Being a guard has to be a thankless job. I doubt if any of the prisoners say, "Thank you so much, Mr. Guard, for keeping me in here to protect society from me." Anyway, some prisoners manipulate guards by planning to have pleasant interactions with them, standing in distinct contrast to the negative ones they usually encounter.

They get to know the guards pretty well, playing on that particular guard's sympathy. When the timing is right, the prisoner asks the guard to send a birthday card to his ailing mother, which is against the prison rules. When the guard does this, there is some kind of rationalization that goes on for the guard to justify his actions to himself, since this is an unethical thing to do. Once this happens, the prisoner knows he's got the guard wrapped around his little finger. He knows that the guard is even more vulnerable to do other things for him in the future. (Remember I said, not all guards or prisoners do this, but it's an example of how little things can undermine the clear thinking of those in authority.)

Politicians and judges are just as human. So are teachers, for that matter. It's probably a lot harder for a teacher to flunk a child of a very involved parent who volunteers for room parties and lavishes the teacher with all types of gifts and compliments, on every occasion. I think that everyone in a position of power or judgment might become vulnerable when there are gifts or favors done. I think that God had the right idea when He said, "*For a gift doth blind the eyes of the wise, and pervert the words of the righteous.*" Definitely something to think about.

Here are some related passages:

> *A wicked man taketh a gift out of the bosom to pervert the ways of judgment. Proverbs, Chapter 17, verse 23.

> *Many will entreat the favour of the prince: and every man is a friend to him that giveth gifts. Proverbs, Chapter 19, verse 6.

....

> *Neither shalt thou set thee up any image: which the LORD thy God hateth. Deuteronomy, Chapter 16, verse 22.*

I trust God to guide me on this one. I do know from everything I have read that God wouldn't want me to have a statue of Buddha or a Greek or Roman god or goddess in my house, even if they are just for decorative purposes.

I don't feel He wants us to pray to any religious article thinking that article is God, Himself. I wear a cross around my neck but I don't pray to it. It just reminds me of what an important part Jesus plays in my everyday life. I have pictures of Jesus in my house. I get a pleasant feeling when I look at them, because they remind me of all Jesus has done for us. I don't pray to the picture or think the picture is Jesus.

You and God alone know whether you are being led astray by these objects or not. Let God be your guide on this one. He will give you good instincts, if you let Him.

....

> *If there be found among you, within any of thy gates which the LORD thy God giveth thee, man or woman, that hath wrought wickedness in the sight of the LORD thy God, in transgressing His covenant, And hath gone and served other gods, and worshipped them, either the sun, or moon, or any of the host of heaven, which I have not commanded; And it be told thee, and thou hast heard of it, and inquired diligently, and behold, it be true, and the thing certain, that such abomination is wrought in Israel: Then shalt thou bring forth that man or that woman, which have committed that wicked thing, unto thy gates, even that man or that woman, and shalt stone them with stones, till they die. Deuteronomy, Chapter 17, verses 2-5.*

This passage is important to me because it lets me know clearly that God doesn't like people being involved with horoscopes or other celestial things. It doesn't sound like God thinks, "I'm not going to get too upset by this. They just like to read their horoscope for fun, which really isn't the same thing." This passage talks about stoning people to death for doing this abomination. The sad thing is there are people who don't even realize that reading their horoscope or calling people to predict their future is directly opposed to their Christian faith.

You wouldn't believe the number of Christians who read their horoscope each day. Most people that I've talked to think that reading their horoscope is harmless, something they do as a joke. It's kind of scary to think how insidious a thing like reading a horoscope can be.

Sometimes people start reading it just for fun. Then it starts creeping into their mind. They think things like, "I probably shouldn't do this thing today because my horoscope said it isn't a good day to do things like this." Then they find themselves not doing things because they didn't read their horoscope that morning and they don't want to make any major decisions until they've read it. They probably don't even realize that they are being led astray by turning to something other than God for guidance. It's worth assessing the little things that we do that allow our focus to be pulled away from God.

Here are some related passages:

And he [Manasseh] did that which was evil in the sight of the LORD, after the abominations of the heathen, whom the LORD cast out before the children of Israel. For he built up again the high places which Hezekiah his father had destroyed; and he reared up altars for Baal, and made a grove, as did Ahab king of Israel; and worshipped all the host of heaven, and served them. 2 Kings, Chapter 21, verses 2-3.

And he put down the idolatrous priests, whom the kings of Judah had ordained to burn incense in the high places in the cities of Judah, and in the places round about Jerusalem; them also that burned incense unto Baal, to the sun, and to the moon, and to the planets, and to all the hosts of heaven. 2 Kings, Chapter 23, verse 5.

....

There shall not be found among you any one that maketh his son or his daughter to pass through the fire, or that useth divination, or an observer of times, or an enchanter, or a witch, Or a charmer, or a consulter with familiar spirits, or a wizard, or a necromancer, For all that do these things are an abomination unto the LORD: and because of these abominations the LORD thy God doth drive them out from before thee. Thou shalt be perfect with the LORD thy God. For these nations, which thou shalt possess, hearkened unto observers of times, and unto diviners: but as for thee, the LORD thy God hath not suffered thee so to do. Deuteronomy, Chapter 18, verses 10-14.

This doesn't lead me to feel that God would approve of watching a "cute" show about a teenage witch. I have noticed that there are more and more TV shows and movies with witchcraft and Satanic themes, lately. There is even a show where someone is trying to contact the dead, which is what a necromancer is, and God considers this an abomination. When we are watching these things on TV or at the movies, we aren't focusing on God. In fact, we are focusing on something that might pull us away from our relationship with God.

Watching these "cute" shows on witchcraft or Satanism may have the potential of making our society more vulnerable to cults. When I was younger, although it probably existed, I never heard of people actually believing in witchcraft or Satanism. It seems like I heard much more about cults after the popular TV show based on a witch that made it look fun to cast spells and have magical things happen. (I can't say that the increase in the popularity of cults is directly related to this TV show but it did, in my opinion, make witchcraft look like a "fun" thing.)

My children used to get frustrated when I asked them not to watch the re-runs of this show, but I would much rather that they be frustrated with me than to be vulnerable to being led astray. Sometimes as parents, we just have to take a stand because we love our children!

Here are some related passages:

And he made his son pass through the fire, and observed times, and used enchantments, and dealt with familiar spirits and wizards: he wrought much wickedness in the sight of the LORD, to provoke Him to anger. 2 Kings, Chapter 21, verse 6.

Moreover the workers with familiar spirits, and the wizards, and the images, and the idols, and all the abominations that were spied in the land of Judah and in Jerusalem, did Josiah put away, that he might perform the Words of the Law which were written in the book that Hilkiah the priest found in the house of the LORD. 2 Kings, Chapter 23, verse 24.

And he [Manasseh] caused his children to pass through the fire in the valley of the son of Hinnom: also he observed times, used enchantments, and used witchcraft, and dealt with a familiar spirit, and with wizards: he wrought much evil in the sight of the LORD, to provoke Him to anger. 2 Chronicles, Chapter 33, verse 6.

And I will cut off witchcrafts out of thine hand; and thou shalt have no more soothsayers. Micah, Chapter 5, verse 12.

> *But the prophet, which shall presume to speak a word in My Name, which I have not commanded him to speak, or that shall speak in the name of other gods, even that prophet shall die. Deuteronomy, Chapter 18, verse 20.*

This passage reminds us to be cautious about the religious advice we listen to. There are many different people out there who say that they know God's Will for us, but these people tell us totally opposite things. Obviously, everyone who says that they know God's Will for us; can't ALL be right. This dilemma confused me for years. I started reading the Bible in 1980, to find out for myself what God's Will was. That way, I could trust the instincts that God gave me as I read the Bible. This is much better than listening to other people's opinions in order to figure out who is right and who is wrong.

....

> *If a man have a stubborn and rebellious son, which will not obey the voice of his father, or the voice of his mother, and that, when they have chastened him, will not hearken unto them: Then shall his father and his mother lay hold on him, and bring him out unto the elders of his city, and unto the gate of his place; and they shall say unto the elders of his city, This our son is stubborn and rebellious, he will not obey our voice; he is a glutton, and a drunkard. And all the men of his city shall stone him with stones, that he die: so shalt thou put evil away from among you; and all Israel shall hear, and fear. Deuteronomy, Chapter 21, verses 18-21.*

I don't want people to get the wrong impression of God because He is both loving and forgiving. I think that God is referring to extreme situations that are similar today. Situations where someone's grown children are addicted to drugs or alcohol and they don't work and are defiant. Some make choices that threaten the lives of others. Some beat their parents, some steal and some abuse or neglect their own children.

I know it would be difficult for any parent to consider this extreme of a consequence-no matter how many faults their adult child had. This passage makes me think about how it would be so much easier for parents to address their children's behavior by setting limitations and having logical consequences while they are still young, so they never get to this point of unruliness.

It seems that some parents are lax about disciplining their children on a consistent basis. I always thought that it was better to make sure that my children grew up respecting laws and were a productive part of society than to have them thrown into prison for stealing to get their next fix. (In this example, the defiant, unproductive adult isn't stoned to death but is dealt with by society through the penal system.) Who wants that for their children?

I know it takes a lot more effort when parents are already tired after a long day at work. Parents may not want to deal with a child who argues with them when they follow through on consequences. Isn't it better to deal with that than to see your child have a miserable life later on, dealing with the law or maybe running from it? They are our children and they're worth the extra effort!!!!

Here are some related passages:

**For every one that curseth his father or his mother shall be surely put to death: he hath cursed his father or his mother: his blood shall be upon him. Leviticus, Chapter 20, verse 9.*

*A wise son maketh a glad father: but a foolish man despiseth his mother. Proverbs, Chapter 15, verse 20.

*But He answered and said unto them, Why do ye also transgress the Commandment of God by your tradition? For God commanded, saying, Honour thy father and mother: and He that curseth father or mother, let him die the death. Matthew, Chapter, 15, verses 3-4.

....

And the LORD said unto Gideon, The people that are with thee are too many for Me to give the Midianites into their hands, lest Israel vaunt themselves against Me, saying, mine own hand hath saved me. Judges, Chapter 7, verse 2.

This is an interesting passage when you know why God said this. Gideon was going to fight the Midianites for God. He called all his soldiers (the Israelites) and a large army gathered. God said, (paraphrased) "If I have the Israelites win the battle against the Midianites while you have lots of soldiers, you won't realize the victory is because I had you overpower them. Instead, the Israelites will think that they had won the battle because of their large army.

"I want you to weed out the majority of your soldiers so that there is only a small band of your soldiers left fighting against the Midianites. Then they will know that only I, the One True God, was in control of having your small band of men win the battle against the huge army of Midianites."

The small band of Israelites did overpower the huge army of Midianites. God staged all of this so that the Israelites would have conclusive proof that He is the One True God. (Feel free to read Judges, Chapters 7 and 8, to find out more about this.)

It wasn't the war part that impressed me so much. It was that God went to such great lengths to show the Israelites that He was looking after them. I think God does this in our everyday lives, as well. I don't think we always stop to realize that it's God taking care of us. I think we chalk it off to coincidence or have some other way of rationalizing it. I think God wants us to open our eyes and see how He works in our lives each and everyday. God isn't just some holy figure way off in heaven, but is intimately involved in every aspect of our lives.

....

And the angel of the LORD said unto Manoah, Of all that I said unto the woman let her beware. She may not eat of any thing that cometh of the vine, neither let her drink wine nor strong drink, nor eat any unclean thing: all that I commanded her let her observe. Judges, Chapter 13, verses 13-14.

The angel of the Lord tells Manoah and his wife this so that she knows that she is to follow these instructions while she is pregnant with Samson. I like this passage because it's like God is providing some obstetric guidance for Samson's mother so that he is born strong and healthy.

....

And when he [Samson] came unto Lehi, the Philistines shouted against him: and the Spirit of the LORD came mightily upon him, and the cords that were upon his arms became as flax that was burnt with fire, and his bands loosed from off his hands. And he found a new jawbone of an ass, and put forth his hand, and took it, and slew a thousand men. And Samson said, With the jawbone of an ass, heaps upon heaps, with the jaw of an ass have I slain a thousand men. And it came to pass, when he had made an end of speaking, that he cast away the jawbone out of his hand, and called that place Ramathlehi. And he was sore athirst, and called on the LORD, and said, Thou hast given this great deliverance into the hand of thy servant: and now shall I die for thirst, and fall into the hand of the uncircumcised? But God clave an hollow place that was in the jaw, and there came water thereout; and when he had drunk, his spirit came again, and he revived: wherefore he called the name thereof En-hakkore, which is in Lehi unto this day. And he judged Israel in the days of the Philistines twenty years. Judges, Chapter 15, verses 14-20.

This isn't the story we focused on in Sunday school about Samson and Delilah. This was before that time in Samson's life. I like this passage because it shows me how powerful God is. Samson was bound and the Philistines wanted to kill him. Sampson was tied up and God made the cords come off of Samson's arms easily, which is the first miracle in this passage. The next miracle is when God allowed Samson to kill a thousand Philistines all by himself with just the jawbone of an ass.

I've seen lots of war shows with one group fighting against the other. The whole screen is filled with people fighting and lots die. In this case, the movie screen would have been filled with a thousand people trying to kill Samson. Samson would be fighting them all by himself with only a jawbone of an ass, a skeleton he found there. Samson killed each and every one of them by himself. Of course, Samson really wasn't alone; God gave him this ability. After this was over, Samson thought he was going to die of thirst. Then, God had the third miracle happen. Water came out of the skeleton (jawbone of the ass) so that Samson could drink the water and be refreshed.

It is easy for me to read right through this passage and not pay any attention to how God had His hand in these situations. This gives me a greater sense of God's involvement in our lives and what He is capable of. If He can have one man conquer an army of a thousand, He can surely take care of our daily needs!

....

And it was so, that all that saw it said, There was no such deed done nor seen from the day that the children of Israel came up out of the land of Egypt unto this day: consider of it, take advice, and speak your minds. Judges, Chapter 19, verse 30.

The rest of the chapter tells about a group of men who abuse and rape a Levite man's concubine (mistress) until she died. God tells us through this Bible passage that we are to speak our minds on issues of this nature.

It might not seem like these things are socially acceptable, but they really are, more so than you think. Think of how easy it is for us to hear about another case of date rape and shrug our shoulders. Our complacent and helpless attitudes toward things of this nature help to perpetuate the growth of these crimes. People start to view it as something that guys do when they are out drinking too much. Well, guess what? Rape or crimes of aggression aren't acceptable under any circumstance! I think we need to raise our children with a clear message on this!

....

And Samuel said unto the people, Fear not: ye have done all this wickedness: yet turn not aside from following the LORD, but serve the LORD with all your heart; And turn ye not aside: for then should ye go after vain things, which cannot profit nor deliver; for they are vain. 1 Samuel, Chapter 12, verses 20-21.

At times we go after vain things ourselves. Some examples would be: wealth, prestige, jobs, social status, etc., which can't bring us Salvation. Sometimes God-fearing people get so focused on their career goals that they lose sight of their faith, their family and their ethics in the name of getting ahead.

Are wealth, prestige and social status really worth it? Is this the lifestyle you really want to model for your children and your grandchildren?

....

And Samuel said, Hath the LORD as great delight in burnt offerings and sacrifices, as in obeying the Voice of the LORD? Behold, to obey is better than sacrifice, and to hearken than the fat of rams. For rebellion is as the sin of witchcraft, and stubbornness is as iniquity and idolatry. Because thou hast rejected the Word of the LORD, He hath also rejected thee from being king. 1 Samuel, Chapter 15, verses 22-23.

This chapter is basically about God telling Saul (through Samuel) to conquer Amalek. They were to destroy everything and <u>not to take anything</u> from there. Well, Saul was an independent thinker. He won the battle but kept the king and the best of the sheep and the oxen after God had already told him <u>not to take anything</u>.

Samuel tells Saul that God isn't happy with him because he took the spoil of the land against His wishes. Saul, being the fast thinker that he was, said the reason that he kept all the best of the sheep and oxen was because he brought them back to sacrifice them to God. Then Samuel tells Saul that God wants us to us to follow Him and do exactly what He asks of us. He goes on to ask Saul (paraphrased), "Which is more important, offering sacrifices to God or doing what He asks you to do?" God wants us to obey Him, not to be independent thinkers and do our own thing, trying to rationalize our actions.

Dorothy Scott

....

> *But the LORD said unto Samuel, Look not on his countenance, or on the height of his stature; because I have refused him: for the LORD seeth not as man seeth; for man looketh on the outward appearance, but the LORD looketh on the heart. 1 Samuel, Chapter 16, verse 7.*

This is when God had asked Samuel to anoint the future king. Samuel looked at David's brothers (David was young and was tending sheep at the time.) Samuel thought surely God had chosen one of David's brothers who were older and stronger, but God had a different idea.

God explained to Samuel that He doesn't look at people by how tall, strong or attractive they are; like men do. God looks at the person's heart. That's how God can tell what type of person we are. It makes me think of Jesus being the one true Equal Opportunity Savior of all! We aren't judged by our race, culture, sex, age, gender, skin color, wealth, height, weight, etc. God looks into our heart and knows who we truly are!

....

> *Then came there two women, that were harlots, unto the king, and stood before him. And the one woman said, O my lord, I and this woman dwell in one house; and I was delivered of a child with her in the house. And it came to pass the third day after that I was delivered, that this woman was delivered also: and we were together; there was no stranger with us in the house, save we two in the house. And this woman's child died in the night; because she overlaid it. And she arose at midnight, and took my son from beside me, while thine handmaid slept, and laid it in her bosom, and laid her dead child in my bosom. And when I rose in the morning to give my child suck, behold it was dead: but when I had considered it in the morning, behold, it was not my son, which I did bear. And the other woman said, Nay: but the living is my son, and the dead is thy son. And this said, No, but the dead is thy son, and the living is my son. Thus they spake before the king. Then said the king, The one saith, This is my son that liveth, and thy son is the dead: and the other saith, Nay; but thy son is the dead, and my son is the living. And the king said, Bring me a sword. And they brought a sword before the king. And the king said, Divide the living child in two, and give half to the one, and half to the other. Then spake the woman whose the living child was unto the king, for her bowels yearned*

upon her son, and she said, O my lord, give her the living child, and in no wise slay it. But the other said, Let it be neither mine nor thine, but divide it. Then the king answered and said, Give her the living child, and in no wise slay it: she is the mother thereof. 1 Kings, Chapter 3, verses 16-27.

This story of Solomon's great wisdom reminds me of when I was little. My sister and I had metal globe banks. (I know this is dating me some.) Our banks were kept at the top of our bedroom closet. I remember climbing on something and taking the money out of my sister's bank, because I wanted to go to the "Candy Store." (I was oblivious to the fact that they sold anything other than candy.)

I was almost out the front door when my mother stopped me. She asked me where I was going and I told her that I was going to the "Candy Store." She asked me where I got the money to buy the candy. Now, I thought I was pretty clever when I told my mother that Sally down the street had given me the money, because there really was no one named Sally. I had made it up. Well, my mother is definitely much smarter than that! She told me that she knew Sally, and Sally had told her that she hadn't given me the money. Boy was my mother ever quick on her feet. I had been caught in the middle of a lie.

I think God is quicker on His feet than even my mother was! He knows what we think and what we do. I don't know why we make these lame excuses. Do we really think that God is truly going to buy them? "Ah, I'm not going to include this income on my tax statement because Uncle Sam gets more than his fair share anyway; besides this was just a side job for a friend." Or, "I really like these fine point pens they have at work. I think I'll take a few-oh yeah, I need them for a work project I'm going to do at home." (I'm guilty of this one.) Why do we even try these things? Who do we think we are fooling anyway? God knows everything and still we find ourselves trying to validate doing things that we know are wrong.

....

And he went up from thence unto Bethel and as he was going up by the way, there came forth little children out of the city, and mocked him, and said unto him, Go up, thou bald head; go up thou bald head. And he turned back, and looked on them, and cursed them in the Name of the Lord. And there came forth two she bears out of the wood, and tare forty and two children of them. 2 Kings, Chapter 2, verses 23-24.

This passage addresses hateful children who torment others. Elisha didn't say, "Oh, poor children. They must have parents who haven't paid enough attention to them." When Elisha cursed them for tormenting him, God had a bear come and destroy them. Although, this passage demonstrates an extremely dramatic consequence for the inappropriate taunting behavior of the children, I think it's important for us to note how this situation was handled.

What would happen today? Have we become so accustomed to rude and tormenting behavior from children that hearing they behaved this way doesn't seem out of place? Isn't that scary? I've seen too many talk shows where kids have been suicidal or wanted to seek revenge because they have been tormented for years by their peers at school. Are we allowing our children to grow up to be rude, insulting and insensitive to others? I don't think we would want God to deal with our children the same way that He did with the children in the passage.

Maybe we need to take a more active role in making sure our children are raised to respect others. Maybe there would be less violence in schools if everyone was committed to enforcing appropriate guidelines with their children from infancy on. Something to think about!

....

Now there cried a certain woman of the wives of the sons of the prophets unto Elisha, saying, Thy servant my husband is dead; and thou knowest that thy servant did fear the LORD: and the creditor is come to take unto him my two sons to be bondmen. And Elisha said unto her, What shall I do for thee? Tell me, what hast thou in the house? And she said, Thine handmaid hath not any thing in the house, save a pot of oil. Then he said, Go, borrow thee vessels abroad of all thy neighbours, even empty vessels; borrow not a few. And when thou art come in, thou shalt shut the door upon thee and upon thy sons, and shalt pour out into all those vessels, and thou shalt set aside that which is full. So she went from him, and shut the door upon her and upon her sons, who brought the vessels to her; and she poured out. And it came to pass, when the vessels were full, that she said unto her son, Bring me yet a vessel. And he said unto her, There is not a vessel more. And the oil stayed. Then she came and told the man of God. And he said, Go, sell the oil, and pay thy debt, and live thou and thy children of the rest. 2 Kings, Chapter 4, verses 1-7.

This passage gives me goosebumps when I read it. It shows the great extent that God goes to in order to take care of us. Miraculously, He made the container of endless oil to take care of this widow and her sons. It makes me think of how foolish I am to worry about bills and finances. If God provided for this widow and her children, He can surely provide for me!

· ·

In this passage, Naaman is a leper. He goes to see Elisha to see if he could cure him of his leprosy.

So Naaman came with his horses and with his chariot, and stood at the door of the house of Elisha. And Elisha sent a messenger unto him, saying, Go and wash in Jordan seven times, and thy flesh shall come again to thee, and thou shalt be clean. But Naaman was wroth, and went away, and said, Behold, I thought, He will surely come out to me, and stand, and call on the Name of the LORD his God, and strike his hand over the place, and recover the leper. Are not Abana and Pharpar, rivers of Damascus, better than all the waters of Israel? may I not wash in them, and be clean? So he turned and went away in a rage. And his servants came near, and spake unto him, and said, My father, if the prophet had bid thee do some great thing, wouldest thou not have done it? how much rather then, when he saith to thee, Wash, and be clean? Then went he down, and dipped himself seven times in Jordan, according to the saying of the man of God: and his flesh came again like unto the flesh of a little child, and he was clean. And he returned to the man of God, he and all his company, and came, and stood before him: and he said, Behold, now I know that there is no God in all the earth, but in Israel: now therefore, I pray thee, take a blessing of thy servant. 2 Kings, Chapter 5, verses 9-15.

Naaman leaves Elisha saying, "That's too easy, I could have bathed in the rivers by my own town. How could something so easy take care of my disease?" (Paraphrased) Sometimes God asks us to do simple things and we don't trust Him.

All we have to do for Salvation is to believe that Jesus is our Savior and to try to live as examples of how He works in our lives. We are "Made in the Shade Christians," because God doesn't ask us to give up everything we own, go into the airport selling flowers, to meditate for hours or to go through great personal sacrifice. Yet many people look elsewhere for God and have been known to jump through all sorts of hoops to find Salvation that is elusive, because they are not focusing on God's simple requirement.

Naaman eventually realized that it was worth giving the simple request a try and it paid off. He was cured from his leprosy by doing what God wanted him to do. I like the way God uses graphic illustrations to demonstrate the lessons He wants me to learn.

....

> *In those days was Hezekiah sick unto death. And the prophet Isaiah the son of Amoz came to him, and said unto him, Thus said the LORD. Set thine house in order; for thou shalt die, and not live. Then he turned his face to the wall, and prayed unto the LORD, saying, I beseech thee, O LORD, remember now how I have walked before Thee in Truth and with a perfect heart, and have done that which is good in Thy sight. And Hezekiah wept sore. And it came to pass, afore Isaiah was gone out into the middle court, that the Word of the LORD came to him, saying, Turn again, and tell Hezekiah the captain of My people, Thus saith the LORD, the God of David thy father, I have heard thy prayer, I have seen thy tears: behold, I will heal thee: on the third day thou shalt go up unto the house of the LORD. And I will add unto thy days fifteen years; and I will deliver thee and this city out of the hand of the king of Assyria; and I will defend this city for Mine own sake, and for My servant David's sake. And Isaiah said, Take a lump of figs. And they took and laid it on the boil, and he recovered. 2 Kings, Chapter 20, verses 1-7.*

This passage makes me realize that God takes all things into consideration. Sometimes I find myself thinking things happen a particular way because that's the way they are meant to be. This passage shows me that although that may be true, it isn't always the way God works. Isn't it funny that I get caught up in trying to figure out how God works? It's kind of like I'm a detective looking for clues, rather than just letting God guide me and show me what He wants.

This passage tells me to continue praying about issues of concern and not to give up hope, because God can decide to turn things around. This is evidenced by God deciding to let the king live fifteen more years after he prayed to Him. God can do anything. He is God! He defies all explanation!

....

> *So Saul died for his transgression which he committed against the LORD, even against the Word of the LORD, which he kept not, and also for asking counsel of one that had a familiar spirit, to inquire of it: And inquired not of the LORD: therefore he slew him and turned the kingdom unto David the son of Jesse. 1 Chronicles, Chapter 10, verses 13-14.*

Saul had his servant contact a woman with a familiar spirit (my Bible refers to her as a witch.) She called Samuel up from the dead to answer Saul's questions, but God did NOT like this, which was the major reason that God had Saul die. Not only did Saul turn to someone who could conjure people from the dead, but he did this rather than turning to God to ask His will.

I'm including this passage because it reinforces my belief that God wouldn't be appreciative of people who get involved in watching TV shows where dead relatives are contacted, even though they try to make it sound positive with some religious connection. We are turning to these shows rather than turning to God. I think God lets us know in this passage that He doesn't take kindly to us turning to anything other than Him. Actually, why would we want to turn to anything else besides God? God takes care of our every need!

....

> *And with them Heman and Jeduthun, and the rest that were chosen, who were expressed by name, to give thanks to the LORD, because His mercy endureth for ever. 1 Chronicles, Chapter 16, Verse 41.*

I'm including this because I like the last half of the Bible verse that states that God's mercy endures forever. It reminds me of the saying, "Blood is thicker than Water."

Although my sister and I live far apart and have different jobs, hobbies and interests, we are always there for each other, through thick and thin, which reminds me of how God's mercy endures forever.

....

> *Now when Solomon had made an end of praying, the fire came down from heaven, and consumed the burnt offering and the sacrifices; and the Glory of the LORD filled the house. And the priests could not enter into the house of the LORD, because the Glory of the LORD had filled the LORD's house. And when all the children of Israel saw how the fire came down, and the*

Glory of the LORD upon the house, they bowed themselves with their faces to the ground upon the pavement, and worshipped and praised the LORD, saying, For He is good; for His mercy endureth for ever. 2 Chronicles, Chapter 7, verses 1-3.

This passage never really hit me before, but when I read it this time it left a stronger impact on me. I started thinking about how God has had to do all of these very dramatic miracles to get people to believe He is the One True God. I guess if I weren't too sure of my faith and I saw fire come down from heaven and burn up a slab of meat, there would be no doubt in my mind that God was responsible for it, even if I had doubted before!

Do people have to have these monumental miracles before they believe in God? It's kind of sad that some of us have a Missouri (the "Show-Me State") mentality. Do I have to have God "Show-Me" miracles before I'm truly willing to believe in Him and not doubt His existence?

God does all types of miracles in my life each and every day. When I was taking a heavy class-load of difficult teacher preparatory classes, I didn't know how I would get through all of them. I had petitioned the college to take 23 units that semester, so that I could have the required classes to start student teaching the next semester. I was praying to God about this on the way home from college one day. God put the thought in my mind that I wasn't supposed to worry about it, because He was going to give me straight A's.

I thought, "How could You do this? These are some of the hardest courses I have ever taken and I don't have enough time to properly study for all of them." Then the thought that God had in my mind was that He could do it, He's God and He could do anything. I relaxed after I thought about it a few minutes. He can do anything, provided I trust Him to. I didn't want to be like Peter who sank when he got fearful, so I asked God for the willingness to trust that He would take care of me.

I would pray a quick prayer over each homework and test question, something like, "God please take care of this one," and the answer or the way to solve the statistical problem would just be in my mind. God did give me straight A's through all of that. It was just like the thought He gave me those many months earlier in the car.

God works in my life in a variety of ways. I don't always say formal prayers to God when I have something on my mind. I just talk to Him and I know God hears me. God answers me in lots of different ways, but I don't hear the actual Voice of God from heaven saying, "Dorothy, this is what you are supposed to do."

Sometimes He answers me by having things happen, like my stalled car starts right after I pray about it. Sometimes He has things not happen, like when my first husband and I didn't get a house we were trying to buy. We were so disappointed at the time, but six months afterward my husband got laid-off of work. Later, I realized that it was a good thing we hadn't gotten the house, because we could have lost everything we owned. When things don't turn out the way I ask, usually God will show me why at a later time, as in this example. Sometimes, God just puts thoughts or ideas in my mind, just like when God let me know that He was going to give me straight A's. Sometimes He guides me by the instincts He gives me. The important thing is that I have to listen to them and not go off in my own direction, ignoring those instincts.

God does all types of miracles in our lives every day, if we would only open our eyes to see them. Do we have the "Show-Me" mentality where we need fire to come down from the sky before we believe in God?

....

And the LORD appeared to Solomon by night, and said unto him, I have heard thy prayer, and have chosen this place to Myself for an house of sacrifice. If I shut up heaven that there be no rain, or if I command the locusts to devour the land, or if I send pestilence among My people; If My people, which are called by My Name, shall humble themselves, and pray, and seek My face, and turn from their wicked ways; then will I hear from heaven, and will forgive their sin, and will heal their land. Now Mine Eyes shall be open, and Mine Ears attent unto the prayer that is made in this place. For now have I chosen and sanctified this house, that My Name may be there forever: and Mine Eyes and Mine Heart shall be there perpetually. 2 Chronicles, Chapter 7, verses 12-16.

And it shall be answered, Because they forsook the LORD God of their fathers, which brought them forth out of the land of Egypt, and laid hold on other gods, and worshipped them, and served them: therefore hath He brought all this evil upon them. 2 Chronicles, Chapter 7, verse 22.

This sounds like sometimes when we have droughts, floods or pestilence like locusts, etc., God is trying to get our attention. I feel like it's His way of saying, "People down on Earth, you are losing your focus on Me. You are getting caught up in worldly things and doubt My existence by taking credit for the things I do." God, who is infinitely merciful, goes on to say that if we turn back to Him, He will forgive us.

....

I want to deviate some from the writing format I've been using, so far. I want to give the background of this chapter in order to condense this. This is about 2 Chronicles, Chapter 10. I hate to include the whole chapter.

Rehoboam, who is Solomon's son, became king after Solomon died. The Israelites sent spokesmen to King Rehoboam to ask him to lighten their work load. They said his father had been much too harsh on them. They asked him to lighten their work load and promised they would be loyal to him in return. He told them to come back in three days so that he could have some time to think about it.

First, King Rehoboam went to get advice from the old men who told him that if he lightened the Israelites work load and talked nicely to them, they would be his servants forever. Then King Rehoboam went to get the advice of the young men (his friends) who told him to tell the Israelites that if they thought his father made their workload heavy, just wait and see how heavy he was going to make it. His friends told him that he was much more of a man than his father. (Paraphrased)

Well, after three days, the Israelites came back to King Rehoboam to get his reply to their request to lighten their workload. He ignored the advice of the older men. *And answered the advice of the young men, saying, My father made your yoke heavy, but I will add thereto: my father chastised you with whips, but I will chastise you with scorpions. 2 Chronicles, Chapter 10, verse 14.* The Israelites rebelled against King Rehoboam.

I wish supervisors and managers would read this passage. It shows that the treatment the boss gives their employees can make the difference of whether the employees are loyal and productive or whether they rebel. The other thing that this passage reminds me of is how easy it is for people to ignore the advice God has given them through the Bible and choose to follow the advice of their friends instead. Obviously, friends don't always have the best of advice, as evidenced in this passage.

....

And Asa in the thirty and ninth year of his reign was diseased in his feet, until his disease was exceeding great: yet in his disease he sought not to the Lord, but to the physicians. And Asa slept with his fathers, and died in the one and fortieth year of his reign. 2 Chronicles 16, verses 12-13.

Bible Passages That Can Influence Your Life

This passage makes me stand up and take note. It becomes apparent to me that God wants us to turn to Him first and foremost when we are ill. I'm not saying that physicians don't have a place, but I get a clear message that Asa didn't turn to God at all. He put his faith totally in physicians, and he died in the natural course of his disease.

In contrast, if Asa had turned to God and put his faith in Him, he wouldn't have died. Sometimes it gets easy to get caught up in the world of science and medicine and to put our total trust in them. I feel that although there have been many medical and scientific breakthroughs; we need to make sure our primary focus is on God. We want Him to guide us to the correct physicians, when needed and to guide those physicians in their actions.

....

And all Judah stood before the LORD, with their little ones, their wives, and their children. Then upon Jahaziel the son of Zechariah, the son of Benaiah, the son of Jeiel, the son of Mattaniah, a Levite of the sons of Asaph, came the Spirit of the LORD in the midst of the congregation; And He said, Hearken ye, all Judah, and ye inhabitants of Jerusalem, and thou king Jehoshaphat, Thus saith the LORD unto you, Be not afraid nor dismayed by reason of this great multitude; for the battle is not yours, but God's. Tomorrow go ye down against them: behold, they come up by the cliff of Ziz; and ye shall find them at the end of the brook, before the wilderness of Jeruel. Ye shall not need to fight in this battle: set yourselves, stand ye still, and see the Salvation of the LORD with you, O Judah and Jerusalem: fear not, nor be dismayed; tomorrow go out against them: for the LORD will be with you. And Jehoshaphat bowed his head with his face to the ground: and all Judah and the inhabitants of Jerusalem fell before the LORD, worshipping the LORD. And the Levites, of the children of the Kohathites, stood up to praise the LORD God of Israel with a loud voice on high. 2 Chronicles, Chapter 20, verses 13-19.

God told Jehoshaphat that his men wouldn't even need to fight this battle, because God wanted them to see the Salvation of the LORD. Now, Jehoshaphat didn't doubt God. He didn't even tell his men to carry spears with them, just in case God didn't pull through. Jehoshaphat trusted God to take care of him, just as we need to trust God will take care of us.

In the following verses, it tells how the men who wanted to fight with Jehoshaphat had hidden themselves in the countryside. Jehoshaphat had singers walk in front of his men saying, *"Praise the LORD for His mercy endureth for ever."* 2 Chronicles, Chapter 20, part of verse 21.

Anyway, the soldiers that were in the countryside preparing to ambush Jehoshaphat and his men, killed each other instead. Jehoshaphat and his men didn't have to lift a finger.

It says in 2 Chronicles, Chapter 20, verse 29, *And the fear of God was on all the kingdoms of those countries, when they had heard that the LORD fought against the enemies of Israel.*

So, God used this battle as a sign to help people realize that He is the One True God, all powerful, and He takes care of His people when they obey Him.

....

Wherefore the LORD brought upon them the captains of the host of the king of Assyria, which took Manasseh among the thorns, and bound him with fetters, and carried him to Babylon. And when he was in affliction, he besought the LORD his God, and humblest himself greatly before the God of his fathers. And prayed unto Him: and heard his supplication, and brought him again to Jerusalem into his kingdom. Then Manasseh knew that the LORD, He was God. 2 Chronicles, Chapter 33, verses 11-13.

This is the most amazing passage! Manasseh used witchcraft, used people who contacted the dead, cast spells, was into Astrology and had his children walk through fire as some ritualistic show of loyalty, which really made God upset. After Manasseh was captured and became humbled, he asked God to forgive him and God did. Pure and simple!

Even if we have made some pretty poor choices in our lives, God will forgive us, just as He did Manasseh if we turn to Him and truly turn our lives around.

....

I really like the Book of Esther. It would be worth reading to find out how Esther and Mordecai were able to protect their people, the Jews, who were persecuted.

....

All the while my breath is in me, and the Spirit of God is in my nostrils; My lips shall not speak wickedness, nor my tongue utter deceit. God forbid that I should justify you: till I die I won't remove mine integrity from me. My righteousness I hold fast, and will not let it go: my heart shall not reproach me so long as I live. Let mine enemy be as the wicked, and he that riseth up against me as the unrighteous. For what is the hope of the hypocrite, though he hath gained, when God taketh away his soul? Will God hear his cry when trouble cometh upon him? Job, Chapter 27, verses 3-9.

This is when Job had suffered many tribulations and his so-called friends were trying to help him. They challenged Job and his beliefs, but Job never wavered. He wouldn't turn away from believing in God, even amidst his tragic situation. I want God to always keep my focus on Him. I never want to turn my back on God or to blame Him for my problems.

....

Lead me, O LORD, in Thy righteousness because of mine enemies; make Thy way straight before my face. For there is no faithfulness in their mouth; their inward part is very wickedness; their throat is an open sepulchre; they flatter with their tongue. Psalm, Chapter 5, verses 8-9.

People's flattery of us does not always reflect their true intent. Here is a related passage:

*Surely men of low degree are vanity, and men of high degree are a lie: to be laid in the balance, they are altogether lighter than vanity. Psalm, Chapter 62, verse 9.

....

O LORD our Lord, how excellent is Thy Name in all the earth! Who hast set Thy glory above the heavens. Out of the mouth of babes and sucklings hast Thou ordained strength because of thine enemies, that Thou mightest still the enemy and the avenger. When I consider Thy heavens, the work of Thy fingers, the moon and the stars, which Thou hast ordained; What is man, that Thou art mindful of him? and the son of man, that Thou visitest him? For Thou hast made him a little lower than the angels and hast crowned him with glory and honour. Thou madest him to have dominion over the works of Thy hands; Thou hast put all things under his feet: All sheep and oxen, yea, and the beasts of the field; the fowl of the air, and the fish of the sea, and whatsoever passeth through the paths of the seas. O LORD our Lord, how excellent is Thy Name in all the earth! Psalm, Chapter 8, verses 1-9.

Reading this makes me think of how foolish it is for me to worry. If God can do all of this, surely He can take care of my concerns.

....

Let the words of my mouth, and the meditation of my heart, be acceptable in Thy sight, O LORD, my strength, and my Redeemer. Psalm, Chapter 19, verse 14.

I have said something similar to this in church for years, but do I always think about what I'm really saying or do I just rattle it off in a routine fashion? I hate to admit it, but sometimes the latter is true. Yet, I would like the words that come out of my mouth and all my thoughts to be ones that glorify God and make Him proud of me.

I also find myself thinking and saying things that don't glorify God and don't make me the best example of my love for Him. Maybe if I put more thought into what I'm saying at church, I might be a better example of what I think and say elsewhere.

Here are some related passages:

And He called the multitude, and said unto them, Hear, and understand: Not that which goeth into the mouth defileth a man; but that which cometh out of the mouth, this defileth a man. Matthew, Chapter 15, verses 10-11.

Do not ye yet understand, that whatsoever entereth in at the mouth goeth into the belly, and is cast out into the draught? But those things which proceed out of the mouth come forth from the heart; and they defile the man. For out of the heart proceed evil thoughts, murders, adulteries, fornications, thefts, false witness, blasphemies: These are the things which defile a man: but to eat with unwashen hands defileth not a man. Matthew, Chapter 15, verses 17-20.

....

GOD, My God, why hast Thou forsaken Me? why art Thou so far from helping Me, and from the Words of My roaring? Psalm, Chapter 22, verse 1.

For dogs have compassed Me: the assembly of the wicked have inclosed Me: they pierced My hands and My feet. I may tell all My bones: they look and stare upon Me. They part My garments among them, and cast lots upon My vesture. But be not Thou far from Me, O LORD, O My strength, haste Thee to help Me. Psalm, Chapter 22, verses 16-19.

When I read this in Psalm, 22, I'm confused and amazed at the same time! David is talking about when Jesus is crucified yet it's many, many years before Jesus is even born. I don't profess to be a theologian, but I remember Jesus saying He had to fulfill the Scriptures. So, I guess David and others told of the details that would happen to Jesus long before He was born. Then, when Jesus had accomplished these prophesies, people would truly know He is the Son of God.

It's distressing that so many people are looking for proof that Jesus is the Savior. It's like they want Jesus to come and touch them on the shoulder and say, "Sally, I want you to quit doubting My existence. Now that you have seen Me, you know that I'm your Savior."

It's sad that they are missing out on a relationship with Him because they don't read the Bible and are not aware of Jesus' love for us through His death and Resurrection. The Bible has so many passages that foretold of the birth, life, death and Resurrection of Jesus and how these Scriptures have been fulfilled that it would be difficult for skeptics to continue to ignore the Truth.

Here are some other passages that foretell of Jesus in the Old Testament:

*Therefore the Lord Himself shall give you a sign; Behold, a virgin shall conceive, and bear a Son, and shall call His Name Immanuel. Butter and honey shall He eat, that He may know to refuse the evil, and choose the good. Isaiah, Chapter 7, verses 14-15.

*For unto us a Child is born, unto us a Son is given: and the government shall be upon His shoulder: and His Name shall be called Wonderful, Counselor, The Mighty God, The Everlasting Father, The Prince of Peace. Isaiah, Chapter 9, verse 6.

*Who hath believed our report? And to whom is the Arm of the LORD revealed? For He shall grow up before Him as a tender plant, and as a root out of a dry ground: He hath no form nor comeliness; and when we shall see Him, there is no beauty that we should desire Him, He is despised and rejected of men; a Man of sorrows, and acquainted with grief: and we hid as it were our faces from Him, He was despised, and we esteemed Him not. Surely He hath borne our griefs, and carried our sorrows: yet we did esteem Him stricken, smitten of God, and afflicted. But He was wounded for our transgressions, He was bruised for our iniquities: the chastisement of our peace was upon Him; and with His stripes we are healed. All we like sheep have gone astray; we have turned every one to his own way; and the LORD hath laid on Him the iniquity of us all. He was oppressed, and He was afflicted, yet He opened not His Mouth: He is brought as a Lamb to the slaughter, and as a Sheep before her shearers is dumb, so He openeth not His Mouth. He was taken from prison and from judgment: and who shall declare His generation? For

He was cut off out of the land of the living; for the transgression of my people was He stricken. And He made His grave with the wicked, and with the rich in His death; because He had done no violence, either was any deceit in His Mouth. Yet it pleased the LORD to bruise Him; He hath put Him to grief: when thou shalt make His Soul an offering for sin, He shall see His seed, He shall prolong His days, and the pleasure of the LORD shall prosper in His hand. He shall see of the travail of His Soul, and shall be satisfied: by His knowledge shall my Righteous Servant justify many; for He shall bear their iniquities. Therefore will I divide Him a portion with the great, and He shall divide the spoil with the strong; because He hath poured out His soul unto death: and He was numbered with the transgressors: and He bare the sin of many, and made intercession for the transgressors. Isaiah, Chapter 53, verses 1-12.

*Behold, the days come, saith the Lord, that I will raise unto David a righteous Branch, and a King shall reign and prosper, and shall execute judgment and justice in the earth. In His days Judah shall be saved, and Israel shall dwell safely: and this is His Name whereby He shall be called, THE LORD OUR RIGHTEOUSNESS. Jeremiah, Chapter 23, verses 5-6.

*And I will pour upon the house of David and upon the inhabitants of Jerusalem, the Spirit of grace and of supplications: and they shall look upon Me whom they have pierced, and they shall mourn for Him, as one mourneth for His only Son, and shall be in bitterness for Him, as one that is in bitterness for His first born. Zechariah, Chapter 12, verse 10.

....

The LORD is my Shepherd; I shall not want. He maketh me to lie down in green pastures: He leadeth me beside the still waters. He restoreth my soul: He leadeth me in the paths of righteousness for His Name's sake. Yea, though I walk through the valley of the shadow of death, I will fear no evil: for Thou art with me; Thy rod and Thy staff they comfort me. Thou preparest a table before me in the presence of mine enemies: Thou anointest my head with oil; my cup runneth over. Surely goodness and mercy shall follow me all the days of my life: and I will dwell in the house of the LORD for ever. Psalm, Chapter 23, verses 1-6.

I like this passage because it's so comforting. Sometimes when I'm afraid in the dark, I think of this passage. (Sometimes when my husband goes out of town for conferences, I hear noises that scare me in the night.)

No, I haven't memorized it all word for word. I don't think a person has to be able to do that in order to be close to God. (It is nice to be able to do that though, because it's like carrying special messages from God with you all the time. Bible passages are handy to know in case a friend needs to be comforted by them.) Even though I don't know this passage by heart, God comforts me when I think about it. Then I don't seem to be afraid anymore.

Here are some related passages:

> *O LORD my God, in Thee do I put my trust: save me from all them that persecute me, and deliver me. Psalm, Chapter 7, verse 1.

> *Lead me in Thy Truth, and teach me: for Thou art the God of my Salvation: on Thee do I wait all the day. Remember, O LORD, Thy tender mercies and Thy loving kindnesses: for they have been ever of old. Remember not the sins of my youth, nor my transgressions: according to Thy mercy remember Thou me for Thy goodness' sake, O LORD. Good and upright is the LORD: therefore will He teach sinners in the way. The meek will He guide in judgment: and the meek will He teach His way. All the paths of the LORD are mercy and Truth unto such as keep His covenant and His testimonies. Psalm, Chapter 25, verses 5-10.

> *Be of good courage, and He shall strengthen your heart, all ye that hope in the LORD. Psalm, Chapter 31, verse 24.

> *The angel of the LORD encampeth round about them that fear Him, and delivereth them. Psalm, Chapter 34, verse 7.

> *The eyes of the LORD are upon the righteous, and His ears are open unto their cry. Psalm, Chapter 34, verse 15.

> *The LORD knoweth the days of the upright: and their inheritance shall be for ever. They shall not be ashamed in the evil time: and in the days of famine they shall be satisfied. Psalm, Chapter 37, verses 18-19.

> *I have been young, and now am old; yet have I not seen the righteous forsaken nor His seed begging bread. He is ever merciful, and lendeth; and His seed is blessed. Depart from evil, and do good; and dwell for evermore. Psalm, Chapter 37, verses 25-27.

*But the Salvation of the righteous is of the LORD: He is their strength in the time of trouble. And the LORD shall help them, and deliver them: He shall deliver them from the wicked, and save them, because they trust in Him. Psalm, Chapter 37, verses 39-40.

*He only is my Rock and my Salvation; He is my defence; I shall not be moved. In God is my Salvation and my glory: the Rock of my strength, and my refuge is in God. Trust in Him at all times; ye people, pour your heart before Him: God is a refuge for us. Selah. Psalm, Chapter 62, verses 6-8.

*This is the day which the LORD hath made; we will rejoice and be glad in it. Psalm, Chapter 118, verse 24.

*Blessed be He that cometh in the Name of the LORD. Psalm, Chapter 118, the first half of verse 26.

*O give thanks unto the LORD; for He is good: for His mercy endureth for ever. Psalm, Chapter 118, verse 29.

*I know that the LORD will maintain the cause of the afflicted, and the right of the poor. Psalm, Chapter 140, verse 12.

*For thus saith the Lord GOD; Behold, I, even I, will both search My sheep, and seek them out. As a Shepherd seeketh out His flock in the day that He is among His sheep that are scattered; so will I seek out My sheep, and will deliver them out of all places where they have been scattered in the cloudy and dark day. And I will bring them out from the people, and gather them from the countries, and will bring them to their own land, and feed them among the mountains of Israel by the rivers, and in all the inhabited places of the country. I will feed them in a good pasture, and upon the high mountains of Israel shall their fold be: there shall they lie in a good fold, and in a fat pasture shall they feed upon the mountains of Israel. I will feed My flock, and I will cause them to lie down, saith the Lord GOD. I will seek that which was lost, and bring again that which was driven away, and will bind up that which was broken, and will strengthen that which was sick: but I will destroy the fat and the strong; I will feed them with judgment. Ezekiel, Chapter 34, verses 11-16.

> *The LORD, is my Light and my Salvation; whom shall I fear? The LORD is the strength of my life: of whom shall I be afraid? Psalm, Chapter 27, verse 1.*

When I'm confused and afraid I'm going to make the wrong decision, I pray and God Lights the way for me. He gives me a feeling of what to do. No, He doesn't say, "Dorothy, this is what you should do." When I talk to Him, my prayers tend to be less formal and more like a conversation with God, except for when I say the Lord's Prayer.

When I'm stressed and God doesn't want me to worry, He gives me a calm feeling I call the Peace Which Passes All Understanding.

After I pray asking God for guidance, I try to listen to the instincts that God gives me. If I get a calm feeling, I move forward on it. If I have an unsettling feeling, I wait because sometimes it's not God's Will or the timing just isn't right. God always sees the Big Picture and knows when the timing is right for us. When I trust the instincts that God gives me, my life seems much more stress-free and things seem to fall into place.

....

> *Be glad in the LORD, and rejoice, ye righteous: and shout for joy, all ye that are upright in heart. Psalm, Chapter 32, verse 11.*

Sometimes, we Christians walk around like our love for Jesus is this private secret that we keep to ourselves, lest anyone think we are religious fanatics. I know that I have been guilty of this myself. God wants us to be excited about all the wonderful things that He does in our lives and not to hide our joy. This is something I still need to focus on.

....

> *Blessed is the nation whose God is the LORD; and the people whom He hath chosen for His own inheritance. Psalm, Chapter 33, verse 12.*

I am no authority on World History, but it seems that predominately Christian countries have been fairly prosperous over time. It seems that when their citizens lose their focus on God (the Father, Son and Holy Ghost), their country doesn't fare as well. Look at our country and the lifestyle choices people are making. Does it seem that people are losing their focus on God?

....

> *The LORD looketh from heaven: He beholdeth all the sons of men. From the place of His habitation He looketh upon all the inhabitants of the earth. He fashioneth their hearts alike: He considereth all their works. There is no king saved by the*

> *multitude of an host: a mighty man is not delivered by much strength. Psalm, Chapter 33, verses 13-16.*

God made all of us with the same kinds of hearts. It's up to us to choose to let Jesus into our heart or not. That will be the determining factor of our Salvation, not how rich, popular, high on the social ladder or how strong we are.

....

> *Cease from anger, and forsake wrath: fret not thyself in any wise to do evil. For evildoers shall be cut off: but those that wait upon the LORD, they shall inherit the earth. Psalm, Chapter 37, verses 8-9.*

Sometimes when people do really hateful and inconsiderate things, I find myself plotting equally hateful things to do back to them. Behavior like that isn't befitting a Christian. I need to turn these draining feelings (they drain my Christianity out of me) over to God, so I can get on with living the life that He wants.

....

> *A little that a righteous man hath is better than the riches of many wicked. Psalm, Chapter 37, verse 16.*

I like this passage. It's saying that it's better to be poor and have Jesus as our Savior than to have all the riches and live a worldly life with no chance of Salvation. I agree. What good does it do to have all the riches in the world, if you lose your own soul?

I remember watching movies that showed people who used to make pacts with the devil to have riches, fame or positions of power. The movies would end with the people realizing that no amount of prestige or wealth was worth losing their soul. Although those are movies, sometimes we make similar decisions by the choices we make in our lives.

Here is a related passage:

> **Be not thou afraid when one is made rich, when the glory of his house is increased; For when he dieth he shall carry nothing away: his glory shall not descend after him. Psalm, Chapter 49, verses 16-17.*

....

> *Create in me a clean heart, O God; and renew a right Spirit within me. Cast me not away from Thy presence; and take not Thy Holy Spirit from me. Restore unto me the joy of Thy Salvation; and uphold me with Thy free Spirit. Psalm, Chapter 51, verses 10-12.*

I have a "Gimme Gimme Christian" relationship with God. I have said these previous verses many times in church, asking God to make me a better Christian. But the next verse says, *"Then will I teach transgressors Thy ways; and sinners shall be converted unto Thee." Psalm, Chapter 51, verse 13.*

I have focused on what I want God to do for me all these years. I want Him to forgive me for all the sinful things I have done. I want Him to give me a new heart and fresh start so that I can go to heaven.

I haven't focused on the things that I should be doing for God, as stated in that last verse, like sharing God's love with others. I hesitate because I think, Big risk! Big risk! But then I wonder, do I want to continue to be a "Gimme, Gimme Christian," focused only on what's in it for me?

....

O GOD, Thou art my God; early will I seek Thee: my soul thirsteth for Thee, my flesh longeth for Thee in a dry and thirsty land, where no water is; To see Thy power and Thy glory, so as I have seen Thee in the sanctuary. Because Thy loving kindness is better than life, my lips shall praise Thee. Thus will I bless Thee while I live: I will lift up my hands in Thy Name. Psalm, Chapter 63, verses 1-4.

I help my students analyze the descriptive writing styles of authors. David would be a great example of this. After reading how much David loves God when he says that his soul thirsteth and his flesh longeth for God in a dry and thirsty land, where no water is, makes me want to have that same dedication in my relationship with God.

....

For a day in Thy courts is better than a thousand. I had rather be a doorkeeper in the house of my God, than to dwell in the tents of wickedness. For the LORD God is a sun and shield: the LORD will give grace and glory: no good thing will He withhold from them that walk uprightly. O LORD of Hosts, blessed is the man that trusteth in Thee. Psalm, Chapter 84, verses 10-12.

David again, eloquently professes his love for God. He says one day of life with God is better than a thousand days of life without Him. He would rather have a lowly job in God's house than to live with all the riches that the wicked have. He tells us how well God takes care of the people who love Him.

This passage helps me to re-evaluate my priorities. I'm looking for a job because we have moved back to the area where our grandchildren live. I haven't gotten a teaching position yet. There are some smaller jobs in the newspaper that I haven't applied for. Part of me doesn't want to go from being a teacher to a position of less significance. I still want to impact the lives of students!

This passage makes me think that I shouldn't minimize jobs. It's hard telling what God's plan is. It says that David would rather be a doorkeeper in the house of God than to dwell in the tents of wickedness. I need to see that any position that God puts in my life has some special significance and I need to be open to it.

....

Thy Word is a lamp unto my feet, and a Light unto my path. Psalm, Chapter 119, verse 105.

This passage has special significance to me because my husband collects light houses. My thoughtful step-sons, daughter-in-law and grandchildren got my husband a light house shower curtain for a gift. When we moved into our house, I decided to paint light houses on the bathroom wall to go with the shower curtain.

My twelve year-old grandson drew the light houses free-hand and I painted them. Being inspired when the painting was completed; I looked for a Bible passage to paint over the door to make a connection between God and the light houses. There were several passages to choose from, although none spoke specifically about light houses. I couldn't decide, so I prayed and asked God for guidance. I decided to use a portion of this passage: *Thy Word is a lamp unto my feet, and a Light unto my path. Psalm, Chapter 119, verse 105.*

When we went to church with our grandsons that evening, one of the songs was *Thy Word Is a Lamp Unto My Feet, and a Light Unto My Path.* At that point, I knew that God had me choose the passage that He wanted. I was so excited that it was hard to wait until after church to tell my husband and grandsons all about it. This passage pops back into my mind, at times when I'm feeling frustrated or discouraged.

....

Teach me to do Thy will for Thou art my God: Thy Spirit is good; lead me into the land of uprightness. Psalm, Chapter 143, verse 10.

Bible Passages That Can Influence Your Life

Sometimes, I get too independent for my own good. I figure that since I'm a Christian and a basically good person, I can see when someone needs help and just take care of it. I'm starting to realize that the "I's" and "Me's" get me no where and I need to start praying for God's guidance, first. Sometimes I have rushed in to help someone, thinking "I" knew what was best for them, only to find out that I had undermined their dignity without realizing it. It sure knocked my "Christian ego" down a few notches and hopefully, I will be more aware of this in the future.

....

He telleth the number of the stars: He calleth them all by their names. Great is our LORD, and of great power: His understanding is infinite. The LORD lifteth up the meek: He casteth the wicked down to the ground. Sing unto the LORD with thanksgiving; sing praise upon the harp unto our God: Who covereth the heaven with clouds, Who prepareth rain for the earth, Who maketh grass to grow upon the mountains. He giveth to the beast his food, and to the young raven which cry. Psalm, Chapter 147, verses 4-9.

This passage had the word thanksgiving in it long before there were any Pilgrims and national holidays. When David talks about thanksgiving, he has the right idea. God provides for us and all the creatures of the world. My focus at Thanksgiving shouldn't be on which recipes to cook, so that my relatives brag on the spread they had at our house. Instead, my focus should consistently be on God, thanking Him for all He does for me. I shouldn't just thank Him on religious holidays. I wonder what it might be like the other way around. God would take care of my concerns on Thanksgiving, Christmas and Easter. The rest of the year, God would put me back on the shelf to wait; because I interfered with all the things He was doing during the year. I sure wouldn't want the tables turned!

Here is a related passage:

Yet I am the Lord thy God from the land of Egypt, and thou shalt know no god but Me: for there is no Saviour beside Me. I did know thee in the wilderness, in the land of great drought. According to their pasture, so were they filled; they were filled, and their heart was exalted; therefore have they forgotten Me. Hosea, Chapter 13, verses 4-6.

....

Praise Him with the timbrel and dance: praise Him with stringed instruments and organs. Praise Him upon the loud cymbals: praise Him upon the high sounding cymbals. Let every thing that hath breath praise the LORD, Praise ye the LORD. Psalm, Chapter 150, verses 4-6.

I realize that some types of music present subject matter and promote beliefs and actions that don't always glorify God. There have been styles of dancing that are less apt to be what God would approve of than others. I think that sometimes we "throw the baby out with the bath water". Here is another time that we are encouraged to sing and dance, showing our love of God. In my opinion, this shows that singing and dancing, in and of themselves aren't bad, especially when they are done to glorify God. Of course, we need to have balance in all things.

....

These are different proverbs that give us food for thought:

*Lying lips are abomination to the Lord: but they that deal truly are His delight. Proverbs, Chapter 12, verse 22.

*A soft answer turneth away wrath: but grievous words stir up anger. The tongue of the wise useth knowledge aright: but the mouth of fools poureth out foolishness. Proverbs, Chapter 15, verses 1-2.

*The lips of the wise disperse knowledge: but the heart of the foolish doeth not so. Proverbs, Chapter 15, verse 7.

*By mercy and Truth iniquity is purged: and by the fear of the LORD men depart from evil. When a man's ways please the LORD, he maketh even his enemies to be at peace with him. Proverbs, Chapter 16, verses 6-7.

*He that handleth a matter wisely shall find good: and whoso trusteth in the LORD, happy is he. Proverbs, Chapter 16, verse 20.

*Wine is a mocker, strong drink is raging: and whosoever is deceived thereby is not wise. Proverbs, Chapter 20, verse 1.

*Even a child is known by his doings, whether his work be pure, and whether it be right. Proverbs, Chapter 20, verse 11.

*A Good name is rather to be chosen than great riches, and loving favour rather than silver and gold. Proverbs, Chapter 22, verse 1.

*The rich and poor meet together: the LORD is the Maker of them all. Proverbs, Chapter 22, verse 2.

*A prudent man foreseeth the evil, and hideth himself: but the simple pass on, and are punished. Proverbs, Chapter 22, verse 3.

Bible Passages That Can Influence Your Life

*Make no friendship with an angry man; and with a furious man thou shalt not go: Lest thou learn his ways and get a snare to thy soul. Proverbs, Chapter 22, verses 24-25.

*Withdraw thy foot from thy neighbour's house; lest he be weary of thee, and so hate thee. Proverbs, Chapter 25, verse 17.

*The full soul loatheth an honeycomb; but to the hungry soul every bitter thing is sweet. Proverbs, Chapter 27, verse 7.

....

Ponder the path of thy feet, and let all thy ways be established. Turn not to the right hand nor to the left: remove thy foot from evil. Proverbs, Chapter 4, verses 26-27.

I remember walking with a friend on a dirt road that ran along the far side of my elementary school. I was rambling on about something as I walked, only to be stopped by the squeals of delight from my walking partner. She had found a silver dollar in my tracks.

I had been so busy focused on something else that I hadn't watched where I was walking, as she had. If I had paid attention to what I was doing and where I was going, I would have been the person who found the treasure.

Well, Christians also have to watch where they are going and whether the choices they are making are leading them astray. The worldly things in life can lead us off our path of faith. If we focus on God's Will for us, as stated in the Bible, we are more apt to find the treasure of Salvation at the end of our road.

....

The soul of the sluggard desireth, and hath nothing: but the soul of the diligent shall be made fat. Proverbs, Chapter 13, verse 4.

This reminds me of the story my grandfather used to tell me when I was little about the Ant and the Grasshopper. The ant worked busily throughout the spring, summer and fall and put food away for the winter while the Grasshopper enjoyed himself and played. Then when the winter came along, the Ant had a plenty of food to last him and the lazy Grasshopper was cold and hungry.

Here is a related passage:

*Slothfulness casteth into a deep sleep; and an idle soul shall suffer hunger. Proverbs, Chapter 19, verse 15.

....

He that walketh with wise men shall be wise: but a companion of fools shall be destroyed. Proverbs, Chapter 13, verse 20.

Well, I have sadly noticed something over my years as a teacher. I have often placed a student who was a good role model next to a disruptive student. I thought the positive role model's example would rub off on the disruptive student. Almost every time, I found the exact opposite to be true. It seems the role model student almost always starts taking on some of the characteristics of the disruptive student, not the other way around.

I think that this often applies to Christians, as well. I think we often take on the traits of the people we hang around. If we associate with people who live their lives focused on God, we are more apt to live in a similar manner. If we hang around people who have worldly values and make lifestyle choices that don't reflect their love for God, then we are more apt to live our lives in a like manner. It boils down to who you think God would want influencing your life.

....

He that spareth his rod hateth his son: but he that loveth him chasteneth him betimes. Proverbs, Chapter 13, verse 24.

Parents often feel guilty for being away from their children with their work and other things that take them away from home. At times, some parents over compensate by giving their children all they desire, overlooking the child's disobedience without realizing how counterproductive it is. If a parent gives in to a child's demands when they are young and doesn't provide appropriate consequences for misbehavior, do you think that child will behave any differently as a teenager or adult? Maybe correcting children and having reasonable expectations for them while they're young would be to their best advantage. Our ultimate goal should be that they grow into responsible, Christian men and women.

....

The thoughts of the wicked are an abomination to the LORD: but the words of the pure are pleasant words. Proverbs, Chapter 15, Verse 26.

Now, I guess I might be able to convince some that my thoughts are always God focused and selfless, but God knows how I really am inside. Fortunately, He forgives me and helps to turn my selfish thoughts and resentments around to be more tolerant and forgiving of others.

Here are some related passages:

*The heart of the righteous studieth to answer: but the mouth of the wicked poureth out evil things. Proverbs, Chapter 15, verse 28.

*A wicked doer giveth heed to false lips: and a liar giveth ear to a naughty tongue. Proverbs, Chapter 17, verse 4.

*Even a fool, when he holdeth his peace, is counted wise: and he that shutteth his lips is esteemed a man of understanding. Proverbs, Chapter 17, verse 28.

*A false witness shall not be unpunished, and he that speaketh lies shall perish. Proverbs, Chapter 19, verse 9.

*A fool utterth all his mind: but a wise man keepeth it in till afterwards. Proverbs, Chapter 29, verse 11.

....

He that refuseth instruction despiseth his own soul: but he that heareth reproof getteth understanding. Proverbs, Chapter 15, verse 32.

When I was a child, my father noticed that I scuffled my feet as I walked. He knew it was a counterproductive trait, so he had me practice walking with an appropriate gait. Being stubborn, I deliberately went back to scuffling my feet. Now that I am older and have recently broken my ankle, I wish I hadn't been such a stubborn child. It would have been nice if I had listened to my father's advice which would have saved me a lot of discomfort. We have the same options in our relationship with our Heavenly Father. To listen, or not to listen, that is the question? (Forgive me for misquoting Shakespeare.)

....

The fear of the LORD is the instruction of wisdom; and before honour is humility. Proverbs, Chapter 15, verse 33.

I enjoy teaching and feel my teaching style has really improved over the years. Our school district allows each school to make nominations for Teacher of the Year. Somehow, I got the distorted notion that I had been nominated for this. Egotistical person that I can be, although most wouldn't know it, I prepared how I would respond when they announced my nomination at a faculty meeting. Ironically, the award went to someone else who was extremely deserving and probably a lot more humble.

Fortunately, no one else knew that I thought I was going to be nominated, which was a big relief but God and I did. This was a humbling experience, to say the least. Hopefully, it leads me to be less self-absorbed in the future.

Here are some related passages:

Every one that is proud in heart is an abomination to the LORD: though hand join in hand, he shall not be unpunished. Proverbs, Chapter 16, verse 5.

Seest thou a man wise in his own conceit? there is more hope of a fool than of him. Proverbs, Chapter 26, verse 12.

Boast not thyself of tomorrow; for thou knowest not what a day may bring forth. Let another man praise thee, and not thine own mouth; a stranger, and not thine own lips. Proverbs, Chapter 27, verses 1-2.

....

Whoso mocketh the poor reproacheth his Maker: and he that is glad at calamities shall not be unpunished. Proverbs, Chapter 17, verse 5.

I remember being with someone who I used to think was a friend prior to this. I realized that they weren't someone I wished to keep company with after this situation. This person put down a guy with long hair in his community who was riding a motorcycle and crashed and got killed, saying it served him right. There was no compassion, only justified indignation at this person with long hair who rode a motorcycle. I don't think it says anywhere in the Bible that only people with short hair, wear suits to work and drive expensive cars are allowed to go to heaven. Actually, Jesus had long hair, but the main point of this is that we aren't to judge others or make fun of their misfortune.

Here is a related passage:

Rejoice not when thine enemy falleth, and let not thine heart be glad when he stumbleth. Proverbs, Chapter 24, verse 17.

....

A fool's mouth is his destruction, and his lips are the snare of his soul. The words of a talebearer are as wounds, and they go down into the innermost parts of the belly. Proverbs, Chapter 18, verses 7-8.

I have seen children at school go to another student and say something like, "Fred thinks you're ugly." The child is crushed by this information. In talking to the student who shared this, I have come to realize that they thought they were doing the child a favor by telling. I have to explain that when they share hurtful things, even though they weren't the one who originally said them, they are actually being hurtful themselves.

Bible Passages That Can Influence Your Life

I have stopped being close friends with some adults who manipulatively work situations to their own good. I have known those who will get a person involved in a discussion focused on putting down another person, as well. Then they go to the other person and say what was said, trying to get in close with that person. It's a, "Did you know what terrible things Fred said about you?" on a grown-up level. This passage doesn't sound like God takes too kindly to this type of behavior.

....

He that answereth a matter before he heareth it, it is folly and shame unto him. Proverbs, Chapter 18, verse 13.

This is good "Open Mouth-Insert Foot" advice. I can't tell you how many times I have embarrassed myself by thinking I knew what someone was talking about. Stupidly, I would interrupt them and put my two cents in; only to find out I wasn't even on the same topic.

....

Wealth maketh many friends; but the poor is separated from his neighbour. Proverbs, Chapter 19, verse 4.

I'm somewhat embarrassed to tell you about this, but here goes. When I was in the seventh grade, I needed to give my little turtle to someone because I was no longer able to keep it. The teacher let me make an announcement to the whole class. There were two people who wanted it. One was the dreamboat of the class who was really popular, but self-absorbed. Then there was a nice person who wasn't in the popular group. I remember thinking that the nice person would have given the turtle a better home, but I ended up giving it to the popular one, instead. I had seen it as my one chance to get the attention of someone popular. It saddens me to have been this shallow.

It also makes me think of how many people are immediately friends of those who have won the lottery, who had little to do with them prior to that.

....

Chasten thy son while there is hope, and let not thy soul spare for his crying. Proverbs, Chapter 19, verse 18.

Sometimes it's all too easy to give in to our children to keep them from nagging us. Their best interest needs to always be in sight as our ultimate goal. I hear children in primary grades talk about graphic, sexual things that they must have picked up from the shows they watch. It may be easier for parents to just let their children watch these shows rather than to have to deal with their children nagging them.

The real question should be, "What does this do to the child?" Little children are exposed to all too much sexually explicit, violent and vulgar language and scenes in the media today. The media isn't going to stop making these shows, so it's up to the parent to value their child enough to monitor the shows they view and put up with some nagging and fits. After all, it's their child's well-being that counts.

....

A man of great wrath shall suffer punishment: for if thou deliver him, yet thou must do it again. Proverbs, Chapter 19, verse 19.

This reminds me of how the police will go to the house of a man beating his wife and just give him a warning. That really doesn't do much. He's going to keep beating her, if not that time, some other time when the stress gets to be too much for him. It also, reminds me of how the court system lets rapists, killers and child molesters out into the public after they have served some time, only to find out that the person raped, killed or molested someone else. A person who could have been saved, if the system had not let that rapist, killer or molester back out.

....

It is a snare to the man who devoureth that which is holy, and after vows to make inquiry. Proverbs, Chapter 20, verse 25.

I can't explain what this passage actually means, only how this relates to me.

I'm not supposed to have sugar because Hypoglycemia runs in my family. It also makes me cranky with those I care about. Anyway, there have been times when someone brought a treat into the Teacher's Lounge to share. I knew it probably had too much sugar in it. I tried to block it out of my mind and eat it as fast as I could. Then I would say something like, "Oh, that was really good. I bet it had sugar in it and I shouldn't have eaten it."

I knew full-well it had too much sugar in it to begin with, trying to fool the people sitting around me. I may have fooled the people that I work with, but you can't fool God!

He and I both knew I was aware of what I was doing all along. Well, I think this Bible verse is saying something similar. You can't fool God by doing something that's against His rules, and then play innocent after the fact, when you really knew you shouldn't have done it.

Here is a related passage:

For thou hast trusted in thy wickedness: thou hast said, None seeth me. Thy wisdom and thy knowledge, it hath perverted thee; and thou hast said in thine heart, I am, and none else beside me. Isaiah, Chapter 47, verse 10.

....

Train up a child in the way he should go: and when he is old, he will not depart from it. Proverbs, Chapter 22, verse 6.

If we take the time and are consistent in raising our children with rules and appropriate consequences, our children will be the better for it, even in their adult lives. For one thing, it helps them have parenting skills when they are raising their own children. As a teacher, I've seen the product of the opposite. There was a period of time, when some parents seemed to think that it was important to cater to a child's every wish and didn't have any consequences for breaking rules. When some of those kids grew up, they didn't know how to raise their own children or how to appropriately discipline them, because those skills were never really modeled for them as they grew up.

....

Speak not in the ears of a fool: for he will despise the wisdom of thy words. Proverbs, Chapter 23, verse 9.

Sometimes we waste our time trying to explain our beliefs to people who just like to be contrary. They could argue with us all day, on any issue. We are just wasting our breath on people like this. They aren't going to be open to any of the things we have to tell them about our love for Jesus.

There are people from a particular religion that comes to my door to talk about God, but they don't believe that Jesus is our Savior. I could stand there all day and talk to them about how the Bible tells us that Jesus Christ is Savior of all, but they won't be open to listening. As a Christian, it's better for me not to debate my religion with people like that.

For one reason, these people may be more persuasive than we are and we may get confused. That happened to me one time. People from this religion were able to quote Bible verses to support the things they were saying, and I started wondering if they were right and I had misinterpreted things.

Later, I got my Bible and read the whole chapter that they had pulled these verses from. That helped me realize that the verses they mentioned were really talking about a totally different issue. Those adults pulled verses from the Bible out of context, making them sound like they supported their argument. If I could get confused by trying to defend my beliefs, then it could possibly happen to you. It's easier to not get into a debate in the first place.

....

> *Withhold not correction from the child: for if thou beatest him with the rod, he shall not die. Thou shalt beat him with the rod, and shalt deliver his soul from hell. Proverbs, Chapter 23, verses 13 and 14.*

The Bible doesn't mean it's acceptable to beat your child when you've had a hard day at work or you've lost your temper. I think this Bible verse is referring to them getting a branch and swatting their child's bottom when they have made significant mistakes to warrant it. I think this was done to motivate them to not make that severe of a mistake again. (My parents used a paddle which used to have a rubber ball attached. My uncle drew a "frownie face" on it, which worked as a deterrent for more serious infractions. My parents didn't do this in a fit of rage. Time out and logical consequences seemed to work for most situations, but there are times when more serious consequences are necessary.)

I think of talk shows that have mothers and fathers as guests who can't control their kids. Their kids seem to control the adults and their household climate. Their children are hateful and self-willed and bully other students at school. The police are now holding the parents responsible for not controlling these children. This Bible verse makes me think it's better to reprimand the children when they are younger than to have to deal with the police later.

Of course, there are children who get into the wrong groups and get involved in drugs and other vices that change the child's whole personality. That's why it's vitally important that parents take an active role in their child's life. It can be difficult when parents work and the child has time to hang around with friends after school. Raising our children by taking them to Sunday school and Church on a regular basis can prove to be beneficial. It is better that children grow up with positive Christian values, rules and consequences. This may give them a better sense of right and wrong that could keep them from being so vulnerable to negative influences. It sure beats having to go to court to explain why your child is unruly.

Here are some related passages:

The father of the righteous shall greatly rejoice: and he that begetteth a wise child shall have joy of him. Thy father and thy mother shall be glad, and she that bare thee shall rejoice. Proverbs, Chapter 23, verses 24-25.

Correct thy son, and he shall give thee rest; yea, he shall give delight unto thy soul. Proverbs, Chapter 29, verse 17.

....

Let not thine heart envy sinners: but be thou in the fear of the LORD all the day long. Proverbs, Chapter 23, verse 17.

I realize that as human beings we sometimes envy all the attention people get in the popular groups. I have found myself thinking that if I were to wear certain clothes or behave in certain ways, then I would get all the same attention. It really isn't worth lowering our standards to lead that type of lifestyle. I don't want to be a "Sell-out Christian," selling out my Salvation for the opportunity to be popular.

....

Hearken unto thy father that begat thee, and despise not thy mother when she is old. Proverbs, Chapter 23, verse 22.

God doesn't only have advice for parents in the Bible; He has advice for children, as well. He wants children to listen to their parents. We aren't to resent our parents or ignore them when they get older when they aren't as convenient to take care of. I don't think He's saying we've done our bit to put our parents away in a nursing home somewhere as long as we pay the bills. I don't have the perfect answer but I've seen the elderly in nursing homes, starved for attention because they haven't seen their children in months or years.

I admired the way my family pitched together to try to keep my grandfather at home where he felt comfortable as long as they possibly could. My great-aunt would take him shopping for groceries. My uncle would come mow his yard and clean around the house and my aunt would look after his legal issues that he was oblivious to. My other uncle took care of his finances. My mother would balance his checkbook, trying to locate the necessary paperwork. Many family members were involved, some living closer and some far away. Everyone helped in whichever capacity they felt able. His aging presented a situation that seemed to pull the family together.

....

Dorothy Scott

> *Hast thou found honey? eat so much as is sufficient for thee, lest thou be filled therewith, and vomit it. Proverbs, Chapter 25, verse 16.*

I really like this because it hits home. When I used to eat sweets, I would think a particular pie or other delicacy was desirable. I didn't think I would get it again for a long time, so I would "sleece" my way around the pie and end up eating almost the whole thing.

Now, if you're wondering what a "sleece" is, it's a word I made up to describe taking a little sliver of pie, cake, etc. It tasted so good that I would take another and another until almost the whole thing was gone. I would feel so guilty for eating that much, I would put my hand on the top crust of the pie and try to push it down so some of the filling would go out the sides. I tried to make it look like there was more pie than there actually was. I thought this would keep my family from knowing what I had done. I used to eat things that were special treats to the point that I made my stomach sick. I'm so fortunate that God has taken care of my compulsive overeating.

....

> *If thine enemy be hungry, give him bread to eat; and if he be thirsty, give him water to drink: For thou shalt heap coals of fire upon his head, and the LORD shall reward thee. Proverbs, Chapter 25, verses 21-22.*

The United States has been involved in trying to deal with the terrorist actions that took place on September 11, 2001. When they were trying to find the terrorists, many were compassionate to the starving people of that country. I heard that they sent food for approximately 6,000 people on a daily basis.

At first when I heard this, I was really frustrated. I thought we are helping the enemy who tried to devastate our country through terrorist acts of violence. Then I realized that I was being very self-centered and decided that it's our Christian duty to take care of all those starving people. Sometimes the human side of me sneaks in and undermines my Christian ethics.

....

> *He that hath no rule over his own spirit is like a city that is broken down, and without walls. Proverbs, Chapter 25, verse 28.*

I would get kids through the years, which had a "reputation" for not being in control of their behavior choices. I think they had been "out of control" for so many years that they thought they'd always be this way and so did some of their families.

After developing a bond with these students, they were more open to following the classroom rules and guidelines. I tried to help them see the improvements they were making to be more "in control" of their actions and choices. At first, they were reluctant to believe that they were capable of this, trying to revert back to old, comfortable ways. After time and continued support to "be the best they could be," they eventually started noticing that they were making more and more good choices and were thinking about the consequences of their poor choices more than they ever had.

It was exciting to see these same children leave my class at the end of the year, taking pride in their ability to be "in control" of their lives and choices. They were better able to bounce back when things didn't go the way they wanted. They left with confidence, which is a distinct contrast from the student who had that reputation of "being out of control."

What a difference consistent parameters make in their lives. Ideally, all families would provide their children with consistent, appropriate rules, not changing them at whim. This would help their children grow up learning to feel "in control" of their actions rather than becoming someone without rule over his own spirit.

....

Answer not a fool according to his folly, lest thou also be like unto him. Proverbs, Chapter 26, verse 4.

Sometimes people treat others like a fishing tournament. The fisherman baits his hook with some challenging remark, just enough to entice us to take the bait by challenging our religious beliefs. Once we bite that lure and get involved in the interaction, the fisherman yanks the pole and starts to reel his catch in. Usually, it's best to resist the opportunity to respond to people when they set us up.

....

Where no wood is, there the fire goeth out: so where there is no talebearer, the strife ceaseth. Proverbs, Chapter 26, verse 20.

I like the visual picture I have with this passage. One way of looking at this passage might be to think of the wood as the person who listens to gossip. The fire is the person who spreads the gossip. If people listen to gossip, it "adds fuel to the fire." If no one listened to these stories, it would put the gossiper out of business; because they do it for the attention it gets them.

Here is a related passage:

> *The words of a talebearer are as wounds, and they go down into the innermost parts of the belly. Proverbs, Chapter 26, verse 22.

....

> When the righteous are in authority, the people rejoice but when the wicked beareth rule, the people mourn. Proverbs, Chapter 29, verse 2.

This reminds me of how I explain to my students about democracies where the people elect the government officials. This is contrasted with some countries where the dictator takes over the country by force. I tell them these dictators usually have their needs as a priority and not the needs of their citizens, who often live in impoverished and inhumane situations.

Here is a related passage:

> *The righteous considereth the cause of the poor: but the wicked regardeth not to know it. Proverbs, Chapter 29, verse 7.

....

> Seest thou a man that is hasty in his words? there is more hope of a fool than of him. Proverbs, Chapter 29, verse 20.

This is talking about our opinion of people who go around babbling every thought that goes through their head. Do you trust people like that to know your deepest, darkest secrets? Do you appoint people like that as heads of corporations? Do you really trust them to be there in a pinch when you really need them? They aren't generally the people we turn to when we need help.

....

> An angry man stirreth up strife, and a furious man aboundeth in transgression. Proverbs, Chapter 29, verse 22.

It seems that some people are always angry. They are abrupt with others and say hateful things rather than try to work things out calmly. They go around upsetting people everywhere they go, leaving a trail of arguments, fights and people with hurt feelings. I learned a long time ago that my life runs a lot smoother when I stay clear of people like this.

....

> Many seek the ruler's favour; but every man's judgment cometh from the LORD. Proverbs, Chapter 29, verse 26.

It reminds me of politics on local level. I remember hearing about local businessmen who bought gifts for those who govern them, hoping to get political favors in return. (Example: Companies were told they had to make costly anti-pollution adjustments to their factories. The newspapers would note companies that were flagrantly non-compliant, without legal repercussions. It was implied that the business had given a politician some gift large enough to overlook the fact that they were dumping waste into the public water supply, etc.) So, this passage says to me that we may try to kiss up to the politicians of the world who might turn a blind eye to our actions, but God really knows what we do!

....

The eye that mocketh at his father, and despiseth to obey his mother, the ravens of the valley shall pick it out, and the young eagles shall eat it. Proverbs, Chapter 30, verse 17.

It doesn't sound like God thinks it's cute when kids are disrespectful to their parents. He's talking about having ravens peck out the eyes of children who are disrespectful to their parents. It doesn't sound like God condones their behavior.

How do children learn to be respectful, anyway? One way is by setting appropriate limits while they're little. If they're allowed to argue with their parents when they're little, do you think they will argue with their parents less when they are 16? If they're allowed to break the rules with no consequences when they're little, do you think they will break the rules less when they are 16? If they are allowed to have a lack of respect for authority figures when they're little, do you think they will be more respectful of authority figures when they are 16? If they are allowed to be self-focused, not thinking of others when they're little, will they be more concerned about the needs of others when they are 16?

If you don't teach them religious principals and allow them to develop a relationship with God when they're little, do you think they will gain these religious principals and develop a relationship with God when they are 16? So, if we don't teach our kids to be respectful when they're little...who will??????????

....

Who can find a virtuous woman? for her price is far above rubies. The heart of her husband doth safely trust in her, so that he shall have no need of spoil. She will do him good and not evil all the days of her life. Proverbs, Chapter 31, verses 10-12.

It goes on to say how she will help provide for her family, but I like verse 20: *She stretcheth out her hand to the poor; yea, she reacheth forth her hands to the needy.*

The next verses continue to list some of the qualities of the virtuous woman, but I, also like verse, 26: *She openeth her mouth with wisdom; and in her tongue is the law of kindness.* There are more qualities listed, and then verse 30 says: *Favour is deceitful, and beauty is vain: but a woman that feareth the LORD, she shall be praised.*

I especially like the last verse that I mentioned. God wasn't saying, "Boy are you lucky to have a wife who is a CEO of a company." Or, "Boy are you lucky to have a wife who is so gorgeous that she looks like a model." God says (paraphrased) that He values women who look after their families, provide for them and are kind and giving to others. In fact, God reminds us that beauty is only skin deep. What really matters is a person's relationship with God and living as an example of that.

Now, we've all met some attractive, shallow people but there are also beautiful women who have a great relationship with God. There are homely, bedraggled women who are shallow and some who have a great relationship with God. We really can't make decisions about people based on their looks. Fortunately, God doesn't judge us by human standards. He knows of our love for Jesus and sees how we lead our lives and what our priorities are.

....

To every thing there is a season, and a time to every purpose under the heaven: A time to be born, and a time to die; a time to plant, and a time to pluck up that which is planted; A time to kill, and a time to heal; a time to break down, and a time to build up; A time to weep, and a time to laugh; a time to mourn, and a time to dance; A time to cast away stones, and a time to gather stones together; a time to embrace, and a time to refrain from embracing; A time to get, and a time to lose; a time to keep, and a time to cast away; A time to rend, and a time to sew; a time to keep silence, and a time to speak; A time to love, and a time to hate; a time of war, and a time of peace. Ecclesiastes, Chapter 3, verses 1-8.

This passage brings back memories of a Simon and Garfunkel song, but this has a deeper meaning. I think the song was popular for many reasons. It made us realize that there are various stages in our lives and different reactions are appropriate, depending on the occasion. I think this passage tells Christians to be flexible, because God will help us handle whatever comes our way. There are going to be births and deaths, wars and peace, etc. How we handle these sets the foundation for how other people, especially the younger generation, handle the trials, tribulations and joys in their lives.

If we get depressed, drink, take drugs, yell at others or mope around all day when we have troubles, what do you think our children are going to do when they have problems in their lives? If we use times of joy to get involved in the excesses of life, including eating, sex, drinking, drugs, etc., what do you think our children are going to do when they have great joy? We need to make sure we handle situations in ways that we would like our children to emulate under similar circumstances.

....

He that loveth silver shall not be satisfied with silver; nor he that loveth abundance with increase: this is also vanity. Ecclesiastes, Chapter 5, verse 10.

When we used to have family gatherings, my grandfather would have all the children and adults gather in the front room for the "Money Game." He would build everyone's anticipation as he jingled all the coins in his pockets. After a hush filled the room, everyone watched intently as he slowly dropped the coins onto the floor. Young and old were trying to mentally tally the coins as they lay there, ever so briefly, before he gathered them up again. Someone would take down everyone's guesses and the person who guessed the exact amount got to keep the money.

I spent my time focused on the money and whether I won or not. Instead, I should have been focused on the "wealth of family interactions" and the extra excitement my grandfather provided, creating a lifetime of memories for everyone involved.

....

It is better to hear the rebuke of the wise, than for a man to hear the song of fools. Ecclesiastes, Chapter 7, verse 5.

This reminds me of when I ask my husband to read over something I've written. He starts looking at it, making comments about corrections he thinks should be made to my paper. It's really very frustrating to me. The thing is-he's right. When I incorporate the corrections he suggests, my paper flows much better than it previously did. Although it's still frustrating to me to have him edit my papers, I know the advice he gives me will be beneficial in the long run.

If I asked someone else for advice on my writing and they told me everything was wonderful regardless of the errors, it would be like hearing the song of fools. They just tell you what you want to hear, but they don't provide the input that is beneficial. I would much rather have the advice of the wise than a "Yes Man," any day.

....

> *For there is not a just man upon earth, that doeth good, and sinneth not. Ecclesiastes, Chapter 7, verse 20.*

My mother used to tell me that there are some who put others down just to make themselves feel better. This saying has comforted me over the years. The thing I never paid any attention to is whether I did this myself.

None of us is perfect, except Jesus. It's funny how easy it is for us non-perfect human beings to find fault in others. It appears that we think that looking down on others makes us better people. NOT...as the kids say!...or No way, Jose!...or Not on your life! I could go on, but you get the idea.

....

> *Also take no heed unto all words that are spoken; lest thou hear thy servant curse thee: For often times also thine own heart knoweth that thou thyself likewise hast cursed others. Ecclesiastes, Chapter 7, verses 21-22.*

As a teacher, the children who came to me crying because someone called them names often were those who were notorious for calling other children names. They could "dish it out," but couldn't handle it when it happened to them.

Isn't it funny that adults are very similar? We come unglued when someone says something rude or hateful to us, when we are often guilty of being rude and hateful to others. Somehow, it seems different when someone else does it. Maybe we can learn to be more forgiving of others, in the same way that Christ forgives us for all our actions.

Our children see how we handle frustrating experiences and will tend to handle things similarly as they grow up. We need to be forgiving, even if someone's just crowded into our parking spot when we had our car all lined up for it!

....

> *Thus is an evil among all things that are done under the sun, that there is one event unto all: yea, also the heart of the sons of men is full of evil, and madness is in their heart while they live, and after that they go to the dead. For to him that is joined to all the living there is hope: for a living dog is better than a dead lion. For the living know that they shall die: but the dead know not any thing, neither have they any more a reward; for the memory of them is forgotten, Also their love, and their*

hatred, and their envy, is now perished: neither have they any more a portion for ever in any thing that is done under the sun. Ecclesiastes, Chapter 9, verses 3-6.

It seems that some people spend their whole lives angry and bitter. They should have gotten the promotion or job that they wanted. They deserved a nicer house or car instead of what they have. I try to stay away from people who are always griping about how things should have been better, because I tend to feel depressed after talking to them.

We have choices in life. We can spend our lives content or always upset when things don't turn out the way we want. When I don't get what I want, although I might be a little disappointed, I recognize that God knows what is best for me. It's a choice we make when we choose to harbor resentments for all the things that don't go the way that we think we deserve. Personally, I don't want people avoiding me because I'm always griping. What's more important, I don't want God avoiding me thinking, "Dorothy's always griping and ungrateful for all I've given her. I think I'll focus on someone else who appreciates what I do for them."

....

Hear the Word of the LORD, ye rulers of Sodom; give ear unto the Law of our God, ye people of Gomorrah. To what purpose is the multitude of your sacrifices unto Me? saith the LORD: I am full of the burnt offerings of rams, and the fat of fed beasts; and I delight not in the blood of bullocks, or of lambs, or of he goats. Isaiah, Chapter 1, verses 10-11.

We all know what happened to the people of Sodom and Gomorrah. I think God is saying that they can give offerings until "the cows come home," but it doesn't buy them forgiveness for their very worldly lives. It reminds me of people who live in the "fast lane" and feel that if they put large amounts of money in the offering plate, it absolves them from the things they do in their lives.

Do you think that God overlooks things like cheating on their spouse, unethical business choices or hateful behavior to others because they've put lots of money in the offering? God wants us to ask Him to forgive us and then, out of love for Him, we are to try to live as examples of how He works in our lives. This "Sin now, pay later tactic" just doesn't work for God.

....

And He shall judge among the nations, and shall rebuke many people: and they shall beat their swords into plowshares, and their spears into pruninghooks: nation shall not lift up

> *sword against nation, neither shall they learn war any more. O house of Jacob, come ye, and let us walk in the Light of the Lord. Isaiah, Chapter 2, verses 4-5.*

This is a very famous passage. There is another passage in the Bible that is the complete opposite, telling people to beat their plowshares into swords and spears. *Beat your plowshares into swords, and your pruninghooks into spears: let the weak say I am strong. Joel, Chapter 3, verse 10.*

These passages tell me that God has times when we are to fight for the causes He wants. Then there are times when we aren't to fight and are to try to maintain peace in all aspects of our lives, if at all possible.

....

> *Therefore thou hast forsaken Thy people the house of Jacob, because they be replenished from the east, and are soothsayers like the Philistines, and they please themselves in the children of strangers. Isaiah, Chapter 2, verse 6.*

It doesn't sound like God approves of His people getting involved in fortune telling and trying to predict the future. He probably isn't any more pleased with people doing things like this, today!

What's even more abominable is that they pleased themselves, in the children of strangers. Does child abuse, child porn, etc. seem less objectionable when it's connected to children who are totally different than we are? During war times, atrocities like this are committed as if the women and children of other countries are sub-human entities, absolving them of any guilt for abusing them. It's an abomination no matter what!

Children aren't to be exploited. Looking at child porn sites on the Internet keeps people in the business of taking advantage of children. Are you helping to perpetuate the problem?

....

> *And the loftiness of man shall be bowed down, and the haughtiness of men shall be made low: and the LORD alone shall be exalted in that day. And the idols He shall utterly abolish. And they shall go into the holes of the rocks, and into the caves of the earth, for fear of the LORD, and for the Glory of His Majesty, when He ariseth to shake terribly the earth. Isaiah, Chapter 2, verses 17-19.*

I remember my father reminding me not to get so high and mighty when I was spouting off about something. I'm glad he drew my attention to it. I don't want God coming to me someday saying, "Dorothy, get off your high horse. You think you're someone special just because you have a Master's degree. If you spent less time focused on your career and your 'stuff,' you'd have more time to focus on Me and what I want for you. It would have been nice if you could have joined Me in heaven, but you had your chance and blew it on worldly things. So sad."

....

> The voice of him that crieth in the wilderness, Prepare ye the way of the LORD, make straight in the desert a highway for our God. Isaiah, Chapter 40, verse 3.

When a new movie comes out on the market, there are some who won't go to see it immediately. They don't just believe the advertisements that the movie producers put out. They are cautious, waiting until they see the movie reviews first to make sure it's going to be good. Well, I think that's why John the Baptist was important. Others had to hear him say that Jesus was our Savior before they would be open to believing. Those that heard John the Baptist profess this were more willing to risk believing in Jesus.

Isn't it strange that some have to hear someone else's opinion before they are willing to take risks? Well, there are people out there who aren't going to get to know Jesus as their Savior unless they hear us share the positive influence Jesus has in our lives. It makes me realize that I have a bigger responsibility than I was aware of. My sitting quietly, rationalizing why it's not a good time to share this information with others may keep someone else from getting to heaven.

Here are some related passages from the New Testament:

> *For this is he that was spoken of by the prophet Esaias, saying The voice of one crying in the wilderness, Prepare ye the way of the Lord, make His paths straight. Matthew, Chapter 3, verse 3.

> *For this is he, of whom it is written, Behold, I send My messenger before Thy face, which shall prepare Thy way before Thee. Verily I say unto you, Among them that are born of women there hath not risen a greater than John the Baptist: notwithstanding he that is least in the kingdom of heaven is greater than he. And from the days of John the Baptist until now the kingdom of heaven suffereth violence, and the violent take it by force. Matthew, Chapter 11, verses 10-12.

....

Woe unto them that call evil good, and good evil, that put darkness for light, and Light for darkness; that put bitter for sweet, and sweet for bitter! Isaiah, Chapter 5, verse 20.

It's sad that having extra-marital affairs has almost become a norm in society. People seem to feel no remorse in doing unethical things in order to climb the ladder of success. People who have great status and wealth are looked upon more approvingly than those who lead good-Christian lives. People who live according to their Christian ethics are often ridiculed and aren't given the same respect as others. God calls it like He sees it! When it comes to determining people's Salvation, no amount of money, status or remarks trying to justify one's actions are going to buy them entrance into heaven.

Here are some related passages:

*Which justify the wicked for reward, and take away the righteousness of the righteous from him! Therefore as the fire devoureth the stubble, and the flame consumeth the chaff, so their root shall be as rottenness, and their blossom shall go up as dust: because they have cast away the Law of the LORD of Hosts, and despised the Word of the Holy One of Israel. Therefore is the anger of the LORD kindled against His people, and He hath stretched forth His hand against them and hath smitten them: and the hills did tremble, and their carcasses were torn in the midst of the streets. For all this His anger is not turned away, but His hand is stretched out still. Isaiah, Chapter 5, verses 23-25.

*And they shall teach My people the difference between the Holy and profane, and cause them to discern between the unclean and the clean. And in controversy they shall stand in judgment; and they shall judge it according to My judgments: and they shall keep My Laws and My Statutes in all Mine assemblies; and they shall hallow My Sabbaths. Ezekiel, Chapter 44, verses 23-24.

*Seek good, and not evil, that ye may live: and so the Lord, the God of Hosts, shall be with you, as ye have spoken. Hate the evil, and love the good, and establish judgment in the gate: it may be that the Lord God of Hosts will be gracious unto the remnant of Joseph. Amos, Chapter 5, verses 14-15.

> *Ye have wearied the LORD with your words. Yet ye say, Wherein have we wearied Him? When ye say, Every one that doeth evil is good in the sight of the LORD, and He delighteth in them: or, Where is the God of judgment? Malachi, Chapter 2, verse 17.*

....

> *How art thou fallen from heaven, O Lucifer, son of the morning! how art thou cut down to the ground, which didst weaken the nations! For thou hast said in thine heart, I will ascend into heaven, I will exalt my throne above the stars of God: I will sit also upon the mount of the congregation, in the sides of the north: I will ascend above the heights of the clouds: I will be like the most High. Yet thou shalt be brought down to hell, to the sides of the pit. They that see thee shall narrowly look upon thee, and consider thee, saying, Is this the man that made the earth to tremble, that did shake kingdoms. That made the world as a wilderness, and destroyed the cities thereof; that opened not the house of his prisoners? Isaiah, Chapter 14, verses 12-17.*

God is condemning Satan's influence on mankind, especially Babylon. Now, if God didn't like that Satan had tried to become like God, don't you think God would be equally displeased when people professing to be Christians want to have "the god power within them?" I'm no expert, but through the things I have read in the Bible, God usually gets pretty upset when anyone is arrogant enough to try to gain the power of God.

....

> *Stand now with thine enchantments, and with the multitude of thy sorceries, wherein thou hast laboured from thy youth; if so be thou shalt be able to profit, if so be thou mayest prevail. Thou are wearied in the multitude of thy counsels. Let now the astrologers the stargazers, and the monthly prognosticators, stand up, and save thee from these things that shall come upon thee. Behold, they shall be as stubble; the fire shall burn them; they shall not deliver themselves from the power of the flame: there shall not be a coal to warm at, nor fire to sit before it. Thus shall they be unto thee with whom thou hast laboured, even thy merchants, from thy youth: they shall wander every one to his quarter; none shall save thee. Isaiah, Chapter 47, verses 12-15.*

God seems to be telling the Babylonians (paraphrased), "You made your bed, now lie in it!" Prior to this, God tried to refocus the Babylonians who were being led astray. They listened to those with power, the sorcerers and astrologers, etc. People were paying attention to them instead of to God. He told them (paraphrased), "When push comes to shove, those people you looked up to are going to hit the road and they won't be there to protect you. But then again, you deserve it because you ignored Me when I tried to help you. I am the Only One who could have saved you. So, sad!"

....

Seek ye the LORD while He may be found, call ye upon Him while He is near: Let the wicked forsake his way, and the unrighteous man his thoughts: and let him return unto the LORD, and He will have mercy upon him; and to our God, for He will abundantly pardon. Isaiah, Chapter 55, verses 6-7.

It's amazing, how forgiving God is. The people had been focusing on astrologers and sorcerers rather than Him, the One True God. God told them that if they realized that they were wrong and turned their act around, He would forgive them and take care of them. Such divine forgiveness is something I haven't always been able to muster.

If people were rude to me, I might be nice to them, but I still remembered that they had been rude to me. Well, this far surpasses any rudeness or disloyalty we might have to endure. God is always willing to forgive us if we ask Him and turn our act around by focusing on His will for us.

....

Behold, ye trust in lying words, that cannot profit. Will ye steal, murder, and commit adultery, and swear falsely, and burn incense unto Baal, and walk after other gods whom ye know not; And come and stand before Me in this house, which is called by My Name, and say, We are delivered to do all these abominations? Jeremiah, Chapter 7, verses 8-10.

I realize that we don't burn incense to idols like Baal, and then go to church, acting like nothing ever happened. Do we do unethical things at work in order to climb the corporate ladder and then go to church and act like nothing ever happened? Do we flirt with people other than our spouse and then go to church acting like nothing ever happened? Do we tell white lies to get ourselves out of financial predicaments with the I.R.S. and then go to church acting like nothing ever happened? Are we rude and talk hatefully to others, even telemarketers, and then go to church acting like nothing ever happened?

It's funny how we can waltz into church acting as if we can pull the wool over everyone's eyes. Maybe we can pull the wool over the eyes of most, but not God who sees and knows who we are and what we have failed to do.

Consider taking the time to tell God that you haven't always behaved the way He would want. Ask Him to forgive you and give you the willingness to be a better Christian in the future. He will do it if you take the time to ask Him to.

....

If that nation, against whom I have pronounced, turn from their evil, I will repent of the evil that I thought to do unto them. Jeremiah, Chapter 18, verse 8.

I remember staying at my aunt's house for a couple of weeks during the summer. We had wonderful fun watching the "Soaps," eating fried egg sandwiches and just spending time together. The girl next door had an above ground pool. I had been envious of her since I had gotten there. At the end of my vacation at my aunt's, the neighbor invited me over for a pool party. I wasn't allowed to go so I ranted and raved around the house, having a "royal hissy fit" because I didn't get my way.

My aunt had been there supporting me all along like God supports us. Then the minute I didn't get everything I wanted, I had a fit and acted like everything wonderful didn't matter anymore. I'm sure she must have been hurt by my ungrateful behavior, the same as God is hurt through ours.

Once I calmed down and realized how unreasonable I was, I apologized and my aunt forgave me, much in the same way that God forgives us, even when we have behaved hatefully. My aunt's forgiving nature, not harboring resentments, allowed us to enjoy our last days of my vacation, creating fond memories to last a lifetime. Fortunately, God doesn't keep a tally sheet of all our shortcomings because Jesus wiped it clean. He doesn't harbor resentments for our sinful deeds. What an awe inspiring and wonderful God!

....

And they built the high places of Baal, which are in the valley of the son of Hinnom, to cause their sons and their daughters to pass through the fire unto Molech; which I commanded them not, neither came it into My mind, that they should do this abomination, to cause Judah to sin. Jeremiah, Chapter 32, verse 35.

What people are willing to do in the name of their beliefs always seems to amaze me. Can you imagine how some people were willing to have their children, their own flesh and blood, walk through fire thinking these acts will get them Salvation? They went to such great lengths when all God asks of us is to <u>believe in Jesus Christ, as our Savior, and try to live as examples of how He works in our lives</u>. He doesn't ask that we sacrifice our children, give all our belongings or money away to have Salvation. His request from us is pretty simple, but I guess it seems too simple for some.

What a shame. Some people can risk their Salvation by getting led astray by cults or they send some TV evangelist all their money so they can get to heaven but they aren't turning to God. All we have to do to get Salvation is underlined in this section. I like to skip the middlemen and focus directly on God.

Here are some related passages:

When the LORD thy God shall cut off the nation from before thee, whither thou goest to possess them, and thou succeedest them, and dwellest in their land; Take heed to thyself that thou be not snared by following them, after that they be destroyed from before thee; and that thou inquire not after their gods, saying, How did these nations serve their gods? Even so will I do like wise. Thou shalt not do so unto the LORD thy God: for every abomination to the LORD, which He hateth, have they done unto their gods; for even their sons and their daughters they have burnt in the fire to their gods. What thing soever I command you, observe to do it: thou shalt not add thereto, nor diminish from it. Deuteronomy, Chapter 12, verses 29-32.

And when the king of Moab saw that the battle was too sore for him, he took with him seven hundred men that drew swords, to break through even unto the king of Edom: but they could not. Then he took his eldest son that should have reigned in his stead, and offered him for a burnt offering upon the wall. And there was great indignation against Israel: and they departed from him, and returned to their own land. 2 Kings, Chapter 3, verses 26-27.

. . . .

Daniel answered in the presence of the king, and said, The secret which the king hath demanded cannot the wise men, the astrologers, the magicians, the soothsayers, show unto the king; But there is a God in heaven that revealeth secrets, and maketh known to the king Nebuchadnezzar what shall be in the latter days. Thy dream, and the visions of thy head upon thy bed, are these... Daniel, Chapter 2, verses 27-28.

You may want to read the rest of the second chapter of Daniel and elsewhere in Daniel to find out what is going to happen in the last days. It has more to do with symbols of countries that are in power or have fallen at particular times in history. I don't truly understand all of that, but I have an uncle who has studied this topic and is very knowledgeable about this.

This passage is included because of the people who turned to fortune tellers, astrologers, magicians, etc. None of these could interpret the meaning of the king's dream, but God could. After Daniel interpreted the dream by trusting the instincts that God gave him, the king realized there is only One True God and it sure wasn't the astrologers, magicians or wizards!

Do you think God would be pleased that the influences of the astrologers, wizards and magicians have worked their way into our lives through the newspapers, books, TV and the movies we choose? Are we spending time focusing on something other than the One True God without even realizing it?

....

God had been telling Jonah to go to Nineveh to tell them to change their ways or they would be destroyed, but Jonah had been reluctant to do it until he was swallowed into the belly of the great fish. After God saved him, he went to Nineveh to do God's Will.

And Jonah began to enter into the city a day's journey, and he cried, and said, Yet forty days, and Nineveh shall be overthrown. So the people of Nineveh believed God, and proclaimed a fast, and put on sackcloth, from the greatest of them even to the least of them. For Word came unto the king of Nineveh, and he arose from his throne, and he laid his robe from him, and covered him with sackcloth, and sat in ashes. And he caused it to be proclaimed and published through Nineveh by the decree of the king and his nobles, saying, Let neither man nor beast, herd nor flock, taste any thing: let them not feed, nor drink water: But let man and beast be covered with sackcloth, and cry mightily unto God: yea, let them turn every one from his evil way, and from the violence that is in their hands. Who can tell if God will turn and repent, and turn away from His fierce anger that we perish not? And God saw their works, that they turned from their evil way; and God repented of the evil that He had said that He would do unto them; and He did it not. Jonah, Chapter 3, verses 4-10.

Some people believe our lives are controlled by fate and we can't do anything to change our lives or our fate. Well, this passage refutes that position. The people of Nineveh lived the high life and didn't focus on God. They turned their lives around after Jonah warned them that they were going to be destroyed and God spared them.

So that means that if we have made some pretty stupid counterproductive choices in our lives, we can apologize to God and turn our actions around. God will forgive us, too, just like He did for the people who lived in Nineveh.

Here are some related passages:

*Bless the LORD, O my soul, and forget not all His benefits: Who forgiveth all thine iniquities; Who healeth all thy diseases; Who redeemeth thy life from destruction; Who crowneth thee with loving kindness and tender mercies. Psalm, Chapter 103, verses 2-4.

*The LORD is merciful and gracious, slow to anger, and plenteous in mercy. He will not always chide: neither will He keep His anger for ever. He hath not dealt with us after our sins; nor regarded us according to our iniquities. For as the heaven is high above the earth, so great is His mercy toward them that fear Him. As far as the east is from the west, so far hath He removed our transgressions from us. Like as a father pitieth his children, so the LORD pitieth them that fear Him. Psalm, Chapter 103, verses 8-13.

*But the mercy of the Lord is from everlasting to everlasting upon them that fear Him, and His righteousness unto children's children: To such as keep His covenant, and to those that remember His Commandments to do them. Psalm, Chapter 103, verses 17-18.

....

Now therefore thus saith the Lord of Hosts; Consider your ways. Ye have sown much, and bring in little; ye eat, but ye have not enough; ye drink, but ye are not filled with drink; ye clothe you, but there is none warm; and he that earneth wages earneth wages to put it into a bag with holes. Thus saith the Lord of Hosts; Consider your ways. Haggai, Chapter 1, verses 5-7.

This passage makes me think of times when anything I have doesn't seem like enough. I have food, but I wish I had better food. I have clothes, but I wish I had better clothes. I have friends, but I wish I had "status" friends. I have a job, but I wish I had a "high level job". I have money, but I wish I had more money.

Am I ever grateful for what I have? I sure wouldn't want God saying, "Dorothy is so ungrateful for all I've given her. If she thinks things are tough now, wait until she sees tough. I'm wasting my efforts here. I'll spend My time helping some other Christian who appreciates what I do more than she does!" Something for me to think about, what about you?

....

These are the things that ye shall do; Speak ye every man the Truth to his neighbour; execute the judgment of Truth and peace in your gates: And let none of you imagine evil in your hearts against his neighbour; and love no false oath: for all these are things that I hate, saith the Lord. Zechariah, Chapter 8, verses 16-17.

Boy, this makes me think of all the times that I secretly hoped that all of the cheerleaders would get fat. What a terrible thing to wish on other people.

....

Yet ye say, Wherefore? Because the Lord hath been witness between thee and the wife of thy youth, against whom thou hast dealt treacherously: yet is she thy companion, and the wife of thy covenant. And did not He make one? Yet had He the residue of the Spirit, and wherefore one? That He might seek a Godly Seed, Therefore take heed to your Spirit, and let none deal treacherously against the wife of his youth. For the Lord, the God of Israel, saith that He hateth putting away: for one covereth violence with his garment, saith the Lord of Hosts: therefore take heed to your spirit, that ye deal not treacherously. Malachi, Chapter 2, verses 14-16.

Some people are able to grab a Bible and quote verses out of it to support their abuse of their wives and children. I want to tell each and every one of you now; God <u>Does Not</u> condone abuse whether it's physical, sexual, mental or any other type of abuse. Anyone who thinks God says those behaviors are permissible in the Bible, is twisting things around (pulling passages out of context) to support their criminal and inappropriate behavior!!! They can possibly hide the abuse from others by trying to justify their actions, but they can't hide it from God.

....

> *And I will come near to you to judgment; and I will be a swift witness against the sorcerers, and against the adulterers, and against false swearers, and against those that oppress the hireling in his wages, the widow, and the fatherless, and that turn aside the stranger from his right, and fear not Me, saith the Lord of Hosts. Malachi, Chapter 3, verse 5.*

God tells us about lots of lifestyle choices that don't meet with His approval. One of the things I was thinking about is the part about not oppressing the hireling in his wages or turning aside the stranger from his right.

I live in an area where there is a large Hispanic population; many coming here directly from Mexico. I see that business owners take advantage of them and it's almost a common practice. The cost of living is high and so are the wages. The businessmen pay the Hispanic workers sub-standard wages, being able to get away with it because these hard-working people don't know the system or the language to dispute this.

I remember driving by a construction site on a Sunday evening, about 7:00 p.m. There were 5-6 Hispanic workers busily digging and installing something at the apartment complex construction site. I was thinking that the vast majority of people wouldn't be working on a Sunday night doing physical labor, especially without being paid overtime. (I highly doubt that these men were even offered any overtime.)

The sad thing is these employees are generally extremely hard workers, but are often treated without the respect they deserve. Even if we aren't the people employing them and paying them the extremely low wages, we might be guilty of not paying them the respect and dignity they deserve as God's people?

....

Ye have said, It is vain to serve God: and what profit is it that we have kept His ordinance, and that we have walked mournfully before the Lord of Hosts? Malachi, Chapter 3, verse 14.

Boy! Are we ever an "I-Me" population, looking out for ourselves as a "What's In It for Me Christian?" My impression is that God wants unconditional love. He doesn't want Christians who are only doing it to look good to other members of society. He doesn't want Christians who are doing it to reap the many rewards God gives His followers. He wants Christians who genuinely love and follow Him and His Word, regardless of the consequences, both positive and negative.

Are we looking at our belief, saying, "Hey, what's it for me to get up each week and go to church?...to be kind to others? to take risks to be examples of our faith in the workplace?" Something to think about!

(Well, this is my last editing before I send this back to the publishers, and I just had to share this with you. I've been telling you throughout this book that I haven't been taking the risks to share my love for Jesus with others. I've always been afraid they would think that I'm a religious fanatic and back away. Writing this book has been an extremely eye-opening experience for me, making me much more aware of my weaknesses as a "Self-absorbed Christian."

Well, about five minutes ago, I was thumbing through the church newsletter while I was munching on something and saw a request. It was asking for a volunteer to do a Bible Study at a local nursing home. I surprised myself and decided to act on it right away before I got cold feet. Unfortunately, the person wasn't there but I left a message saying that I would be willing to lead the Bible Study and asked that they call me back.

The more I got to thinking about it, I thought this book would probably be ideal to use for the Bible Study. Nope, I'm not trying to sell more books, although additional sales will help whichever charity I choose to donate the proceeds to. What I was thinking is that I have this book on my computer. I could copy several pages each week and enlarge the print to make it easier for the people in the nursing home to read. We could talk about how they relate to the passages. Although I haven't listed every passage in the Bible that relates to a given topic, I occasionally have other passages that support a great many of them. This may take us off into different directions.

You realize that I'm talking this all out with you, processing it as I write. I think I like this idea, because I know that the passages I have listed in this book come from the King James Bible. Then I don't have to be concerned about which study guide to pick, worrying if another author's point of view matches my belief in Jesus as my Savior.

I'm starting to get excited about this whole new adventure. I almost feel a little teary eyed. When I started this book, I said that I would see where God leads me and within minutes of being finished with the final editing, I read the request in the newsletter. Not two weeks earlier where I would have thought that I still had too much to do or two months later, when I might have slipped away from my resolve to take more risks. God had me read it minutes before finishing. God works that way in my life and can work that way in your life too, if you let Him. I know you're a captive audience, but thanks for being here with me as I grow in my relationship with God. He has positively influenced my life through reading the Bible on a daily basis and He can do this for you too. Thanks again. D.S.)

....

And now we call the proud happy; yea, they that work wickedness are set up; yea, they that tempt God are even delivered. Then they that feared the Lord spake often one to another: and the Lord hearkened, and heard it, and a book of remembrance was written before Him for them that feared the Lord, and that thought upon His Name. And they shall be Mine, saith the Lord of Hosts, in that day when I make up My jewels; and I will spare them, as a man spareth his own son that serveth him. Then shall ye return, and discern between the righteous and the wicked, between him that serveth God and him not. Malachi, Chapter 3, verses 15-18.

I was just talking about how some business people take advantage of the Hispanic workforce. Management talks behind their backs, talks down to them and takes advantage of them financially, treating them like sub-standard human beings. Now, these workers may or may not realize that they are being treated poorly, because some of them don't understand the language.

Do you think we can pull the same thing on God and get away with it? Think again! He knows when we have a perfect opportunity to share our belief with others, but we are too embarrassed to mention it. He knows when we take advantage of others or make fun of them. He knows when we put work before Him and our families. He knows when we only turn to Him in dire trouble, but we forget about Him until the next traumatic situation. He knows when we harbor hatred, jealousy and resentment toward others.

Although He is very forgiving, God will remember these things, using them to help determine if we are one of His "Jewels" or not. Are you one of His "Jewels"? It's never too late to reassess your actions and to change them around. Reading this book has given you the opportunity to see things from a different perspective. You have a choice. You can decide to start reading the Bible on a daily basis or you can ignore what you have read. I pray that God opens your heart to be willing to do His will.

....

> *For, Behold, the day cometh, that shall burn as an oven; and all the proud, yea, and all that do wickedly, shall be stubble: and the day that cometh shall burn them up, saith the Lord of Hosts that it shall leave them neither root nor branch. But unto you that fear My Name shall the Sun of Righteousness arise with healing in His wings; and ye shall go forth, and grow up as calves of the stall. And ye shall tread down the wicked; for they shall be ashes under the soles of your feet in the day that I shall do this, saith the Lord of Hosts. Malachi, Chapter 4, verses 1-3.*

This makes me think of when I'm driving the speed limit and someone in my car gets annoyed. They tell me that I need to just "blend in" with the others (going the same speed that others are driving, so as to not be noticed). At times, I let people persuade me to go faster to "blend in" with the flow of traffic, still knowing I'm driving at a speed that's against the law.

Are we, as Christians, finding ourselves "blending in" with a lifestyle speed of the people we associate with, so our actions go unnoticed? Do we use God's Name in vain because everyone else does? That way we don't stand out in a crowd as a Christian. Do we do unethical things at work because everyone else does them? Well, we are exceeding God's speed limit for our lives and we know it. Even if we "blend in" with lifestyles similar to others, we have to make a decision. Do we want to be one of God's "Jewels" or just "blend in" with the traffic of lifestyle choices that won't get us to Heaven?

You have a chance to make a monumental change in your life and to show your commitment to God. No, you don't have to shave your head and sell flowers on street corners! You just have to make a conscious effort to live as an example of God's influence on your life. If you listen to the instincts that God gives you instead of listening to the urges of society to "blend in" with the traffic of life, you will attain the ultimate goal of Salvation through Jesus.

I want to, again, explain that I do not profess to be an expert on the Bible. Read the passages noted and see what God is saying to you through them. I have read the Bible from cover to cover sixteen plus times now, and every time I read a passage, I get something totally new from of it. God gave me a feeling that I should share how reading the Bible on a regular basis has positively influenced my life and deepened my relationship with Him, and may do the same for you.

I apologize if I have offended anyone, because that isn't the intent of this book. There were times I thought about not writing particular things, not wanting to offend people I care about or for fear of antagonizing the media and the business world. If I had done that, I would just be "blending in" with the traffic of life instead of genuinely expressing how God has influenced my life.

It is my desire that you will come to relate to the Bible in a way that is personally significant to you. If nothing else, I hope that this gives you things to think about as you use the instincts that God gives you while reading your Bible.

D. S.

About the Author

Dorothy Scott has a unique way of explaining how selected Bible passages can influence the reader's life. Her fifteen years of teaching experience, M.Ed. and a quest for accuracy, led her to read the Bible from cover to cover to locate the often quoted saying, "god helps him who helps himself." Although surprised with her findings, she enjoyed reading the Bible so much that she continued to read it sixteen plus times. The author states that each time she reads the Bible; she gets whole new insights from it. It is her desire that readers will become empowered to relate to the Bible in a more personal way, as they read *Bible Passages That Can Influence Your Life*.

As you read the book, look for some of the interesting types of Christians that the author refers to throughout the book.

- Show Off Christian
- Have Your Cake and Eat It Too Christian
- Back Seat Driver Christian
- Dragging Your Feet Christian
- Freeloader Christian
- Hold Grudges Against Others Christian
- Just When It's Convenient Christian
- Blind Christian
- Self-righteous Christian
- Looking for Jesus in All the Wrong Places Christian
- Old Maid Christian
- Bird in the Hand Christian
- Gimme Gimme Christian
- Luke-warm Christian
- Selective Listening Christian
- Do as I Say, Not as I Do Christian
- Sell-out Christian
- Put Their Money Where Their Mouth Is Christian
- Made in the Shade Christian
- What's In It for Me Christian
- Self-absorbed Christian

Printed in the United States
63846LVS00003B/123